ALL THEATER IS
REVOLUTIONARY THEATER

ALL THEATER IS REVOLUTIONARY THEATER

BENJAMIN BENNETT

CORNELL UNIVERSITY PRESS

ITHACA AND LONDON

First published 2005 by Cornell University Press

Printed in the United States of America

Library of Congress Cataloging-in-Publication Data

Bennett, Benjamin, 1939–
   All theater is revolutionary theater / Benjamin Bennett.
     p. cm.
   Includes bibliographical references and index.
   ISBN 0-8014-4309-1 (alk. paper)
   1. Theater—Philosophy.   I. Title.
  PN2039.B455 2005
   792'.01—dc22   2004017458

Cornell University Press strives to use environmentally responsible suppliers and materials to the fullest extent possible in the publishing of its books. Such materials include vegetable-based, low-VOC inks and acid-free papers that are recycled, totally chlorine-free, or partly composed of nonwood fibers. For further information, visit our website at www.cornellpress.cornell.edu.

Cloth printing   10 9 8 7 6 5 4 3 2 1

For Renate Voris

κἀνταῦθα δὴ τὰ δεινὰ κινηθήσεται.
καὶ γὰρ ταλάντῳ μουσικὴ σταθμήσεται—

Wozu die sauere Arbeit der dramatischen Form?

CONTENTS

ACKNOWLEDGMENTS

I am grateful as usual to my friends and colleagues and students at the University of Virginia for their constant assistance—sometimes deliberate, sometimes unwitting—in developing this book's material. For specific suggestions and challenges I am indebted to Jeffrey Grossman and David Kovacs, to Hans-Thies Lehmann, who was visiting professor here and to whom chapter 9 is in part a tribute, to the editors and consultants at Cornell University Press, and of course to Renate Voris, to whom this book is dedicated.

Chapter 3 is developed from an article, "Brecht's Writing against Writing," in *The Brecht Yearbook* 17 (1992):164–79. Chapter 6 appeared as "Hofmannsthal's Theater of Adaptation," in *A Companion to the Works of Hugo von Hofmannsthal*, ed. Thomas A. Kovach, pp. 97–115 (Rochester, N.Y., 2002). And chapter 8 began life as an article, "Performance and the Exposure of Hermeneutics," in *Theatre Journal* 44 (1992):431–47. *Theatre Journal* is published by Johns Hopkins University Press. I am grateful to the editors and publishers concerned for permission to use this material. In addition, a shorter version of chapter 4 was delivered as a lecture at Harvard University in October 2001, and a version of chapter 5 at Rutgers University in April 2002. In both cases I received valuable criticism from the listeners.

I am grateful, finally, to the University of Virginia for technical support, research funds, and free time for writing; to Robert M. Grossman for assistance in preparing the proofs and the index; to the staff of the German department, Brenda Ayres and Melody Palmer, for assistance with technical and administrative matters; and of course to my wife, for living with this project and supporting it as she has so many others.

ALL THEATER IS
REVOLUTIONARY THEATER

Introduction

I speak frequently in the following pages of revolutionary, progressive, liberal, and conservative tendencies in various artistic and discursive forms. It must be understood that I am not referring to ways in which particular texts make or influence particular political choices. (In fact, in two of the cases cited, the work of a socially conservative author is shown, by virtue of its genre, to be ultimately revolutionary in its tendency.) My argument concerns the manner in which the history of artistic and discursive forms, at the entirely basic level of genre, is already involved in framing the very inventory of political choices that are available or even conceivable in a particular cultural situation. At issue are thus very long-term phenomena that cannot be studied either in direct historical documentation—to what genre could such documents possibly belong?—or by their historical results, which, even assuming one could somehow get a sense for them, could not be profiled in relation to alternative possibilities. Hence the very general political terminology. But is the idea of "genre" not also too general to support the extraction from it of political consequences? Perhaps in most cases. But the distinction of "drama" from other literary genres, I argue, is unique both in its clarity (hence our ability to work with it) and in its fundamental incongruity (hence our ability to detect its historical tendency).

Genre

The basic idea of genre, however, remains a problem. For to the extent that we can either observe or imagine genre as an operative force in discourse, its operation will *always* be, in a broad sense, conservative. In itself, this is a simple enough proposition. It is quite adequately developed, for instance, in James Thurber's "The Macbeth Murder Mystery," where we recognize that we cannot participate in a coherent conversation about *Macbeth* without first permitting our perspective upon the play to be governed by highly specific generic conventions; and that if those conventions were somehow forgotten, and if the only available generic choice for a reader were the murder mystery, then *Macbeth*, quite simply, would *be* a murder mystery. In either case, the need for a prior sense of the text's genre imposes very narrow limits upon how new or original a view of it we can adopt; we have no choice but to read as others have read before us.

But this point, if it is valid at all, is valid for all types and levels of discourse, which means that the idea, in this form, of a "conservative" operation of genre is in practice (hence politically) meaningless, since there is no corresponding liberal alternative to measure it against. Therefore, chapter 2 requires a good deal of argument to make plausible that specifically *in literature* (meaning poetic or imaginative literature) there is after all a politically "conservative tendency" that has to do with the way literary genres are established and recognized and used.

And that argument, once it leaves behind the level of maximum generality at which political questions cannot arise, becomes (like the idea of genre itself) quite complicated and open to misconstruction. In particular, the existence of a conservative tendency associated with literary genre does not imply that literature as a whole *is* conservative in the sense of exerting directly, even over the long term, a conservative influence in politics. On the contrary, it is empirically evident that literature since the eighteenth century has been generally liberal, often enough revolutionary, in intent, and for all we know—how could we measure it exactly?—has been liberal or revolutionary in effect. My own personal inclination, moreover—as the reader will recognize from the tribute paid in chapter 2 to a number of leading liberal North American critics, beginning with Lionel Trilling—is to develop as best I can whatever liberal possibilities literature may offer. One form of this book's main question, in fact, would have to be: Where are the deepest and best anchored liberal possibilities in literature to be found, and how are they constituted, given what I think we still have to admit is the undeniable conservative tendency associated with literary genre?

There are, it is clear, any number of ways in which the liberally inclined production of literature, as well as the liberally inclined criticism or theory of literature, can circumvent the problem presented (in my view) by the concept of genre. But what attracts me to the group of liberal critics I have mentioned, and of which I imagine myself a member, is precisely that they do *not*—or at least do not always or on principle—circumvent that problem, but show a willingness to confront it directly, in a liberal sense. And the results of this confrontation are of great significance. In chapter 2, beginning with what seems to me a culminating instance of liberal-leaning genre theory (as formulated mainly by Northrop Frye), I trace the implications of this theoretical initiative and argue that for all its conceptual ingenuity, for all its interpretive achievements, for all its continuing importance in the overall project of literary studies, it fails in the end to hold together *as theory*; that in fact the mechanism of its failure lays bare a fundamental corruptness in the very concept of "literature" as redefined and developed since the eighteenth century; and that both the insuperable difficulties of genre theory and the corruptness of literature as a concept are related to the hopeless but unavoidable attempt to understand drama as a literary type. What we have here is something like a Thermopylae of modern literary thought, the assertion of a demonstrably untenable position, but with sufficient tenacity and in sufficient detail to permit the issues and insights to emerge by which the basic task—of finding revolutionary possibilities in the very teeth of the problem of genre—becomes manageable after all.

As my title suggests, I think it has become clear that the site of those revolutionary possibilities is the dramatic theater—not in the sense that there is something inherently revolutionary about theatrical performance, but in the sense that when theater and literature are joined together by main force into a supposed single poetic genre, into the radically incongruous entity we call "drama," it is this basic incongruity, in its refusal to be adequately theorized, that disrupts the operation of literary genre in a manner that I contend is revolutionary.

Drama and Theater

I do not adopt the untenable position that either the theater as an institution, or theatrical performance, or any particular instance of either one is inherently revolutionary. The theater as an institution does not generally arise and operate for any sustained period without being at least tolerated, if not actually promoted, by a structure of relatively stable social and political institutions. And if the dependence of understanding upon an established system of genres tends to favor the conservative inclinations in a body of readers, how much more so in a body of theatergoers. Surely theatergoers are more likely than readers to be bewildered initially by the work of art, the performance, that bombards them with sensory stimuli at its own pace, leaving no room for readerly reflection. And how shall this bewilderment be checked, if not by a clear prior sense of the genre of performance in question? (A related issue, the importance of the ever present possibility of *distraction* in the theater, arises in the argument of chapters 8 and 9.)

These considerations apply to all theaters in all periods. But the unique feature of Western theater is that it is understood as the single criterion for distinguishing a major poetic type, which we call "drama." Non-Western theaters are of course often enough used as vehicles for poetic or literary works of various genres—as indeed Western theaters also often stage works not originally classified as drama—but only in the West (or, in other cultures, only under Western influence) is theater used as the *definition* of a single, clearly distinguishable poetic type. It is not at all clear how the theater manages to function thus—I discuss this problem later in some detail—but function it does nonetheless. We are practically never in any doubt when asked, for instance, whether a particular work is "narrative" or "dramatic." Even if we happen to have seen *Nicholas Nickleby* on the stage, we will immediately say "narrative"; and we will be equally confident in categorizing as "dramatic" plenty of texts that we have only ever read in books.

How does it happen that we find ourselves thus in the absurd situation of employing as a literary definition something that is not literary at all but (depending on how you look at it) either a social practice or an architectural form? This question, I maintain, concerns a true radical anomaly and so does not admit of a theoretical or systematic answer. Its answer must be strictly historical; it must be true that at some point in history, for reasons that had nothing to do with the systematic unfolding of poetry, the supposed poetic category of "drama" was invented and has been sustained ever since by nothing but the force of Western tradition.

Once we put the matter in these terms, the concrete shape of the problem becomes clear. We still cannot say exactly *how* theatrical drama comes into being, but the *when* and the *where* are no longer at all obscure. Everything that we recognize today as drama traces its origin to sixth-century Attica, where tragedy, reputedly the invention of Thespis of Icaria, is accepted and developed in Athens itself under Peisistratus. And it is, as far as I can see, undoubtedly under Peisistratus—who was concerned, at the very least, to gain the reputation of a preserver, promoter, and regularizer of the whole of Greek poetic tradition from Homer on—that the fateful association of the dramatic theater with a supposedly discrete poetic type was made.

As I say, this piece of knowledge, assuming it is that, does not enable us to understand exactly how that association arose. The sixth-century documents upon which such an understanding would have to be based are not available to us. In fact, as far as I know, there is really only one extant document that gives any significant information about the internally incongruous condition of drama in its early period. It is a relatively late document, from fourth-century Athens, and it provides its information only negatively, by failing in the attempt to work out a consistent theory of contemporary drama as a poetic type. But its author—as was admitted even by the teacher whose doctrine he repudiated—was a man of uniquely powerful intellect, and its reasoning is strong enough to speak to our modern concerns even without meaning to. Which is why the main argument of the present book has to begin, as it does in chapter 1, with a discussion of Aristotle's *Poetics*.

Again, theatrical drama is not amenable to a strictly abstract theoretical treatment, because no part of its nature, of its operation or properties, can be separated conceptually from the concrete historical circumstances of its origin and development.

It may be objected, finally, that my title speaks of "all theater," whereas the argument I have outlined concerns only Western theater. My reason for not making fine distinctions here is that in the twentieth and twenty-first centuries, those distinctions have become obsolete. Western ideas of drama and theater have by now triumphed globally, not in the sense that all theaters in the world have adapted themselves to European models—which is of course far from the case—but rather by way of the universal application, or imposition, of the Western concept of "literature," which I contend brings with it automatically the specific notion of "drama" it has inherited from the Greeks. We now routinely speak of African and Asian literatures, or of the literatures of indigenous peoples who have had practically no contact with Western culture. But "literature" is not a culturally neutral term. That it is, on the contrary, a specifically European notion, that its meaning is inseparable from its history, and that it expresses a definite bias with respect to the genres of novel and drama are matters I go into later on.

Performance

Performance is what makes theater theater and so is inherently part of this book's concern, but only in a limited sense. At no point below—except once indirectly, in the case of Robert Wilson—do I discuss any actual theatrical performance, for to do so would only obscure my main argument. Performance *as such* is crucial in that argument, and chapter 8 below attempts to show how performance as such counteracts the genre-related conservative tendency that finds its way into philosophical hermeneutics. But the anticonservative or revolutionary tendency in any actual performance—if one could demonstrate it—could never be made to illustrate this point adequately, for it would always depend much more heavily and obviously upon specific contemporary circumstances. And by looking at performances in different historical circumstances, one could always find counterillustrations.

This idea, that performance as such is crucial in understanding the revolutionary aspect of theater, whereas the effect of actual performances is not, is not only a methodological point in what follows but also a substantive point. Crucial to the whole argument of part 2 is the recognition in chapter 7 of Denis Diderot's exemplary status, in his understanding that the specific philosophical and social effect of drama requires *that* it be performed but implies no standards for, or limits upon, *how* or *how well* it is performed.

This idea is anticipated in a related argument on Hugo von Hofmannsthal in chapter 6 and is developed in chapters 8 and 9. Chapter 3 argues for a level of theatrical effectiveness in Bertolt Brecht's work that is not dependent on acting techniques; chapter 4 shows that under certain historical circumstances a work's liberating theatrical effect can be entirely predetermined—though not yet achieved—by its text; and the discussion of Georg Büchner in chapter 5 offers something like a model case, the case of a theater "that never was," in which no actual performance was ever staged or ever will be, yet still a theater that turns out to be historically effective in creating the conditions of meaningfulness for a body of literary work. There must be a theater, performance must happen *somewhere*, for Büchner's plays to be understood, but no actual theater and no practicable criteria for performance are required or even possible.

I do not claim that this strand of argument settles the matter of performance. It simply avoids most of the questions raised by contemporary performance theorists; in fact, I have tried to set up the subject matter of this book so as to make those questions, for the moment, immaterial. But of course, this does not make them go away, and it may be useful to note that there are a couple of important points where my argument impinges on them.

Especially the issue of the *transitivity* of performance concerns me. When one speaks of performance, does one always imply the presence of an object—normally a "text" or "work"—that the performance is a performance *of*? If so, then exactly in what sense: as the object of interpretation, of reproduction or reiteration, of ontological completion? If not, then how can the performance achieve sufficient historical substance to become an object of study? W. B. Worthen, in a very important and comprehensive article from 1998, organizes an unexpectedly wide range of performance-theoretical initiatives with reference to just these questions.[1]

My own view of the matter is in a sense simpler than Worthen's. There is such a thing, there needs to be such a thing, as intransitive performance; but I maintain that performance is never intransitive in the first instance, because we cannot regard an action as "performance" to begin with without recognizing it as *interpretive*. We never merely *see* a performance; we also always *see through* it, even if we cannot assign a clear category to what our seeing through is aimed at. Intransitive, or what I call "absolute" performance, therefore, as Antonin Artaud well knew, is never simply given but must always be achieved. Chapter 3 treats the "performance of writing" in a strictly transitive sense. But beginning in chapter 6, with a discussion of Hofmannsthal's practice of dramatic adaptation, I attempt to show how absoluteness is compassed not by ignoring or avoiding the interpretivity of performance, which is impossible, but by fully understanding and exploiting that interpretivity. Chapter 8 opens a discussion of the political dimension of this issue, and chapter 9 treats the consequences, in a society dominated by mass media, of failing to keep the issue in view.

Perhaps, one might argue, it is only a matter of definitions here. Surely "performance" can be defined so as to include instances that more or less demonstrably lack the component of interpretation. But I think we show a certain lack of cultural honesty if we permit ourselves unlimited freedom in the choice of definitions. In particular, I think it is true not only that the conceptual systematicity of literature is disrupted by the influence of the theater but also that our idea of the theater, hence inescapably the reality of the theater for us, is irreversibly impregnated (or contaminated, if you prefer) with the process of writing, with literacy, with "literature" in a strict etymological sense—hence with the quality of interpretation. Again, this is not an abstract theoretical assertion. It involves the recognition that Western theater cannot be conceptually detached from the conditions of its origin, as a historical accident, in sixth-century Greece—or that if we do forcibly carry out such a detachment, we simply loosen our thinking to the extent that anything becomes plausible. This point, that the origin of Western theater is radically literate, or literary, is argued (I think conclusively) in a major book by Jennifer Wise, which is discussed in chapter 2.[2]

These are the reasons for my insistence on understanding "performance" in a manner that always implies the attribute "interpretive," even in cases (such as are treated in chapter 9) where nothing corresponding to an original text or interpretandum can be identified. Of course, it is possible to use the term in ways unconnected with the evolved condition of Western theater; but without the theatrical metaphor at its center, performance studies can hardly even be said to exist. And of course one can find—even in Europe, before the model of Greek and Roman theater fully asserts itself—things that might be called predramatic theater. But to infer the continued existence, or even the possibility, of a nondramatic, strictly nonliterary theater would be to underestimate hopelessly the extent to which such concepts and institutions are historically conditioned. Even Worthen's article, though it does not explicitly favor the position I have adopted, offers evidence for the basic interpretivity of performance—as it were, performatively—by exhibiting the insuppressibility of the *question* of the performed object.

Do I, finally, by positioning myself as I have, necessarily part company with Artaud and all the energetic theater theory his work has stimulated? Not at all. Fifteen years ago, in a comparable context, I said, "I am an Artaudian."[3] I confirm that insistence now. To suggest that Artaud, himself a committed professional writer, was fanatically opposed to the textual, or to literature, in every conceivable meaning of the idea, would be absurd. And in chapters 3 and 4, by developing a parallel with Brecht, I attempt to show exactly the scope of his opposition to the involvement of text in the theater.

The Overall Argument

The two chapters in part 1 provide historical and theoretical background for the individual illustrative arguments in part 2. Chapter 1, as I have said, attempts to show that in the *Poetics,* even Aristotle's organizational intellect is defeated by the task of justifying logically the established Athenian idea of drama as a single discrete poetic type. Chapter 2, on "genre and drama," treats a number of widely disparate topics, some of which I have already mentioned; but all its arguments are focused on showing that drama, by way of its indissoluble association with the brute materiality of theater, disrupts fundamentally, and opens to the possibility of revolution, the otherwise at least potentially closed system of Western literature.

Part 2—chapters 3 through 9—uses particular instances to develop the historical and theoretical material of part 1 in the direction of a political understanding of the relations among literature, drama, and theater. Chapters 3 and 4 are concerned to provide this development with a sound basis in modern theater history. In both chapters the argument is referred to the point that Brecht and Artaud, for all the obvious differences between them, share a single basic idea of the nature of drama and of the mission of the theater in their time. Within this historically limited frame of reference, I argue, it is possible for more or less conventional literary analysis to show how specific plays—first Brecht's own *Leben des Galilei,* then Frank Wedekind's *Frühlings Erwachen* and T. S. Eliot's *Murder in the Cathedral*—exhibit the revolutionary tendency of Western theater. Chapter 5 approaches the matter from exactly the opposite direction. It shows how Georg Büchner, a historically isolated and eccentric author, faced with the problem of finding a literary avenue for the pursuit, and for the adequate criticism, of revolutionary sentiments, is driven to recapitulate the whole history of Western poetry and literature by inventing and applying his own theory of theatrical drama, without benefit of any significant personal contact with the real theater of his time.

From chapter 6 on, the question of the achievement of absolute or intransitive performance becomes central; and with respect to the relation between actor and role, the initial argument on Hofmannsthal develops suggestions from chapters 4 and 5, especially with reference to Büchner. Hofmannsthal, it happens, in trying to formulate his idea of acting and identity, makes reference to Diderot's *Paradoxe sur le comédien,* and much of chapter 7 is then taken up with a close reading of that text. For Diderot, I argue, the theater is a means of coming to grips with ideas that lie entirely outside the organized conceptual inventory (the possibilities for meaning in texts) of modern European languages, especially the idea of "nature" in a sense sufficiently strict to make it useful in establishing a political program. In Diderot's theory—as in Hofmannsthal's practice and Büchner's—there is thus a strong separation between the meaning of the text and the meaning of the play. The political dimension of this point is then developed with respect to George Bernard Shaw, and the philosophical dimension (questions of personal identity and its lack) with respect to Samuel Beckett.

Chapter 8, on hermeneutics, is mainly theoretical and attempts a general explanation of how it happens that performance, while remaining basically interpretive, can leave behind altogether the domain of textual meanings and become in a sense absolute. The conservative tendency associated with the operation of literary genre is here seen in relation to a built-in political bias in the whole discipline of hermeneutics, including its self-critical component; and the basic opposition that I argue for, between hermeneutics and performance, supports the idea of a revolutionary tendency in the dramatic theater. This chapter concludes with a short discussion of Jean Genet, which, together with the discussion of Beckett from chapter 7, is used to define the idea of limiting cases of drama that chapter 9 takes as a starting point. In this final chapter, the ideas and arguments of the entire book are tested against the example of a contemporary theater that appears to have exhausted and severed its connection with the history of "drama." Precisely here, I argue, the treatment of theatrical drama from chapter 2 on has the effect of profiling—in the theater of Robert Wilson, for instance—an artistically and politically *problematic* quality that entirely escapes other approaches, a fabric of problems that also includes the question of the history and the destiny of totalitarianism.

Part One

CHAPTER ONE

Aristotle's Defeat

A good deal of our habitual thinking about drama is at least indirectly shaped and colored by the thought of Aristotle's *Poetics*. Especially, I suggest, the habitual *difficulties* in our notion of drama are often Aristotelian in character. For despite spending much of his life in Athens, Aristotle, within two centuries or so of the invention of Attic tragedy, not only fails to achieve a clear critical grasp of that form but seems also to experience unaccustomed embarrassment in his conceptual approach to it.

The Focus on Drama and Theater

Aristotle begins (1447a13–18) by asserting that "epic poetry, tragedy, comedy, dithyrambic poetry, and most flute and lyre music" are all forms of "imitation," which differ from one another in three ways: τῷ ἐν ἑτέροις μιμεῖσθαι (by imitating "in" different things, usually taken to mean, in different "media"), τῷ ἕτερα μιμεῖσθαι (by imitating different objects), and τῷ ἑτέρως μιμεῖσθαι (by imitating in a different manner). The second of these types of differentiation, when later elaborated upon (48a1–18), turns out not to have much significance for the theory of art. The objects of imitation, says Aristotle, are "men acting," and these men differ from one another mainly by being either better than we, similar to us, or worse than we. But the first and third types of difference appear to engage real questions of artistic technique, and the only problem they present immediately is *how to distinguish between them*, between the "medium" and the "manner" of imitation. (The question becomes more obviously difficult if we accept the actual manuscript reading for the first type of difference: τῷ γένει ἑτέροις μιμεῖσθαι, "by imitating through the use of categorically different means.") If either the first or the third type were omitted, the two remaining would correspond to the ideas of form and content. Why does Aristotle insist on three types? Our sense of an imbalance here is increased by the addition, at the end of the sentence, of the words, καὶ μὴ τὸν αὐτὸν τρόπον, "and not in the same manner," which obviously attach themselves only to the phrase immediately preceding, "by imitating in a different manner," and so lend special emphasis to this type of difference.

What is even more interesting about the question of the "manner" of imitation is that only *one* example of its application is given. For the question of the "medium" of imitation, Aristotle begins by identifying three media, "rhythm, language, and harmony" (47a22)—to which he afterwards adds "melody and meter" (47b25)—and shows how these concepts help one understand the differences among practically all the musical and poetic genres one can think of, plus the art of dancing. In the case of "objects" of imitation, he not only gives numerous examples of how types of poetry may be differentiated but also extends the discussion to include painting, dance, and music (48a5–10). The question of "manner" of imitation, however, is exhausted in a single short passage:

> Yet a third difference concerns how (in what manner) one may imitate each of these various objects. For imitation in the same medium and of the same objects can be carried out in that either (1) the imitator [speaker] sometimes narrates and sometimes as it were becomes a different person [namely, in using direct speech, speaking in the person of a fictional character], or else (2) the imitator speaks as the same person, without changing, or else (3) the imitators [i.e. actors] all speak in the persons of the living and acting characters themselves. (48a19–24)[1]

The question of "how" imitation is effected is thus applicable *only* to the set of distinctions in which drama is differentiated from nondramatic poetry.

There is of course a clear reference here to the tripartite analysis suggested by Plato in book 3 of the *Republic* (392C–394C), which distinguishes (1) strict narration (διήγησις), where the poet speaks only in his own voice, (2) "imitation" (μίμησις) or direct-speech dialogue, where the poet speaks as if he were this or that character, and (3) a style like Homer's, where the two basic possibilities are combined. But precisely the comparison with Plato, the different emphasis and ordering, shows Aristotle to be more attentive to the separation of theatrical drama from other artistic types. In Plato, a work in which one speaker did nothing but reproduce "mimetically" the speeches of a dialogue would be generically indistinguishable from drama, whereas Aristotle speaks of "imitators" (plural) in a manner that makes clear that the individual parts are distributed among them. Indeed, in the immediate sequel, which begins as a summary of his whole argument "from the beginning," Aristotle suddenly loses this focus and wanders into a historical-etymological meditation on the origins of dramatic and theatrical forms (48a24–b3).

Drama as a Poetic Type

But if Aristotle has a special interest in defining theatrical drama (including both tragedy and comedy) as a form, why does he insist on the distinction between "medium" and "manner" of imitation? Why not simply recognize theatrical representation, or representation by parts distributed among actors, as yet one further "medium" of imitation? Later, when he distinguishes the six constituent "parts" of tragedy—μῦθος, ἤθη, λέξις διάνοια, ὄψις, μελοποιία (50a7–12): plot, characters, diction, thought, spectacle, song—he states that three of these have to do with objects of imitation (obviously plot, characters and thought), two with the "medium" of imitation (diction and song, as stated explicitly a short while earlier [49b33–34]), and one with the "manner" of imitation—which must be ὄψις, or spectacle, the visual aspect of the performance. Here again, therefore, the single "part" of tragedy that makes it specifically dramatic or theatrical is associated with "manner" of imitation. And here, even more than in the case of the distinction of dialogue from narration, one wonders why the characteristic mark of drama is not classified as a "medium" or "means" of imitation. Must one assume that "media" of imitation—rhythm, language, harmony, melody, meter, diction, lyric singing—are restricted to the domain of the audible, as opposed to the visible? Then how does one explain Aristotle's suggestions that his system can be extended to such arts as dance and painting?

Despite the antiquity and corruptness of Aristotle's text, I think there are a few far-reaching conclusions to be drawn right away. First, the whole category of "manner" of imitation is invented *for the sole purpose of defining or separating dramatic form*. Second, the only possible reason for this invention of a third type of difference among arts—which disrupts what would otherwise be the simple and perspicuous duality of form and content—is that Aristotle wishes, at all costs, *to avoid classifying theatrical representation as a "medium" or "means" of imitation*. And third, the reason for this avoidance can only be the consideration that giving theatrical performance (with different actors taking different roles) the same status as "rhythm," "language," and "harmony," as a medium or means of imitation, would incline us to think of drama as an art *separate* from that of poetry simply sung or recited; it would become difficult to understand drama as a *kind* of poetry. It is of cardinal importance to Aristotle, I will argue, that as close a relation as possible be maintained between drama and epic. Therefore, in discussing "medium," the most powerful criterion for differentiating arts, he leaves theatrical representation entirely out of account; and with regard to epic, he concentrates on differentiating it from nonpoetic uses of hexameter (47b13–20), thus stressing its nearness to the musical-poetic arts (47b24–27) which include tragedy and comedy.

In other words, Aristotle uses a special category to distinguish drama, and an *intrapoetic* category, precisely in order to reduce the importance of the distinction and preserve the subordination of drama to poetry as species to genus. Hence the obvious gradation in importance of the three basic types of difference: first, "medium," with the longest explanation and a range that obviously covers all forms of artistic imitation; second, "objects," with a somewhat shorter explanation and a similarly large range, except that poetry is where it is most obviously applicable; third, "manner," with the very brief explanation quoted above and a range that includes *only* poetry—indeed (as far as we can tell from the explanation) only epic and dramatic poetry. Hence also the repeated insistence that spectacle (ὄψις), which distinguishes drama as the theatrical form it after all is, is the least essential or artistic "part" of tragedy (50b17–21, 53b1–8).

Drama as the Highest Poetic Type

Now Aristotle makes no secret of his overriding interest in drama as a form, or of his opinion that drama is not only a type of poetry but the highest type. (In this he opposes Plato, who regards "imitative" discourse—the direct presentation of characters' speech—as maximally corrupting.) As grounds for his praise of Homer, he twice explicitly uses the concept of "drama" (μιμήσεις δραματικὰς ἐποίησεν . . . τὸ γελοῖον δρα-ματικοποιήσας [48b35–38]), and he later discusses in detail how Homer's unique excellence as a poet includes especially the quasi-dramatic staging of his characters (60a5–11). Evidently, he means to portray the history of poetry as a gradual development in which the example of Homer taught "epic" or "heroic" poets to become tragedians, and taught "iambic" or lampooning poets to become writers of comedy, "because these forms [tragedy and comedy or, in general, dramatic forms] are larger and more worthy of honor than the others [that preceded them]" (49a5–6). And of course his final chapter (61b26–62b15) is devoted to demonstrating that tragedy is a higher form of art than epic.

The trouble with this gradualist view (κατὰ μικρόν [48b22–23, 49a13]) is that it stumbles on the fundamental difference, the gap that must be jumped, between poetic art and theatrical art, the difference that Aristotle minimizes by relegating it to the domain of "manner" and by reducing the artistic significance of theater's visual component. (Or if, perhaps, he does *not* regard tragedy and comedy as fundamentally theatrical, why does he even mention the differences that define theater—the visual aspect of the work and the use of multiple "imitators"—in the first place?) Even in the present and recent past of Aristotle's Athens, where poetry is still more prominently a performed art than an art recorded in writing, the fundamental difference obtains (one is tempted to call it a difference in "medium") between poetry that is sung or recited by an individual or a chorus (or by a chorus plus leader) and a poetic work of fiction in which the lines spoken by different characters are assigned to different individual performers. And my point is that the difficulty of regarding drama as a poetic type produces serious problems in Aristotle's thought, problems that we have inherited.

Why not simply regard "drama" and what we now call "literature" as *separate* arts? Or why not—as in many Eastern cultures, before their ideas of theater are influenced from the West—simply regard drama as one of several possible expressive devices by which a literature of poems or stories may from time to time be embellished? After all, we do routinely adapt nondramatic works for our stages. Why insist on a genre distinction between works that may someday be adapted and works that are "originally conceived" for the stage? Do the latter always (or even usually) make "better theater" than the former?

For some reason or reasons, Aristotle insists on regarding the theatrically realized forms of tragedy and comedy as distinct types of poetry—indeed, as the culmination of poetry's essential and historical unfolding. And for some reason or reasons, we—we Europeans—are strongly inclined to follow him in this, not only in theory but also in our practical articulation of literary history, whose national high points (the reigns of Elizabeth I and Louis XIV, the *siglo de oro*, Weimar Classicism) tend to coincide with periods rich in drama. The "reason or reasons" in each of these various cases—apart from the effects of imitation or historical influence—will almost certainly be different; I will try to say something later about those reasons in modern Europe.

In Aristotle's case, one can only speculate; but a hunch from which to start speculating is fairly obvious. For if theatrical drama and poetry are separate arts, then the specifically Attic institution of the dramatic theater remains merely a local achievement, whereas if drama is the latest and most perfect form of Greek poetry as a whole, then Athens is the privileged vessel of that poetry, the only true heir to Homer. To attribute such thinking directly to Aristotle, who was not a citizen of Athens, would go too far; but to imagine Aristotle's working in an intellectual atmosphere saturated with that originally patriotic (but perhaps no longer obviously patriotic) idea of drama, to imagine his simply accepting that idea as a received fact and then working to understand it, is not at all unreasonable. In any case, Attic drama itself, on the level of content—in *The Eumenides*, for example, and in *Oedipus at Colonus*—exhibits a clear tendency to present Athens as the point of culmination or adjudication for myths that are not basically Attic, thus to appropriate those myths in a manner that would parallel the appropriation by drama of poetry as such. Or perhaps it is important that the idea of drama ("imitative" discourse) as a culminating form of poetry lends useful emphasis to Aristotle's fundamental disagreement with Plato about the value of "imitation" in general, his insistence on imitation as an educative tendency (48b5–19) rather than a corrupting force; this aspect of the relation between drama and poetry helps explain Aristotle's use of τοὺς μιμουένους (48a23–24), "the imitators,"as the accusative agent of μιμεῖσθαι in a context where the reference must be to actors.[2] And if Aristotle means, as he apparently does, to castigate both the excessive theatricality of tragedy in his own time and an excessive critical focus on the material theater (61b32–62a6), then, again, the idea of drama as entirely contained within the domain of poetry—hence the idea of a now lost or sullied poetic essence of tragedy—obviously serves his purpose.

The Basic Conceptual Problem of Drama

In any event, Aristotle is clearly pulled in two directions here. He is obliged (for reasons I discuss below) to keep in focus the theatrical aspect of tragedy and comedy; yet at the same time, in order to establish these forms in the vicinity of epic, as strictly poetic types, he must insist that their basic effect does not depend on the theater (50b19-20, 62a17–18). He is exposed (as we are, in his wake) to the basic conceptual difficulties that result from trying to define a poetic genre by asking who says or sings the words and under what concrete circumstances, difficulties which of course only become worse as poetry becomes more strictly literary. The only conceivable way to avoid these difficulties altogether would be to detheatricalize drama—to find a way, somehow, of thinking "drama" without thinking "theater." Gerald F. Else, for example, tries to rescue Aristotle's consistency by attributing to him exactly this sort of conceptual legerdemain. He takes ὄψις to mean not "spectacle" but "the decking out of the characters' appearance," and he relates it to the αἰσθήσεις, "sense perceptions," that Aristotle later asserts (54b15–17) are a necessary part of poetic art (ἐξ ἀνάγκης ἀκολουθούσας . . . τῇ ποιητικῇ). Then he continues:

> We shall see that these are the (a) visual and (b) audible manifestations which are *necessarily involved in the presentation of a drama as an action performed by (dramatic) persons*. Notice that I say "persons," not "actors"; for the point at issue is not performance on a stage, by living actors, but a feature inherent in the drama as such. It is inherent in the drama of *Othello* that Othello is a Blackamoor, or in that of *Lear* that Lear is a kingly old man. The concept of these characters—and it is a concept implicit in the idea of a drama—is that they will 'look' or appear in such and such a way: as a Moor, not a white man, a king, not a commoner, etc. Moreover, the characters must be thought of ("seen," i.e., by the poet: 17.55a24, 27) as being in

certain places, moving in certain directions, being on or off stage at certain times, etc. These are necessities that the dramatist cannot dodge, a condition which he has laid upon himself by the act of writing a play, and which must necessarily affect the way a reader—independently of any actual performance—will visualize it. It is a necessity which impinges upon the dramatist because in writing a play he has stepped across the line that separates the pure universal . . . from its embodiment in a given dramatic person (Oedipus, Antigone, Dicaeopolis). (Else, p. 234)

As ingenious and impassioned as this position may be, it is also hopeless. In the first place, the "sense perceptions" Aristotle talks about are (as he says) necessary to *poetry in general*, not just (or even preeminently) to drama. That sense perceptions are "necessary" for poetry and ὄψις is "necessary" for drama does not imply that ὄψις belongs to those sense perceptions. In the second place, Aristotle is certainly right about sense perceptions in all poetry, not only drama. In fact, the eidetic quality, the ability to "see" a fictional scene or object, is *more* needed by the epic or narrative writer than by the dramatist (who after all can rely on the stage to do some of his sensory work for him). Is Queequeg, for example, somehow less racially and visually conceived than Othello? Or to remain in Hellenic antiquity, we might compare the scene in Homer where Hector and Andromache meet at the Skaian gate (*Iliad* 6.466–81) with Sophocles' travesty of it in the *Ajax* (530–82). In Homer, the whole interest of the scene is visual, the nodding plumes on Hector's helmet that frighten the child, and the sudden bright laughter of the otherwise doom-burdened parents when they recognize the cause of his fright. In Sophocles, by contrast, the interest is verbal, the grim prophetic tone of Ajax's speech to his son. And in the third place, since in Else's view (though he avoids saying so) ὄψις ought to be as important in epic as in drama, what can the "parts" (μέρη) be that tragedy possesses but epic lacks (49b16–20)? Else does a reasonably convincing job (pp. 595–98) of explaining away the phrase ἔξω μελοποιίας καὶ ὄψεως (59b10) in Aristotle's discussion of "parts" of epic; and his explication (pp. 523-36) of the idea of "parts" in relation to "types" (εἴδη) of tragedy (55b33–34) probably goes as far as humanly possible toward restoring the sense of the passage in question. But none of this—even if we accept his deletion of καὶ τὰς ὄψεις (62a16) in Aristotle's summary of the advantages of tragedy—compensates for the complete absence of evidence that ὄψις, in this text, has anything but its normal reference to what is *actually* visible, thus to the single "part" of drama that is clearly and radically absent in epic: the unfolding upon a visible stage of an action distributed among actors. Precisely Aristotle's minimizing of the "artistic" importance of ὄψις operates against Else here, since (on Else's hypothesis) there would be no reason to minimize the importance of eidetic imagination. We really have no choice but to translate the crucial passage as follows:

> Since people acting [not a narrator] make the imitation, it follows of neces-
> sity that in some sense a portion of tragedy consists in the proper ordering
> of visible effects [ὁ τῆς ὄψεως κόσμος]. (49b31–33)

It is true that Aristotle attenuates this point as much as he can. (As I have
said, he is pulled in two directions.) But however uncomfortable it makes
him—by producing the conceptual difficulties I have spoken of—he does
nevertheless admit, as he must, that you cannot think "drama" without
thinking "theater," without referring to the experience of an actual visible theater.

I do not quote Else at such length merely because his notion of "the
drama as such" is so clearly vulnerable. I quote him because his is the
best and most thorough attempt that I know of to rescue strict conceptual consistency in the *Poetics*. And by discussing the failure of that
attempt, I hope at least to approach the goal of demonstrating a negative, of showing that conceptual consistency is simply not achievable in
the Attic and Aristotelian—and thence ineradicably European—tradition of regarding drama as a type of poetry or literature. My reasons for
opening this whole book with a discussion of Aristotle are similar. I do
not mean to diminish him as a thinker or observer. Far from it. My point
is that *even* Aristotle cannot complete the task he sets himself in the *Poetics*. Let us attempt, therefore, to put together as much of his actual argument as we can.

Theater as "Praxis"

Of crucial importance is the comparison between drama and epic, and Aristotle is careful to give epic its due. Shortly after making the point that even
in narrative poetry the plots should be "dramatic," as in tragedy, and
focused on a single compact "action" (59a17–20)—and that perhaps even
Homer's poems exceed the proper measure of length, which is given by the
aggregate time of tragedies presented at a single hearing (59b21–22)[3]—he
appears to change direction:

> Epic poetry, however, has a great and unique ability to extend its length.
> For in tragedy it is not permitted to imitate a number of separate actions
> understood to be happening simultaneously; but only the one action
> shown by the actors on the stage may be imitated. In epic poetry, by con-
> trast, since it is narrative in form, it is possible to present several actions
> that take place simultaneously, actions by which, if they fit the overall
> scheme, the weightiness of the poem is increased. This procedure thus has
> the advantage in magnificence, and also in variation for the listener and in
> variety of episodes. For strings of similar episodes, by satiating us quickly,
> make tragedies fail on the stage. (59b22–31)

What he is doing is what he does again at the end of his treatise (61b27–62a4): presenting the strongest possible argument in favor of epic in order to demonstrate the superiority of tragedy by then refuting that argument. Here, after a few sentences in praise of heroic meter (59b31–60a5), he suddenly turns the tables on his hypothetical opponent by showing that in spite of the supposedly clear advantages of epic or narrative form, Homer himself, in his method, strives in the direction of the dramatic in that he puts himself forward as little as possible, instead permitting his scenes and especially his characters to speak for themselves (60a5–11).

Then follows a complicated and somewhat murky discussion of miraculous and illogical elements in poetry (60a11–b2) from which, for present purposes, two important points emerge. First, although wonderful or astonishing motifs give pleasure (60a17) and so are useful in all poetry, and although they therefore have a place even in tragedy (60a11–12), still a limit must be imposed on them—at least the central plot should be free of the illogical (60a27–31)—since otherwise what had been wonderful tends to become ridiculous. But second, precisely the concrete visibility of the dramatic stage helps establish this limit by making the ridiculous potential of an astonishing scene more quickly apparent (60a12–17). What Aristotle does, in other words, is take the supposed advantage of narrative, its greater scope, and reveal in it a source of artistic *danger* that is best counteracted by the stage-imposed discipline of drama in its actual visibility.

That this twist in the argument is in fact central in Aristotle's thinking is shown by a number of other passages where success or failure on stage is offered as *evidence* of basic artistic soundness. Euripides' stage successes prove the correctness of having tragedies end unhappily (53a23–30). Stage failures provide proof of the artistic doctrine of the single and compact plot (56a15–19). And stage presentation trips up the poet who fails to visualize his action thoroughly (55a22–29). The actual visible theater thus operates as a kind of touchstone for artistic correctness and even artistic merit. Aristotle, that is, unlike Else, takes the bull by the horns, faces the problem of the theater's physical visibility, and attempts actually to use that quality in arguing the poetic advantage of drama.

But the idea of the theater as a poetic touchstone is not alone sufficient to obviate or circumvent the conceptual difficulties that arise in the attempt to incorporate ὄψις, or theatrical representation, into the definition of a poetic genre. To complete the argument, one further step is needed, which Aristotle takes by insisting repeatedly that tragedy is the imitation *of an action* (μίμησις πράξεως, e.g., 50a16–17), not the representation of a person or people (50a16), and that if people are represented, it may only be by way of the action in which they are involved (50b3–4). For this doctrine implies that people should never be represented *except as interacting members of groups,* because an "action" or πρᾶξις, as this concept is understood in the *Poetics*, is never the action of one person but always the interaction within a group of people. Once the idea of "imitation of an action" has been introduced (49b24), we practically never hear of the persons in tragedy except in the plural: "persons acting" (πράττοντες) "make" the imitation (49b31); action must be done "by some agents" (49b37); character is that by which we say of what sort "the agents" are (50a5–6); tragedy imitates "the agents" by way of the action (50b3–4); and when the matter of which actions (πράξεις) produce pity and fear is broached, the first question is how the *people* involved are related to one another (53b15–17). Even in the discussion of how a man's moral and public standing should be related to his good or ill fortune—where the singular is more appropriate, since the various participants in a single action will differ in these respects, and where Aristotle does in fact come around to the singular halfway through (53a1–12)—the habit of thinking of dramatic characters in the plural still asserts itself in the opening sentences (52b34–37). And at the one point where we hear of "actions of one person" (πράξεις ἑνός, 51a18), the meaning is clearly those various actions in which, at different times and with different coparticipants, the one person may be involved. There is, finally, one occurrence of πρᾶξις in a nontechnical sense—that is, not referring to the whole of what a tragedy or a tragic plot imitates—in the passage where *pathos* is defined as "a deadly or painful action, like cases of killing, extreme pain, wounding and the like" (52b11–13). But even here, nothing suggests the absence of interaction.[4]

The full importance of this rule, however—that people should never be represented except as interacting members of a group—appears only when we recognize that for Aristotle it applies not only to tragedy but to *all poetry* or, at the very least, to all narrative and dramatic poetry. This point follows logically from the stipulation that narrative, like tragedy, is the imitation of an "action" (51a15–36, 59a17–b7), provided we agree that "action" means interaction in a group. But drama in the theater, assuming it to be a poetic form, is the one such form in which the imitation is *carried out* by just such a group—as opposed, for example, to a choral group that acts only in unison. Indeed, it is not even clear that the concept of "imitation" is strictly valid in cases where one person (or one voice) imitates the "action" of several people. It may be true that Homer approaches dramatic form when, after a short prelude, he immediately introduces his fictional persons (60a9–11); but if even that short prelude and its governing authorial voice can be dispensed with, if we have *nothing but* the interacting people who "make" and "imitate" the action (49b31, 60a8–9), then the form is that much more perfect. Therefore, if the doctrine of "imitation of an action" applies to all poetry, then the problem of understanding drama as a poetic genre has in a sense been solved. For it follows now that *all poetry* tends toward the condition of imitation by interacting members of a group, so that the actual fulfillment of this condition in drama has a strictly poetic value and can operate as a poetic definition.

All poetry tends or strives toward the condition of theatrical representation. But this theorem does not by any means imply, and does not need to imply, that the *effect* of poetry in the theater is more complete or perfect than in other expressive or representational situations. Again, Aristotle insists that even in the case of dramatic tragedy, the full power of the work should be available without a theater, without *opsis*, to someone who merely hears the story (50b19–20, 53b1–11). Theatrical effect, in other words, is not the issue; the actual effect of poetry on actual spectators is not a measure of anything. If it were, then the hypothetical argument in favor of epic, on the grounds that it is the "less vulgar imitation" (61b26–62a4), appealing generally to a better class of auditor, would be valid. The theater does not need to show any particular effectiveness in order to establish its position in relation to poetry. Its position, its excellence, and its necessary eventual reality are all *logically* given by the nature of poetry, by the doctrine of "imitation of an action." The only expectable empirical consequence of this logic—as we have seen—is the operation of the real theater as a touchstone for poetic merit.

The Inescapable Contradiction

Faced with an extremely thorny problem—how to include physical theatricality in the definition of drama as a poetic form—Aristotle thus develops a wonderfully ingenious theory: all poetry imitates action, but all action is interaction among people, so that drama, where the imitation is actually carried out by people interacting, discharges the poetic task most perfectly. But even this argument breaks down in the end; it breaks down even in Aristotle's own terms, for it leads to a contradiction that he himself implicitly acknowledges.

How can the idea that tragedy should show a change from good to bad fortune (53a13–15) be reconciled with the idea that the best form of tragic plot is the one in which the tragic act, the *pathos* or moment of suffering, is *prevented* by the characters' recognition of what they are about to do (53b34–36, 54a4–9)? Commentators try to wiggle out of this contradiction in various ways, usually by suggesting that the doctrine of an ending in misfortune applies to the plot as a whole, whereas the doctrine of a prevented *pathos* applies only to the climactic scene.[5] But in neither of the two conflicting passages does Aristotle give the impression of limiting the applicability of what he says. If we are honest about it, it is hard to see how we can avoid either simply accepting the presence of a contradiction or else perhaps conjecturing that the text incorporates and confuses two different stages in Aristotle's thought, two different versions of the argument.

And yet this last possibility presents difficulties of its own. For on the one hand, the idea that the best tragic plot moves from good fortune to bad is not only a fairly clear consequence of the doctrine of pity and fear (52b30–53a12) but also practically indisputable on empirical grounds (53a17–30). And on the other hand, that in the best plot *pathos* is prevented by recognition is an idea indispensable on *logical* grounds. Commentators have suggested that by advocating the prevention of *pathos*, Aristotle mainly wants to keep the abominable (τὸ μιαρόν: 53b39, 54a3) at as great a distance as possible. But the doctrine of *praxis* as interaction takes us further by providing a *technical* reason for the ranking of plots. For if the tragic deed is actually carried out and is followed by a recognition, then the recognition, in a sense, occurs *outside* the "action," since the tragic deed will have eliminated at least one of the most important participants in the action. There may still be several people interacting after the deed, but the most important and tragic interaction, the potentially deadly relation between kinfolk, will be gone. If, however, the recognition prevents the *pathos*, then that recognition belongs much more fully to the interaction that is *praxis*. The ranking of plots is thus logically implied by the doctrine of "action" as interaction, and the contradiction it implies is therefore integral to the argument, not merely an accidental feature that may have been changed from one version to the next.

Indeed, the doctrine of "action" as interaction, which had apparently solved the conceptual problem of drama and poetry, produces not only a logical contradiction but also critical difficulties with respect to what is obviously one of Aristotle's favorite works, Sophocles' *Oedipus the King*. For this is a play in which interaction among the characters is a decidedly secondary feature. Everything revolves around the single central figure; it is as if we were experiencing the play from inside Oedipus' head. "Here," says Else (p. 420), "through a feat of virtuosity which was not likely to be duplicated, the poet has managed to sublimate his plot-structure into a *pure nexus of recognition*." Everybody who reads the play recognizes this. But if Aristotle had read the play in this way, he would have had to consider it a play without a *praxis*, a strict artistic impossibility, which is obviously not his view. How, then, does Aristotle read *Oedipus*?

An answer to this question—assuming that the play must have a πρᾶξις and either an achieved or an intended πάθος—is suggested by Else. The *pathos*, says Else (pp. 349, 353, 357, 409, 420-21, etc.), is Oedipus' killing of Laius, even though it does not occur within the play's actual scope. Thus the plot conforms to Aristotle's second-best type—achieved *pathos* followed by recognition—not to the best; and what makes it at least comparable to the best type, as exemplified by *Iphigenia among the Taurians*, is "the attenuation of the *pathos*" (Else, p. 420) that results from having the tragic deed (the killing of Laius) done at a distance, outside the play, ἔξω τοῦ δράματος (53b32).

But this argument is untenable. In the first place, in all the other passages where Aristotle speaks of things "outside the play" (54b3) or "outside the tragedy" (54b7) or "outside of the whole plan, outside the myth" (55b7–8) or "outside the main story" (60a29), he means things that *should* be kept outside the play in order not to corrupt the unity and logic of its action. In the second place, two of these passages refer to things that *were* fortunately and correctly kept out of the central action of *Oedipus the King* itself:

> Among the incidents of the story there should be nothing illogical [ἄλογον], and if there is, then it should be kept outside the tragedy as it is in the *Oedipus* of Sophocles. (54b6–8)

> The plot should not be put together out of illogical elements, but, if possible, should have nothing illogical at all; or if it does, then the illogical should be outside the main story, as *Oedipus* has in it the hero's ignorance of how Laius died, but [this failure to learn is] not inside the drama. (60a27–31)

But if Else's view is correct, if the killing of Laius is really the work's *pathos*, hence a component of the central action, then Oedipus' "illogical" failure to learn how Laius died, since it follows the killing, would also belong to the "action," which Aristotle obviously denies.

The logical and critical situation thus seems hopeless and, in fact, probably is. But for the sake of leaving no stone unturned, I suggest one further possibility for interpreting the *Poetics*, a possibility that both circumvents the contradiction and offers a way for Aristotle to read *Oedipus*: the contradiction between ideas of the best form of plot disappears if we can demonstrate a case in which *both of the apparently contradictory conditions are completely fulfilled*. And it is conceivable that this case is exactly the one, exactly the text, we would expect: *Oedipus the King*. There is of course no question that *Oedipus* shows a change from good to bad fortune. The question is, how would Aristotle read the *plot* of that play? That is, if one reads *Oedipus* looking specifically for tragic *interaction*, what does one find? The answer is simple. The play shows Oedipus threatening to kill Creon (*OT*, 623–24) without knowing that the latter is his blood relative; but then he learns the truth about himself, hence also about Creon, and the *pathos* (the killing of Creon) is prevented by his recognition of the true situation. I do not mean to suggest that this is an acceptable reading of this particular tragedy. The motif of Oedipus' threat against Creon does not have anything like the structural prominence and centralness that would be required. But for Aristotle's purposes, this reading of Sophocles would have had the enormous advantage of vindicating his whole argument.[6]

Again, the chances that this is a correct reading of the *Poetics* are extremely small. And even if it is a correct reading—which would preserve him from logical contradiction—Aristotle's argument would still be defeated by the critical absurdity it implies. It is defeated at every turn, as I have said, by the inevitable difficulties that arise from trying to regard drama strictly as a genre of poetry. Without these basic difficulties, Aristotle would not have had to manufacture a poetic function for ὄψις, in the shaky idea of visibility as a poetic touchstone. And he would not have had to develop an idea of "action" that either leads to contradiction or else implies criteria for a dramatic plot so constraining that only one play in the entire literature could be construed (by misreading it) as satisfying them. If he had been able to do without the idea of an *essential* connection between theater (the mark of drama) and poetry, he would have been able to say simply, with Lucas, that *Oedipus* is "the best type of play" (poetically), whereas "*Cresphontes* and *IT* [*Iphigenia among the Taurians*] contained each a finer scene" (theatrically) (Lucas, p. 155). He went as far as he could, by saying that the *effect* of tragedy is produced even for someone who merely hears the story. But he could not go the step further that would have marked only the story as "poetic" and would have relegated its division into roles for multiple imitators to the status of a mere vehicle of transmission.

It is possible, as I have suggested, to speculate on why Aristotle could not take that step, on how the idea of drama as a poetic type gets established in his background and in his own thinking. But speculation on this point—on whether, for example, the integration of drama into the history and nature of poetry is a premise or a conclusion in Aristotle's thought—is not my project here. The argument I make is that, once established in Attic practice and Aristotelian theory, the idea of drama as a structurally integrated element of the whole of poetry exercises a conceptually corrupting influence and, perhaps for that very reason, a useful influence, on all of European literary tradition.

CHAPTER TWO

Genre and Drama:
The Historical and Theoretical Background

I begin here by pointing out, as in chapter 1, difficulties and inconsistencies in an established body of critical thought. As in chapter 1, however, nothing but the deepest respect, plus a kind of generational gratitude, is implied toward the thinkers of that thought and toward their courage in confronting the radically insurmountable problems of their discipline.

The Difficulty of Genre

In 1972, Paul Hernadi opened his book *Beyond Genre* by saying, "Interest in genre has been growing among contemporary critics of various persuasions."[1] I doubt, frankly, that that statement was true at the time it was written, and I am fairly certain that it is not true now—at least if we take "interest in genre" to mean a focused theoretical interest in the concept itself, not in particular examples. For the study of genre, compared with other critical or theoretical approaches, offers (depending on one's point of view) either the greatest promise or the greatest danger of *explaining* literature, of circumscribing its domain. Genre, if it could be shown to exist as a complete system of types, would imply an exhaustive definition of literature, a boundary beyond which literature could not pass without ceasing to be itself. And this hypothetical achievement conflicts very strongly with our sense of the history of at least Western literature as a repeated *overstepping* of its own boundaries, our insistence upon as much historical "originality" as possible in what we recognize as the literary or the poetic.

Critics therefore tend to be of two minds with regard to genre. On the one hand, it is difficult to justify *not* being particularly interested in a complex of questions that promises maximum insight into what Hernadi calls "The Order of Literature" (pp. 183–85). But on the other hand, we cannot help remembering that the recent history of our literature is positively littered with the ruins of intellectual edifices that had pretended to establish, in one way or another, its limits. Therefore we are careful to attenuate our systematizing, to stress the fluid distinctions between our concepts, the permeable or flexible quality of our outer boundaries. Hernadi follows this procedure in his summarizing section, "The Modes and Perspectives of Discourse" (pp. 156–70), which maps literary discourse into the space of difference between "vision" and "action" and culminates in a quadrangular diagram (p. 166) that includes a place for practically any literary form one might think of. "I hasten to add," he says then, "that the modes of discourse are not always clearly distinguishable" (p. 168). And at its outer edges, his diagram demonstrates not the limits of literature but rather the possibility of *gradual transitions* between the literary and such categories as "assertive discourse," "pantomime," and "other arts," including cinema, music, architecture, sculpture, painting, and photography (pp. 168–69).

But if Hernadi attenuates his system, as he does, to the point where it exerts no pressure on literature, where it simply accommodates everything and makes no attempt to pin down what literature actually is, then why construct the system in the first place? Lacking the concentrating force of definition, the system inevitably expands and becomes a general system of aesthetic philosophy, not different in kind (and in fact not a great deal different in content) from Hegel's in the *Vorlesungen über die Ästhetik*, except that Hegel—in the firm belief that art's historical destiny has been achieved[2]—is not inhibited from pursuing his project with the sort of maximum systematic rigor that Hernadi (for instance) insistently disavows. Again, therefore, what is Hernadi trying to accomplish?

The same question could be asked of the larger and more famous work that in many ways serves Hernadi as a model, Northrop Frye's *Anatomy of Criticism*. No reasonable person would deny that the *Anatomy* is a work about literature and, in fact, mainly about literary genre, which, broadly speaking, is the topic not only of the Fourth Essay, where it is named, but also of the First and the Third. But Frye himself, for all his elsewhere obvious reasonableness, does deny that his work is about literature. He insists that it is, instead, about "criticism," which he distinguishes from the "art" of literature by saying: "Physics is an organized body of knowledge about nature, and a student of it says that he is learning physics, not nature. Art, like nature, has to be distinguished from the systematic study of it, which is criticism." And yet further: "Criticism, rather, is to art what history is to action and philosophy to wisdom: a verbal imitation of a human productive power which in itself does not speak."[3]

These assertions are troubling. Wilhelm Dilthey's notion of "Geisteswis-senschaften" (usually translated, in English and French, as "human sciences") may have its shortcomings, but it does clearly imply a powerful critique of the very idea of "human productive powers" that "do not speak"—which idea, incidentally, is also undermined by the vision of a "verbal universe" (Frye, p. 350)—and I am not sure that even a Northrop Frye is justified in simply ignoring that critique.[4]

Why does Frye so emphatically adopt such an untenable point of view? Given what we have recognized about Hernadi's dilemma, the answer is clear: Frye does not want to be in the position of having to hedge or qualify his systematic arguments, or apologize for them. But as a theorist of literary genre, which he indisputably is, what choice does he have? In a stroke of either genius or gross irresponsibility—or both—he solves the problem by going ahead with the construction of an extremely detailed and tightly woven system while simply denying (unfoundedly) that it ever was or will be a system *of* literature in the first place. His own inevitable unhappiness with this situation appears eventually when he does after all make the gesture of hedging his position, in what he now calls a "Tentative Conclusion," especially its very last paragraph, where (in the course of comparing his project, interestingly enough, to the reading of *Finnegans Wake*) he concludes:

> Some such activity as this of reforging the broken links between creation and knowledge, art and science, myth and concept, is what I envisage for criticism. Once more, I am not speaking of a change of direction or activity in criticism: I mean only that if critics go on with their own business, this will appear to be, with increasing obviousness, the social and practical result of their labors. (p. 354)

Even leaving aside the quibble about who, if not Frye himself in his "Polemical Introduction," has most recently "broken the link between creation and knowledge"—not to mention the question of whether the words "appear to be" are a treacherous slip of the pen—we are still deeply puzzled, as with Hernadi, about what is meant to be accomplished here. If the sum of what we learn is to "go on with our own business," then why was the whole immense project undertaken to begin with?

Genre and the Conservative Tendency in Literature

There has to be an answer to that question, but it will not be an answer in the form we would expect. I think we will find it necessary to explain what Frye and Hernadi are doing, and others like them, not in terms of a goal aimed at but rather in terms of a kind of maddening itch that needs to be scratched, a problem that cannot be solved yet cannot in conscience be left alone. Frye and Hernadi, like most North American critics, are basically liberal in temper, and the notion of genre is therefore deeply disturbing to them—as it is, for that matter, to me. For "genre," among other things, names an inveterate *conservative* tendency in literature. Genres cannot be invented; they operate as genres, as basic guides for how to read texts, only by *already* being there, prior to the text in question. Genres cannot be overturned or destroyed; if I deliberately flout the rules of a particular genre, then I am still *invoking* precisely that genre as a guide to understanding me. Genres evolve over time, of course, but not in ways we can predict or control. Genre thus has the character of tradition, but only in the sense that we experience tradition as *confining*; and the more we think about genre, the more we are worried by the prospect of having to admit that literature itself, as a whole, is nothing but tradition in just this sense. How can literature ever be significantly original or revolutionary, or even progressive, if our very first step in understanding a text, the mere identification of a "literary" text, involves a recognition of its belonging integrally to an extensive body of established fact for whose description we routinely use such metaphors as canonicity and immortality?

I am of course using the term "genre" loosely here, in a manner that encompasses our common idea of literary types, the structured articulation of literature suggested in books such as Frye's and Hernadi's, and the hermeneutic notion advanced by Friedrich Schleiermacher and developed by (for instance) E. D. Hirsch.[5] But I excuse my procedure on the grounds that the integrity of genre as a concept is not yet at issue here. I am talking about genre as a broad area of thought that either attracts or awakens our concern about a strongly conservative aspect of literature, and I am trying to keep things as simple as possible. I do not, for instance, mean to refer to anything like the agonistic quality of poetic tradition as Harold Bloom presents it in *The Anxiety of Influence*. Our relation to genre can never be agonistic; genre has not the kind of face, character, identity that might make it an adversary. It is simply there, as a weight, a confining limit on what literature *can* say, a kind of ghostly editor who alters not a single word yet manages to give us back our manuscripts (when we reread ourselves) with everything truly revolutionary expunged.

T. S. Eliot, it is true, who uses the term "tradition" more or less in my loose sense of "genre," sees the matter in a less troubling light: "The existing monuments form an ideal order among themselves, which is modified by the introduction of the new (the really new) work of art among them. The existing order is complete before the new work arrives; for order to persist after the supervention of novelty, the *whole* existing order must be, if ever so slightly, altered; and so the relations, proportions, values of each work of art toward the whole are readjusted; and this is conformity between the old and the new."[6] But this fanciful, unverifiable, and I think strained view of tradition—with its conspiratorial insistence on the "really" new—like Hans-Georg Gadamer's comparably unverifiable and strained argument on "hermeneutic conversation,"[7]—is in my opinion really only a denial of the obvious, a scratching of the itch of genre.

Literature, Discourse, Communication: Is Literature Conservative?

And yet, if the hermeneutic notion of preunderstanding, or interpretive hypothesis, is a main part of what I mean by genre, then the specifically literary quality of the argument appears to evaporate, because genre in this sense affects and limits the understanding of *all* discourse. And to call all discourse "conservative" would be silly, since there could be nothing liberal or revolutionary, on the same scale, against which to measure it.

This objection is met by the consideration that there are different manners and degrees of "understanding discourse" and that literature (practically by definition) is that area of discourse where we make the greatest demands on our understanding; where we insist on understanding better, more deeply and completely, with more perfect unanimity, than elsewhere, and where we expect our understanding to be correspondingly rewarded; where meaning is expected to take something close to the form of prophetic vision or Sir Philip Sidney's "heart-ravishing knowledge."[8] It is in literature, therefore, that we—as writers or as readers—suffer most intensely the limits of understanding, especially the operation of genre, which means that in the field of literature we find it difficult, in strict honesty, even to *pretend* to adopt a political or cultural position that is not conservative. And pretense is entirely crucial in the relation of discourse to political and social practice, pretense in the sense of that suspension of the critical faculty (Nietzsche calls it "illusion") without which no decisive action can ever be undertaken. All discourse that aspires to the quality of action, all revolutionary or even merely liberal discourse, is characterized by this pretense, by an impatient and peremptory *Ça ira* that cuts short (by a head, so to speak) the endless brooding of discourse upon itself which is literature.

This point is perhaps a gloomy answer but, I think, a correct answer to the question posed long ago by Lionel Trilling:

> If we . . . consider the contemporary literature of America, we see that wherever we can describe it as patently liberal and democratic, we must say that it is not of lasting interest. . . . The sense of largeness, of cogency, of the transcendence which largeness and cogency can give, the sense of being touched in our secret and primitive minds—this we virtually never get from the writers of the liberal democratic tradition at the present time.

And since liberal democracy inevitably generates a body of ideas, it must necessarily occur to us to ask why it is that these particular ideas have not infused with force and cogency the literature that embodies them.[9]

The trouble is that literature's largeness and cogency, in Trilling's sense, are indissolubly bound up with its discursive scrupulousness, its hesitancy (in this one respect) about pretending, its attentiveness to an understanding of genre that saps the energy of liberalism. The effect of the eloquence in Trilling's dream of "an active literature" (p. 293) is thus to exhibit and in a sense energize the problem of genre, precisely in its insolubility.

This argument does not support the conclusion that literature simply "is" conservative, in the sense of being absolutely inconsistent with revolutionary or liberal thought. (At most we can speak of a conservative "tendency" in literature.) For the operation of genre, on which such an apodictic conclusion would have to depend, is understood only as a logical *necessity* and can never be ascertained as a *fact*. Facts are by definition communicable, and within the framework of what genre could one conceivably communicate the factualness of genre as such? (This problem is a corollary of Jacques Derrida's argument in "La Loi du genre.")[10] Of course, particular genres of literature, or of extraliterary discourse, are in an obvious sense facts, about which any amount of communicable knowledge can be developed. But the quality of those genres as an indispensable *condition of communication* always escapes that body of knowledge, always tantalizingly recedes from the realm of the factual.

And questions of communication and communicable meaning arise at every turn in the discussion of genre as a problem. Hirsch says, for example: "Now a genre is a kind and shape of utterance whose norms and conventions have been partly fixed through past usage. Every communicable utterance belongs to a genre so defined, and in communicated speech there can be no such thing as a radically new genre, for so-called new genres are always, by linguistic and social necessity, extensions and variations of existing norms and conventions" (p. 262). The immediately recognizable bearer of liberal hopes in these sentences is the word "partly," which is meaningless, being based on no conceivable method of measurement. But perhaps there is a more genuine hope in the question of communication. For if we could have literature *without* presupposing communication, if we could have "largeness and cogency" *without* the postulate of communicability and hence without the logical necessity of a conservative operation of genre, then perhaps we could have an "active" literature after all. I will come back to this matter later on.

Types of Genre

Nowadays, the terminology of "works" and their "genres" has been supplanted in much criticism by the idea of "text," which—when its use is based on a real distinction from other concepts, not merely on the dictates of fashion—refers not to a discrete unit of writing but to the particular instance of a larger *process* of meaning-production in the form of social or cultural or intellectual history. But even if texts, in this understanding, appear capable of a kind of historical agency, an "active" role in society, still the problem of genre is thus merely avoided, not solved. For the notion of a liberal or revolutionary literature is meaningless in practice except insofar as literature leaps a categorical divide between writing and brute reality. ("Leben die Bücher bald?" [When will your books come to life?] asks Friedrich Hölderlin scornfully of those who think this divide easily bridged.)[11] And such a divide is simply *absent* in theories of the textual domain as a historical or social process. The question is simply begged.

But if, at least, there are avenues of inquiry that avoid the problem of genre, and if in fact such avenues, like the notion of textuality, can prove definitely fruitful and on occasion positively revelatory in their own right, then we are brought back to the question of how the procedure of a Frye or a Hernadi can possibly be justified. And only one type of answer appears possible, provided we hold these authors in the esteem to which the interpretive and theoretical details of their work entitle them: both books must be understood as deliberately *refusing* to avoid the question of genre, as deliberately setting out to meet the matter of genre head-on, to analyze it in detail and lay it out for us to see, thus to place it—in whatever degree—under our control, rather than simply submit to its controlling operation in our discursive, especially literary practice. But since we have also seen that a project of this sort cannot possibly be carried out with any reasonable approximation of success, again we must ask, what hope motivates Frye and Hernadi to press on nonetheless?

It is, I think, a hope based on a kind of categorical legerdemain, which we can understand by dividing the concept of genre into three types. The first we might call *historical-prescriptive*, referring to all those traditionally hallowed poetic forms for which at least approximate rules can be written down: for example, the sonnet (fourteen lines, originally and still frequently hendecasyllables, with a prescribed rhyme scheme, on the topic of love), or the epic (long narrative poem on heroic material, usually in hexameters). Genres of this type (at least from our point of view) are defined *arbitrarily*, not systematically. To ask why the sonnet has fourteen lines and not fifteen is the same as to ask why Olympic sprinters race 100 meters and not 107. That 100 is a round number stands in an entirely arbitrary relation to the actual business of running. The rules of the genre are simply a prescribed task that the poet undertakes in competition with other poets.

The second type encompasses genre in the sense that creates the problems I have been discussing, and I call it *hermeneutic*. A hermeneutic genre is more or less the same thing as a preunderstanding, or an interpretive hypothesis, as long as these are understood to be historically or publicly established, not mere individual fancies. Unlike historical-prescriptive genres, hermeneutic genres (it appears) *must* eventually form a system. Otherwise, there would be radical and unaccountable disjunctions between what we understand as the "understanding" of different types of text. Of course, there are differences between modes of understanding; but the unity of language (or of a particular language), the quality of language as a single large system (assuming it has this quality), guarantees that those differences can never wholly obscure the fundamental relatedness of what they separate. And yet, on the other hand—for reasons I have already discussed—the system of hermeneutic genres, however necessary it may be, can never actually be plotted or ascertained as a fact. It remains beyond our conceptual grasp, because no single genre of utterance can communicate it.

And finally, we may distinguish the *structural* type of genre, where genres are defined and related to one another according to criteria derived from a systematic analysis of discourse or of literature. The most obvious example is the tripartite division of literature into epic, lyric, and dramatic types, which are systematically distinguished (in Frye's version of the system) according to whether the poet and the audience are aware of each other (epic), or the audience is concealed from the poet (lyric), or the poet is concealed from the audience (drama). Frye himself adds a fourth type, "the genre of the written word" (p. 303), which he calls "fiction," but the systematicity remains, since in fiction, poet and audience are in a strong sense concealed from each other. And systematicity is the key here, a symmetrical and transparent systematicity that consoles us for our inability to achieve a similar view of hermeneutic genres.

Once we start looking at genre in this way, it becomes fairly clear that Frye and Hernadi both violate the boundary between structural genre and hermeneutic genre, or perhaps, rather, try to reduce the latter to the former in order to gain systematic control over it.[12] That something of this sort is actually present in of the minds of both can be seen from a telling similarity between what Frye says at the very beginning about his book's usefulness and what Hernadi says on the same topic at the very end. Frye says:

> The gaps in the subject [literary criticism] as treated here are too enormous for the book ever to be regarded as presenting *my* system, or even my theory. It is to be regarded rather as an interconnected group of suggestions which it is hoped will be of some practical use to critics and students of literature. Whatever is of no practical use to anybody is expendable. (p. 3)

And what he means by "practical use" (or perhaps we should say, what he *has to* mean) is spelled out a bit more clearly by Hernadi:

Surely, theoretical constructs . . . are but distant pointers to the living reality
of literary works. Yet they may provide a flexible conceptual framework for
the historical study of more concretely definable generic traditions. And
they can, I think, help explicate and evaluate any given work of imaginative literature as a presentation and representation of human action and
vision. (pp. 184–85)

Both men, after making the ritual gesture of denying—as plausibly as they
can—the systematicity of their highly systematic thought, then insist that
their work must be justified by its "practical" usefulness, which can only
mean its usefulness *in the practice of interpretation*, which in turn implies that
they are after all offering their system-generated concepts as *hermeneutic*
genres. Do not regard my work as systematic, each one is saying, because
there can never be a communicable and usable system of hermeneutic genres, which my work nevertheless is.

The Illogic of Literature

Whether this situation is disgracefully illogical or gloriously illogical,
whether it is a sign of basic corruptness in literary thought or the sign of a
tragic defiance in the face of stern necessity, it is in either case thoroughly
illogical and thoroughly typical. It is the kind of situation literary thought
tends repeatedly to get itself into. Nor does it appear very difficult, from the
point we have reached, to understand why this should be so. For the conservative tendency in literature, associated with genre, must inevitably collide
with the liberal or progressive tendency that is manifest in such ideas as
genius and originality, or in the idea—more or less Theodor Adorno's[13]—
that art in general, hence literature, is in a sense fundamentally "opposed to
society" and so harbors the possibility of a radical social critique.

   In fact, even the discussion of genre shows a progressive aspect, in the
picture of literary history that was prevalent for much of the nineteenth and
twentieth centuries, according to which a new age or epoch is born when
the "rules" of literature (the constraints associated with historical-prescriptive genre) are broken by a rising generation of writers. If we manage to
understand those rules as the expression, or somehow the equivalent, of
subliminal cultural determinants—if, in other words, we permit ourselves a
certain confusion of historical-prescriptive with hermeneutic genre—then
the invalidating of traditional constraints in literature can be regarded as a
historically progressive activity, a contribution to future-shaping. There are
some very important and very excellent works of literary criticism that are
not free of this particular bending of concepts: for example, Erich Auerbach's *Mimesis*, where the various incarnations of high and low style are
clearly genres in my broad sense of the term.

The more we think about the penchant for self-contradiction or self-opposition in literary studies, the more inevitable it appears. For although the very idea of "literature," in the modern sense, does not arise until the eighteenth century and is not widely accepted until the nineteenth, still, at the same time, "literature" is meant to be understood as the direct historical continuation of everything in the Hellenic-European tradition that had been known as "poetry." Homer, we say—without blushing—belongs to the history of literature, which is more or less like saying that Icarus belongs to the history of aviation. Of course we are careful to concede that literary tradition contains breaks or discontinuities. German Romantic writers saw the difference between classical antiquity and Christian Europe as crucial; for Harold Bloom the crisis is marked by Descartes, for T. S. Eliot by Milton, for Foucauldians by Kant, and Roland Barthes draws a line in the middle of the nineteenth century. But if the idea of a discontinuous tradition is to make any sense at all—and no one is rash enough to deny the historical discontinuity of literature—then it can never be understood in a radical sense; it can never do without the recognition of a basic level of uninterrupted connectedness in the tradition it refers to. Otherwise, how could one speak of a "tradition" in the first place? In particular, how could one even identify "literature"?

And if we ask after the presumed level of historical continuity that gives literature what we take to be its identity, we are brought back inescapably to the notion of genre. Attempts have been made to describe the perennial "spirit" of literature, or the necessary figural or metaphorical mechanism of literary language, but such ideas are always far too debatable to serve the purpose of basic identity foundation. What gives literature, for us, the character of literature, through the ages, is nothing but that we posit as a definition (that we enclose within a more or less arbitrary boundary) a collection of specific identifiable *types* of writing, a collection in which we accept a certain amount of evolution over time but which never undergoes violent disruption. That the boundary of literature is arbitrary is evident, especially, in our disagreement about exactly where it is located—a disagreement that appears mainly in relation to prose forms, since practically all verse, or all writing traditionally classified as "poetry," is included automatically. (Aristotle would have balked here.) But precisely in the period where the actual concept of "literature" arises, an extension of its boundary deep into the realm of prose is unavoidable, since this is also the period in which—for any number of cultural reasons—the novel establishes itself once and for all as a leading vehicle of poetic expression.

It follows, in turn, from the arbitrariness of their selection, that the genres that make up literature are of the historical-prescriptive type. They continue to exist, or to develop, mainly because they *have* existed, not because they possess some radically human or logically derivable reason for existing. And this fact creates a problem, for at least two reasons. In the first place, it is an instance of the conservative tendency in literature and so conflicts with the liberal or liberalizing tendency that is already present in the conceptual shift by which "literature" is born. In the second place, the quality of arbitrariness conflicts with the needful operation of literary genres in *making sense* out of a history, a tradition supposedly dating back to Homer, which otherwise (without somehow making sense) would simply not be there.

The result of all these considerations is, first, that the notion of genre is a prominent part of literature's self-understanding, that the question of genre therefore cannot be permanently avoided or suppressed, that practitioners of literature—be they poets or critics—must always yet again find themselves confronted with that question; and, second, that the historical-prescriptive type is not sufficient to discharge the function assigned to genre in the development of "literature" as a historically anchored reality. It follows, since hermeneutic genre resists any direct conceptual approach, that literary thinkers have no choice but to experiment in the area of *structural* genre, which means we have come full circle and are faced again with the problems faced by, and presented by, authors like Hernadi and Frye.

The Corruption of Literature

It would not be correct to say that we are talking here about "aporias" in literary thinking. For whereas aporia is normally a quality of concepts and their formal relations, the illogic of literature is rooted in the *historical* situation in which the concept "literature" is first formed, which is to say that it characterizes literature less as a concept than as an *institution*. And aporia cannot characterize an institution in the same way it does a concept. Well-known aporias arise in the development of the concept of origin, for instance, especially as it is applied to language. But these logical difficulties do not prevent us from using the concept; in fact, they give the concept a clear contour and structure, marked by internal tension, which can then be employed to suggest critical arguments in related conceptual areas. In the case of an institution, however, a comparable internal tension, the tension of contradiction, becomes negative and ultimately destructive. The more nearly *material* quality of an institution's existence, and the need for its conceptual aspect to have a chronologically plausible history, cannot tolerate illogic. Therefore, when an institution like literature, characterized at its origin by illogic, is nevertheless favored by historical accidents that establish its existence more or less permanently—as literature is favored by the usefulness of the fiction of "national literature" in forging a cultural shape for modern European bourgeois nation-states—then that institution, from the moment of its birth, is corrupt and self-deceived.

This reasoning does not of course imply that writers on or of literature are corrupt as individuals. On the contrary, the same combination of characteristics that marks literature as corrupt, a deep-seated illogic plus an established institutional permanence, can be interpreted quite differently, as the signature of an especially challenging and eminently "human" discipline of knowledge: its permanence an indication of how deeply ingrained it is in our culture, if not perhaps in our very nature; its illogic an invitation to our creativity and judgment, in preference to the more mechanical mental faculties. And it is clear that all the authors quoted above would be at least inclined or tempted, in perfect honesty, to subscribe to this view of literature.

But then, how can we tell the difference? Why is it necessary to take the dimmest possible view, to draw extreme conclusions from our encounter with logical difficulties in thinking about literature? There are, in any event, plenty of modern writers who manage to combine their literary activity with a thoroughly radical grasp of literature's corruptness. One thinks immediately of Nietzsche, and of a number of French writers: Artaud and André Gide certainly, Stéphane Mallarmé, perhaps even Gustave Flaubert. And one thinks of Goethe, for whom the wrongness or corruptness of literature emerges from its inevitable association with various European manifestations of nationalism. "Literary Sansculottism" is how it occurs to Goethe to describe the assignment to literature of the function of producing modern national "classics."[14]

Of course, it helps to have Goethe on your side, but for the purpose of distinguishing between the view of literature as corrupt and the less desperate view in European and American literary education, I think the argument I have suggested about aporia and institutionality is sufficient. And in order to see how literary corruptness plays out in practice, we might turn to a well-known passage from Paul de Man's "Literary History and Literary Modernity." De Man does insist that the illogic of literature is an aporia and in fact envisages a literary history "that would be able to maintain the literary aporia throughout, [to] account at the same time for the truth and the falsehood of the knowledge literature conveys about itself." Then, a few sentences later, he continues:

> The relationship between truth and error that prevails in literature cannot be represented genetically, since truth and error exist simultaneously, thus preventing the favoring of the one over the other. The need to revise the foundations of literary history may seem like a desperately vast undertaking; the task appears even more disquieting if we contend that literary history could in fact be paradigmatic for history in general, since man himself, like literature, can be defined as an entity capable of putting his own mode of being into question. The task may well be less sizable, however, than it seems at first. . . . To become good literary historians, we must remember that what we usually call literary history has little or nothing to

do with literature and that what we call literary interpretation—provided only it is good interpretation—is in fact literary history. If we extend this notion beyond literature, it merely confirms that the bases for historical knowledge are not empirical facts but written texts, even if these texts masquerade in the guise of wars or revolutions.[15]

The fundamentally liberal impulse of literary thought is apparent here in the opposition against an overriding and unchallenged idea of truth that would unquestionably entail rigid conservatism as a consequence. But the vocabulary already signals a dilemma, since the very definitions of truth and error make "favoring" the latter inconceivable. And de Man's response to this dilemma—which is the problem of how to imagine literature *in* history, where the opposition of truth and error cannot happen without a referential (or "genetic") component that would obstruct their supposed simultaneity—is to turn the situation inside out and imagine history, all history, as happening *inside* literature, inside the domain of "written texts" and "interpretations," provided the latter are "good" interpretations: that is, provided they insist on exactly that version of anthropology which, by understanding man as an "entity" similar (if not equivalent) to literature, makes them themselves into the very fabric of human history as a whole.

Thus the liberal impulse of literature is corrupted at its root. For as I noted above in connection with the idea of textuality as a way of historicizing the condition of the individual piece of writing, literature cannot be liberal or progressive, let alone revolutionary, except in the presence of a categorical divide between the literary domain and brute physical or political reality. To the extent that literature assimilates reality to itself—or even itself to reality—its character is ineluctably conservative, its activity focused on maintaining and elaborating its identity *as* literature. Only to the extent that it is categorically different from reality can literature be thought of as mounting a significant critical challenge to that reality. "Die Sprache ist das Haus des Seins" (Language is the house of Being), says Heidegger, and appears thereby to have established a special philosophical power and privilege for poetry, or for literature in general. "Das Sein . . . bleibt verborgen. Aber das Weltgeschick kündigt sich in der Dichtung an, ohne daß es schon als Geschichte des Seins offenbar wird" ("Being remains hidden. But world-destiny announces itself in poetry, without yet being revealed as the history of Being).[16] And like de Man, Heidegger has thus taken the one step too far that cripples poetry, or literature in general, leaving a strictly conservative advocacy as the only possible political component of its meaning.

This, I think—although neither of them would have explained it in exactly these terms—is basically why Frye and Hernadi after him commit themselves to the impossible project of merging structural with hermeneutic genre. For the resulting *system* of hermeneutic genres promises to have the effect—if perhaps only the temporary effect, until its inevitable flaws are exposed—of shaping and situating literature *in* the world (rather than situating the world in literature), thus keeping open, if perhaps only temporarily, the possibility of literature's critical or restorative or revolutionary operation *on* the world. This is criticism as a kind of Thermopylae, but its hope is ultimately empty. Literature is as corrupt for Frye as it is for de Man, even if there is a fairly clear difference in temper between the theorist who concludes simply that we should "go on with our own business" and the theorist who, in saying substantially the same thing, adds a requirement—that our interpreting be "good"—by which our own business can be subjected to external authority after all.[17]

Literature is a kind of infernal machine. It comes into being, in the age of a nascent "aesthetics," side by side with the idea of artistic *autonomy*, the idea that art, not shackled by any need to prove its utility in real society, is capable of a visionary transcendence of mundane social norms, which seems to imply that it has a unique revolutionary potential. But precisely the autonomy of literature—assuming that this attribution is valid— implies that its self-identity can have no anchor outside itself, which means that literature, in order to continue being the revolutionary force it supposedly is, must understand itself by way of the collection of established genres that constitutes it—if it does not go de Man's or Heidegger's one step further and claim historical *hegemony*, which turns out to have the same effect—so that precisely its revolutionary vigor engenders inevitably its conservative helplessness.

One obvious question affects this whole argument. When we say that literature is characterized by illogic, the consequence of corruption does not follow unless we mean "literature" in exactly the same sense in which we recognize literature *as an institution*. But I maintain that we do mean literature in this sense. Literature as an institution is not sustained, for example, by the modern publishing industry or by the modern reading public. These two elements of society may, respectively, produce and consume literature, but they do so indiscriminately; literature is for them only one product among many. Literature's quality as an institution in its own right, by contrast, depends entirely on the position and stature accorded it in our systems of education, which is to say that it is sustained (and created) as an institution by nothing but the repetition and development of exactly the type of critical reflection that produces its illogic. Or to put it differently, there is no clear separation between theory and practice in literature— whatever Frye might say to the contrary. The practice of literature could not produce works that would be recognized as "literature" (which means that the practice would in effect not exist) if readers were not taught in school to carry out such a recognition. And even if we cannot establish firm criteria for distinguishing "literature" from other sorts of writing, we can still say that one indispensable quality of the "literary" work is that it be on some level *serious*, which means that it must give the impression of reflecting carefully upon its own form and purport, that it must have, in other words, a theoretical dimension.

Drama Is Not a Literary Type

But what does all this have to do with drama or theater? To answer this question, one must begin with a clear grasp of the sense in which drama both *is not* and yet also *is* an integral part of "literature" as the latter has come to be understood in the European history of writing. Since the end of the eighteenth century, in the wake of theoretical speculations by such figures as Goethe and Hegel, we have developed the habit of relating theatrical drama to literature as a whole by way of this or that system of structural genres, even if "genre" is not always the word used to describe the system in question. Aristotle, we have seen, already feels obliged to manipulate his concepts so that the system of types of imitation situates drama as a subtype of poetry. And Frye argues no less illegitimately in his system of "radicals of presentation," where he defines drama, in relation to epic, as that form in which the author is concealed from the audience:

> In drama, the hypothetical or internal characters of the story confront the audience directly, hence the drama is marked by the concealment of the author from his audience. . . . In *epos*, the author confronts his audience directly, and the hypothetical characters of the story are concealed. The author is still theoretically there when he is being represented by a rhapsode or minstrel, for the latter speaks as the poet, not as a character in the poem. In written literature both the author and his characters are concealed from the reader. (p. 249)

For all its intelligence from sentence to sentence, the argument here, as a whole, seems to me to create insurmountable problems for itself. Does Frye mean concealment in a strictly visual sense? Then his system does not work for lyric poetry, where "the concealment of the poet's audience from the poet" is merely something that "the lyric poet normally pretends" is the case. And if we move even the slightest bit away from simple visibility as a criterion, then the question of whether we are actually "confronted directly" by the *characters* of a drama arises, whether those characters are not after all more deeply concealed by the interposition of interpreting actors than they would be by the simple text. And even if we attempt to retain the criterion of visibility (and find something else to do with lyric), we still have to ask about the status, for example, of the stage adaptation of a novel. Frye responds:

> We have to speak of the *radical* of presentation if the distinctions of acted, spoken, and written word are to mean anything in the age of the printing press. One may print a lyric or read a novel aloud, but such incidental changes are not enough in themselves to alter the genre. For all the loving care that is rightfully expended on the printed texts of Shakespeare's plays, they are still radically acting scripts, and belong to the genre of drama. (p. 247)

The novel adapted for stage presentation, in other words, is still "radically" a novel. But if the novel happens not to be a very good one, and the stage version turns out to be brilliant, will we not be tempted to conclude that the original author had produced something "radically" dramatic without knowing it?

With respect to Frye's account of "radicals," I think it is clear that we must ask, as with Aristotle, why he insists on regarding drama as a basic literary type in the first place. If we remove drama from the equation, the need for the criterion of visibility vanishes, and one could construct a simple scale of rhetorical possibilities, using as a criterion the extent to which the author pretends to be (or writes as if he were) aware of his or her real ultimate audience, along with, perhaps—as a refining factor—the extent to which the utterance pretends to acknowledge the audience's awareness of its author.

And if the criterion of visibility, in any form, only disrupts the system of literary genres and so is of no use in classifying drama, the criterion of "mode of enunciation" produces conceptual disorder even more quickly.[18] The idea that all drama belongs to that class of utterances in which the author speaks never "as himself" but always in the person of one of a number of more or less fictional characters is historically an evident overstraining of Plato's famous argument in book 3 of the *Republic*. Plato's focus is upon the concept of imitation, upon how that concept must be applied in education, and, by consequence, upon the indirect or tangential educative effects of different types of poetic discourse (394D–398B). He does not claim to have established a system of clearly distinguished types of "enunciation"; his concepts do not permit any such claim. If one interrogates those concepts on any but a relatively superficial level, one finds it difficult, for example, to distinguish between the case of an author who uses the "imitative" dialogue form and that of a strictly "diegetic" author who from time to time says such things as, "To look at the matter from another point of view . . ." or "It could be objected that. . . ." After all, if it is still the author who is "enunciating," how is the dialogue-persona not reducible to a figure of speech? At least in the *Republic*, such a reduction must be possible, for otherwise that text itself would not exemplify that "unmixed imitation of the fair or reasonable [τοῦ ἐπιεικοῦς]" (397D) which it advocates.

And if we ask now why any number of modern thinkers still attempt to make fundamental discourse theory out of Plato's ad hoc pedagogical distinction between speaking as oneself and speaking as someone else—as if one ever *really* spoke, let alone wrote, "as oneself"—the only possible answer is, to make room for drama in a theoretically founded system of poetic genres. Not that this end would be accomplished *even if the theory were sound*, for drama is not pure dialogue and never has been. The earliest examples in our tradition contain long choral odes for which the fictional identity of the chorus is obviously only a pretext, and indispensable parts of the plot are more often than not supplied by "messengers," whose function is patently narrative. Then, later, come texts with detailed stage directions which eventually blossom—as with Shaw (see chapter 7)—into short, witty essays. Shall we dismiss these pieces of language as immaterial in determining the work's genre? By the same token, we could dismiss everything but direct quotation and the reporting of characters' thoughts in a novel. And suppose, in a play with no stage directions at all, a character named "Oedipus" or "Clytemnestra" appears before us. Is the name not already itself a stage direction, the communication, from author to audience, of a necessary background for the dialogue? And in a play where the characters are not known to us from myth or history, do we not listen in a special way for the details of "exposition"—characters' calling each other by name, title, or kinship designation, and such like—so that these details become in effect stage directions or a narrative framework? And even if we succeed, after all, in developing for drama a modern version of Aristotle's idea of the text's tending in the direction of imitation by a group, it is hard to see how our argument will not already have been gone one better by M. M. Bakhtin's view of the multistyled and multivoiced novel.[19]

What all this boils down to is plain: drama is not a literary type. This is plain even without going back to the point I suggested in connection with Aristotle, that you cannot think "drama" without thinking "theater," and that "theater" names not by any stretch of reasoning a literary category but rather an institution whose substance is situated in brutally real architecture and organization—an institution that would not exist if stone were not piled on stone, person not subordinated to person, in a particular way.

> For there is nothing whatever that is rhetorically or formally unique about a dramatic text; there is no characteristic or set of characteristics, or complex of "family resemblances," by which we would recognize a dramatic text as something different from a narrative text, *if we did not know about the institution of the theater*, if the theater, as an institution, were not already there to be "meant" as the text's vehicle. Otherwise a character's name, followed by a colon and some clearly fictional words, would be an entirely transparent shorthand for the sentence, "X said . . . ," and we would

immediately understand that the general literary type is narrative. [And yet,] we also reserve a special *literary* category for texts that are distinguished by nothing except what we recognize, somehow, as a fundamental association with the theater.[20]

This passage is from my own book, *Theater As Problem*—to which the present argument is a sequel—and I reproduce it here because I cannot think of a better way of saying what I said then. And my point now, as then, is that the "somehow" by which we distinguish drama from other literature is always in truth arbitrary, never a distinction of type that is generalizable in literary terms.

On the Contrary, Drama Is in Fact a Literary Type

And yet it is preposterous to suggest that drama, *as* theatrical drama, is not part of literature. Drama is in fact *by definition* a part of literature, insofar as it is the very nature of "literature"—as the concept first arises and as it is codified in histories of national literature—to include indiscriminately, as part of its larger range, all traditionally sanctioned poetic forms, including "drama." How, in any case, could we have ever developed the habit of talking about "scenes"—or, more generally, about a "scenic" quality—in narrative, or about the "tragic" or "comic" quality of fictional works, or about "pace" or "climax" or the management of "narrative time," if we were not making understood comparisons with drama, if it were not perfectly natural for us to think of literature, and to assume that others think of literature, as being staged in the mind, thus effortlessly including actual drama as a type?

On a somewhat more complex conceptual level, I will appeal one more time to my argument in *Theater As Problem*:

Drama is unquestionably a [literary] genre in the deep sense, in fact a genre par excellence. For it operates not only upon our preunderstanding within its own particular domain, but also, directly and crucially, upon our preunderstanding, our attitude, our situation, our mode of existence, with respect to the literary at large. Drama, especially, is the locus of: the happening of the literary as a human *act*; the maintenance of the "outside" and of semiurgic indeterminacy as literary conditions; a constant resistance to the organic metaphor for literary form, and to the idea of uniformity of response. (p. 256)

The question of literature's "outside" is one I have already discussed, in connection with the point that a categorical divide between social reality and the literary realm is presupposed by any reasonable idea of a revolutionary potential in literature. And where can literature actually achieve contact with that "outside"—which it tends normally either to exclude or to absorb—if not in the form, at once thoroughly literary and brutally real, of theatrical drama?

The other ideas alluded to in the passage above are the subject of much discussion in *Theater As Problem* but are not difficult to understand in themselves. "Semiurgic indeterminacy" means the impossibility of deciding whether the meanings of drama should be classified as signification or as reference: signification being that semiurgic or sign-working process (normally recognized as dominant in literature) in which the signifier is *prior* in operation to the signified, which latter itself always has the character of a sign, not that of a somehow nonsignifying reality; reference being that process (normally thought of as characterizing daily experience) in which the sign *responds* to a prior "referent," which has, at least relatively, the character of preexisting reality. The important point about signification and reference is that each represents a *complete* theory of meaning that excludes the other, so that when theatrical drama appears to require that the two operate together, the result is a radical challenge to the very idea of communicable meaning. And I have noted above that such a challenge offers hope of circumventing the conservative tendency that is built into the concept of hermeneutic genre. Again, this is a matter I will return to in greater detail.

The organic metaphor for literary form, the idea that every true or good literary work is somehow a strict natural unity (which unity then forms the object for a type of uniform readerly response that is equally natural and prior to all interpretive disagreement) is an idea that belongs clearly to the conservative side of literary theory. The work's unity and self-containment become the single ultimate goal of all reading and interpretation, and the practice of literature is reduced to the worship of a pantheon of classical instances whose very nature—even if, as Eliot imagines, they shift position slightly from time to time (think Dante in Limbo) to accommodate a newcomer—is to be unchanging. But the application of the organic metaphor to drama is always thwarted, first, by "the ontological defectiveness of the dramatic text" (*Theater As Problem*, p. 61), our inevitable recognition—based on our assumptions about the work's relation to the theater—that the text, as we read it, as *mere* text, is constitutionally incapable of delivering to us everything that the work in truth *is*, including the physical immediacy of performance. (It may be that no particular reading of a novel or a poem ever grasps the work in its perfect entirety, but not because the text is constitutionally prevented—prevented by its nature as text—from being read perfectly.) And if, on the other hand, we exchange our situation as readers for that of spectators, the inherently provisional quality of dramatic performance obstructs, from another angle, our hypothesized view of the work as a perfected object and now insistently reminds us that all art—like the event in the theater—is in truth a relatively arbitrary collective *act* in which our own participation is at once (paradoxically, not to say impossibly) both contingent and constitutive.

But even if it follows from these considerations that theatrical drama is deeply involved in the development and self-conception of literature, the further conclusion that drama is a *genre* of literature is not necessarily justified. At least not if we require a precise and exclusive understanding of the concept of genre, an understanding, for example, that would enable us to distinguish, with John Snyder, among "genre," "semigenre," and "nongenre."[21] As I have said above, however, it seems to me preferable that we take genre in a very broad sense and then distinguish its "types," by which we really mean different ways of looking at the same basic but elusive phenomenal area, an area in which we only disorient ourselves by attempting to conceptualize it precisely. To repeat, the central "type" is hermeneutic genre, which means those entirely fundamental prejudgments (or interpretive hypotheses) by which we make texts intelligible to ourselves—especially literary texts, where we expect a maximum density and range and completeness of meaning. But although we can grasp theoretically the necessary operation of hermeneutic genre, we can never identify such genres in practice, since our doing so would imply our complete control over the conditions of our own understanding, and so would violate precisely the founding theorem of the concept of hermeneutic genre. Therefore historical-prescriptive genres are interesting as visible and discussible models of what we assume is the concealed operation of genre in our own reading, while structural genres model hermeneutic genres in the sense that the latter, we theorize, must ultimately form a system. Obviously the boundaries between these types are fluid—their whole purpose is to be fluid—and an insistence on rigid conceptual distinctions would only confuse matters.

From this conceptually relaxed perspective, finally, what possible objection is there to regarding drama as a literary genre? Drama, again, is by definition at least a part of literature and has certainly been thought of as a genre for long enough (at least since Aristotle) and has certainly participated in the modeling operations that constitute the relations among types of genre. If we do not think of it as a genre, we shall have to invent an entirely new category for it, ad hoc.

All Theater Is Revolutionary Theater: Drama and Literature

We probably have no choice but to reserve a special category for drama after all. The arguments against regarding drama as a part of literature are simply too strong. It follows therefore, as I have said, that in a strong sense drama both is and is not a literary type, which means that drama operates as an undermining or refutation of the very concept of literature by exposing the manner in which that concept, once institutionalized, produces a contradiction.

I have already discussed, in broad theoretical and historical terms, the instability or questionableness of the concept of literature. With respect to the theory of genres, and the collision between liberal and conservative impulses, I have sketched the illogic of literature and remarked upon the possibility of inferring a fundamental corruptness in literature as an institution. I have noted that although "literature," in its present sense, comes into being as a concept only in the eighteenth century—when for various reasons it becomes convenient to include in a single category all the traditional poetic genres plus a number of relatively popular prose forms, especially the novel—still, that new category loses little time in claiming for itself the whole history of imaginative European writing (and pre-scribal forms as well) back to classical antiquity. There is thus ample reason—even without considering drama—to worry about the integrity of the concept of literature. But drama has the effect of focusing this worry upon a simple and manifest contradiction, a contradiction, in fact, whose existence is not merely conceptual but has a concrete social and physical dimension in the institution of the theater.

Two further points now need to be recognized. In the first place, the disruptive operation of drama affects only the *integrity* of the concept of literature, not necessarily any particular elements of that concept's *content*; in particular, it does not affect the application to writing, or to language, of the idea of an autonomous artistic sphere, which preserves the possibility of a radical social critique and a revolutionary advocacy in literature. In the second place, drama's disruption of the concept of literature is also a disruption of the *institution*. For as I argued above, the concept and the institution of literature are much too deeply involved with each other to permit the latter to escape disruption by drama; in fact, it is precisely that quality of the concept that drama attacks most directly, its integrity, which is most needed as a basis for the idea of historical continuity on which the institution of literature (in educational practice) is founded. Thus the effect of drama upon literature is equivalent to *a liberation of literature's revolutionary potential*. (If literature is imagined as a nonintegral concept, without the integrity that permits it to become an institution, then it is a potentially revolutionary impulse.) The infernal machine of literature, the vicious historical circle we looked at above, can thus be turned inside out. Precisely the conservative tendency of literature, which includes the insistence of literature upon thorough historical continuity as a guarantee of its questionable existence, necessarily embraces the poetic tradition of including drama as a type and so swallows its own revolutionary poison.

All theater, in other words, is revolutionary theater. I say "theater" here, rather than "drama," because I think it is clear that in the Western tradition, theater is *not* any longer (if it ever was) the simple performance vehicle that it is in most Eastern instances, at least before they are influenced by the legacy of Thespis and Aristotle. The theater, I claim, is always for us basically the *dramatic* theater; it is as thoroughly corrupted *by* literature as it is corrupting *in* literature. Obviously this is not a theoretical point, and I attempt to give it critical substance—and so justify my title—in part 2. The first two chapters there, in different ways, seek to show the basic literary quality of Artaud's antiliterary theatrical initiative. The argument of the chapter on Diderot, Shaw, and Beckett has as a corollary that there is no generic gap whatever between Beckett's plays without words and his plays with words. And the concluding chapter, on Robert Wilson's "theater of images," shows that these works, if they can be judged strictly nonliterary, thus also become basically nontheatrical.

It is, in any event, principally the theater—the fact that you cannot think "drama" without thinking "theater"—that produces the contradictory and potentially revolutionary force in drama. It is the theater, therefore, that I call revolutionary, especially since revolution means ultimately revolution in brute social reality, a domain with which literature actually has contact only by way of the theater. This point, as I have developed it so far, *is* a theoretical point, and I think a sound one. But it certainly cannot be left theoretical. By its nature, it requires as much empirical and critical content as can possibly be given it. This is the need I try to meet in part 2, where I hope it will be found perhaps especially interesting that although two of the authors I treat, T. S. Eliot and Hugo von Hofmannsthal, are strongly conservative in their social views, I argue that their work for the theater takes on a revolutionary character *by* being theatrical.[22] All theater—whether it will or no—is revolutionary theater.

The question arises, does Western drama have the same revolutionary tendency throughout its history? Before the concept of "literature" is invented, with its aim to unite all the traditional poetic genres in a single category that also includes a number of relatively new types, is drama's relation to the poetic at large already basically revolutionary? The answer to this question is probably no. Drama, again, becomes revolutionary by attacking the *integrity* of the concept of literature, which quality is inseparable from the conservative political tendency of literature as an institution. But before the invention of literature, the general domain of the poetic is not well enough organized—or at least does not sufficiently *lay claim* to conceptual integrity—to offer the same kind of target. (Bakhtin, like many others, forces the concept of "literature" onto the whole history of European writing, which enables him to say [p. 4] that at times of "'high' literature [that is, the literature of ruling social groups] . . . the whole of literature, conceived as a totality of genres, becomes an organic unity of the highest order." This assertion, with reference to pre-eighteenth-century Europe, is baseless. The idea of conceiving literature as a totality does not arise—obviously—until the concept of literature arises. There are of course always "hierarchical" relations among poetic genres, but in the absence of "literature," these relations do not form anything like an "organic" system.) In preliterary Europe, drama is certainly an *anomaly* among genres—as it is already for Aristotle, for all his unwillingness to admit it—and its persistence nonetheless *as* a recognized genre testifies to the fundamentally conservative operation of genre even without the concept of literature. But the conservatism of the poetic is not organized enough to be directly threatened by drama until it is organized as "literature."

And yet there are, after all, indications, long before the invention of literature, of a revolutionary tendency associated with drama. For if we shift our terms for a moment and understand "literary" in the literal sense of "having to do with letters or writing," then in sixth- and fifth-century Greece, drama is the *only* poetic form to which that designation can be applied. All the other forms in current or past use at that time had existed independent of their written versions, whereas drama, in the sense of theatrical drama, *could not have arisen except in the presence of widespread alphabetic literacy.* This point—that drama, so to speak, is uniquely "literary" *avant la lettre*—receives its most complete and convincing treatment in Jennifer Wise's book *Dionysus Writes.* At the end of a thoroughly detailed and ingeniously constructed argument, Wise summarizes:

> The practice of literary criticism, inaugurated by the writing down of Homer's epics; the decontextualized study of poetry, made possible by the literate classroom; the reconceptualization of conflict initiated by the writing down of law, and the emergence of a literate economy of exchange—all of these literate developments made crucial contributions to the rise of theatre and its displacement of an epic storytelling model. . . . [It is] clear from the outset: that from their inception theatre and drama were structured according to the same set of social and poetic principles and therefore cannot be described as two separate art forms; and that we can no longer accept those theories which portray literacy and literacy practices as peripheral to, let alone destructive of, the art of the stage. As a genre dependent on the manipulation and exchange of decontextualized, arbitrary signs . . . theatre is indeed an art of writing.[23]

Alphabetic literacy is not a *sufficient* condition for the emergence of dramatic theater (there are plenty of counterexamples in history, and I do not think that an even approximate parallel to what happens in sixth- and fifth-century Greece can be shown anywhere), but Wise demonstrates beyond a doubt that alphabetic literacy is a *necessary* condition for theater.

Another of her points, however, is more important for my purposes. It is pretty generally recognized that drama from Aeschylus onward [and probably also before Aeschylus, back to Thespis] is specially marked by its tendency to set inherited material on its ear. All the plays that treat of mythological material (and that is most of them) share a distinct taste for criticizing, altering, questioning, and transforming the traditional stories they treat. . . . Homeric deities and heroes are no longer the extratemporal, godlike stuff of praise poetry but, essentially, contemporary Athenians subject to ridicule and abuse, and to representation in iambics. If Thespis' plays were anything like this, it is no wonder that Solon was shocked. (pp. 87–88)[24]

Wise's contribution to the discussion here is to associate the irreverent and iconoclastic—thus in a sense the revolutionary—tendency of Greek drama with its character as a creature of written language:

Having been reduced to writing, the epic tradition of the Greeks came to be redefined as a storehouse of stories amenable to division and alteration, criticism and innovation. Whereas the lyric poet Stesichorus was believed to have been struck blind in punishment for having "sinned in matters of mythology" (*Phaedrus* 243) the dramatists of the fifth century had gained the freedom through literacy to treat the epic tradition more or less as they pleased. (p. 82)

Owing to the growth and spread of literacy, Greek poetry is enabled to carry out a lacerating move of self-examination—a critical move with respect to the conservative inertia of epic tradition and myth—and the vessel of this revolutionary tendency is the one distinguishable form that is born in the very lap of literacy, the dramatic theater.

Does history repeat itself? Does the formation of the concept of "literature," more than two millennia later, represent another self-examining move in the development of poetic forms, now in the guise of a supposed self-integration? And where else should we now expect the slumbering revolutionary potential of the poetic to be goaded once more into existence, if not in the dramatic theater?[25]

Drama and the Novel

Many readers will be inclined to answer that last question by asking, what about the novel? The really exciting event, in the arena of genre, that accompanies the formation of the idea of "literature" historically, is the novel's coming into its own and assuming a dominant position among poetic forms. And surely the novel, in the upheaval and confusion it causes in the very idea of genre, is more a revolutionary force than the by now thoroughly tamed practice of drama.

The novel does unquestionably, in a sense, come into its own in the eighteenth century—although we have just seen that it is certainly not true, as Bakhtin and many others suggest, that "of all the major genres, only the novel is younger than writing and the book" (Bakhtin, p. 3)—and the novel does then become a "dominant genre" (p. 5) in the sense that other genres conform to it and become "novelized" versions of themselves. But none of this implies that the novel is a revolutionary or even a liberal force. In chapter 4, in fact, I argue that precisely the principal "novelized" characteristic of literature, in the period 1850–1950, constitutes the conservative inertia against which revolutionary drama must assert itself, especially in the work of Brecht and Artaud. And I contend, in general, that the effect of the growth and dominance of the novel as a form, since the eighteenth century, is to consolidate and entrench in cultural practice precisely the conservative aspect of literature.

It does not by any means follow, of course, that any particular novel or novelist is conservative in temper. There are certainly as many liberal or revolutionary novelists as there are conservative dramatists, like Hofmannsthal and Eliot. My argument has to do only with the historical situation and tendency of the form as such, and my basic contention is that this situation and tendency can be understood quite independently of the opinions of particular authors. Bakhtin, for example, argues:

> The novelization of literature does not imply attaching to already completed genres a generic canon that is alien to them, not theirs. The novel, after all, has no canon of its own. It is, by its very nature, not canonic. It is plasticity itself. It is a genre that is ever questing, ever examining itself and subjecting its established forms to review. Such, indeed, is the only possibility open to a genre that structures itself in a zone of direct contact with developing reality. Therefore, the novelization of other genres does not imply their subjection to an alien generic canon; on the contrary, novelization implies their liberation from all that serves as a brake on their unique development, from all that would change them along with the novel into some sort of stylization of forms that have outlived themselves. (p. 39)

The novel, in other words, is a genre in the sense that genre is inherently *elusive*, refuses to be pinned down or delimited, which means that the novel approximates an institutionalized version of *hermeneutic* genre, genre as the inevitable preunderstanding that guides and limits our idea of the meaning of texts. That this is what Bakhtin is talking about is confirmed by his idea of "a genre that structures itself in a zone of direct contact with developing reality," which means a genre in relation to which the very existence of the text is equivalent to its real, communicable *meaning*— as opposed to cases in which meaning is simply given by genre, and the text's existence is equivalent to its form. But hermeneutic genre, as we have seen, or the presumption of communicable meaning as the substance of text, is precisely the point at which the conservative aspect of literature appears and unfolds.

It is true, to open another issue, that "heteroglossia" in Bakhtin's sense—the subjection of text to context, the untheorizable particularity of meaning in any actual utterance—is a thorn in the side of hermeneutics ("Individuum est ineffabile," Dilthey concedes), an interruption in the traditional continuity of meaning and thus an anticonservative element to the extent that it operates in literature. But heteroglossia in the novel, however more developed it may be there than in other discursive genres, is still basically itself a *theoretical* quality of the text, whereas it achieves unsurpassable actuality in dramatic performance. When Hamlet encounters Ophelia after his "To be or not to be" monologue, and she asks him, "How does your honour for this many a day?" he replies, "I humbly thank you; well, well, well." Even in the text, there is ambiguity here. Is Hamlet merely saying how he is, or does his repeated "well" express suspicion about the odd coincidence of running into Ophelia alone, hence a recognition that the interview may be overheard? But even without this complication, consider how many real factors on the stage influence the meaning of "well" in the simple sense of "I am well." How "well" is Hamlet really (is he pale, flushed, normal? are his gestures nervous, sluggish? are his clothes carefully chosen, rumpled, defensively fastidious?), and what are the relations among how he really is, how he thinks he is (how he speaks the word "well"), and how Ophelia thinks he is (in her reaction to his words)? It is true that the same level of heteroglossia could be achieved by putting any fictional dialogue onto the stage. But what actually happens in the theater is not at issue here. My point is that Western poetic tradition since the Greeks—hence the very definition of "literature"—associates theatrical performance, however arbitrarily, with one particular poetic type and so assigns preferentially to that type, to drama, the progressive or subversive or revolutionary potential of heteroglossia. It may be that among literary types restricted to the form of text, the novel most closely approaches the condition of perfect heteroglossia. But this means simply that in the actual history of poetic forms, the novel is a "dramatized" genre.

It will be objected, finally, that drama never has the effect of breaking down the *boundaries* of other genres, that it does not disrupt the existing *system* of genres as the novel does. Bakhtin insists "that the novel gets on poorly with other genres. There can be no talk of a harmony deriving from mutual limitation and complementariness. The novel parodies other genres (precisely in their role as genres); it exposes the conventionality of their forms and their language; it squeezes out some genres and incorporates others into its own peculiar structure, reformulating and re-accentuating them. . . . Behind [this process] one must be sensitive to the deeper and more truly historical struggle of genres, the establishment and growth of a generic skeleton of literature" (p. 5). But as he himself points out here, the novel's disruption of the system of genres does not represent anything like drama's attack on the very concept of literature. On the contrary, it represents a *defense* of the integrity of literature, the establishment of a new and better founded, no longer merely systematic, "generic skeleton"—which means, clearly enough, what I called above an institutional approximation of hermeneutic genre itself. And earlier, in discussing Hernadi and Frye, I argued that the attempt to rescue systematic genre—that aspect of literature which is most evidently undercut by the novel—does not by any means express a conservative attitude but is rather the last resort of a committed liberal opposition against the implacable conservatism of a literature in the sway of hermeneutic genre.

Again, therefore, the novel—however new or constantly self-renewing it may be—is always ultimately conservative *as a form*. And if we are interested in finding a genuinely progressive dimension in the modern literary situation, we must seek according to the maxim: all theater is revolutionary theater.

❀

Part Two

CHAPTER THREE

Brecht's Writing against Writing

It would be in a sense unfair of the reader to require me to show a clear instance of revolutionary operation in modern drama. What do we mean by revolution in particular cases? Is the documented influence of this or that play upon one person, or upon a small group of people, sufficient? How do we distinguish the effect of dramatic form as such from that of the play's content in any particular case? Still, I think I have put myself under the obligation to come as close to showing an instance as can possibly be expected. I shall try to discharge that obligation in discussing Bertolt Brecht's *Leben des Galilei*.

Brecht versus Artaud?

Brecht and Artaud both envision a comprehensively revolutionary theater that will not only revolutionize its own form but also, in the process, contribute to a revolutionary movement in the society that engenders and employs it. The literary theater of complacent moral psychology, against which Artaud polemicizes, supports and justifies an oppressive bourgeois culture in much the same way that what Brecht calls Aristotelian theater does. Theater specialists, even those most deeply engaged in the theoretical aspect of their study, do not generally find it difficult to recognize the parallels here. Herbert Blau speaks of a special uncompleted quality of theory that "one sees in the shifting certitudes and ideological nuances of Brecht and in the enfevered slippages, concussions, and cardiac arrests in the nervous system of Artaud's thought."[1] But a considerable number of recent theorists of literary revolution, or literary theorists who are concerned with revolution, find they can follow Artaud only at Brecht's expense. Susan Sontag, in trying to align Peter Weiss (whom she likes) with Artaud, is embarrassed by Weiss's acknowledgment of a debt to Brecht: "How *could* one reconcile Brecht's conception of a didactic theater, a theater of intelligence, with Artaud's theater of magic, of gesture, of 'cruelty,' of feeling?"[2] Jacques Derrida, writing on Artaud in "The Theater of Cruelty and the Closure of Representation," takes the occasion to dismiss summarily all "theater of alienation" yet manages, unwittingly, to conclude his long anti-Brecht paragraph with a sentence that could be taken to summarize Brecht's whole project: "And the *act* of political revolution is *theatrical.*"[3] Even where Artaud and Brecht are mentioned separately, the same valuation often holds. For Julia Kristeva, Artaud is a central figure in the pantheon of poetic revolution, whereas Brecht, as far as I know, is not mentioned in her work.[4] Adorno, on the other hand (as far as I know), does not mention Artaud but takes a generally negative view of Brecht.[5]

The most important reason for this way of looking at Brecht and Artaud, in some literary theorists, is Artaud's explicit, radical rejection of the literary *as such*, especially his opposition to the tyranny of text in the theater. Writing and the tradition of writing, the apparent unchanging rigidity of the written word, assumes for Artaud the role of a principal cultural obstacle to revolution. Writing seems to feed and build only upon itself; especially in the field of literature, where the specific claim of nonreferentiality is common—a claim by which literature denies itself any productive leverage in an "outside" world—writing can never mean anything fundamentally different from what it *has* meant. Therefore, although it may be strictly impossible to *escape* the tyranny of writing, a significant revolutionary initiative (especially in literature) must at least *resist* and so *expose* that tyranny, which Artaud unquestionably does. Brecht, on the other hand, appears to be more nearly a mere writer among writers. His work does attack certain specific literary and dramatic canons but does not appear to challenge the literary system at the level where canons are formed.

There are of course serious theoretical problems in Sontag's argument "against interpretation," and even Kristeva's much more consistently theorized opposition of the semiotic to the symbolic fails to account fully for the co-optiveness of the symbolic order, the absorption of her own text along with the texts she appeals to (like Artaud's) into literary tradition. But exactly this type of problem (which bedevils a great deal of literary theory) engenders a strong preferential interest in Artaud. Derrida, for example, whose scrupulousness keeps him perched precariously on the brink of an outright capitulation to the history of writing, attempts in *Writing and Difference* to create a resonance between his own text and Artaud's in order to use the latter's (so to speak) clinically extreme refusal to capitulate as a means of stabilizing his own endeavor. The quest for radical cultural or intellectual renewal always runs the risk of an unwitting capitulation in the domain of the tradition of writing, and to the extent that we are aware of this risk, the entirely uncowed and uncompromised radicality of Artaud's writing appears as a kind of beacon to navigate by.

On its surface, Brecht's writing seems too simple and popular to offer the same sort of paradoxical comfort that Artaud's does. But does this imply that Brecht's revolutionary project fails to confront the danger of capitulation to the tradition of writing? I use *Leben des Galilei* as a text for discussing this question because among Brecht's plays it is the one in which writing and the tradition of writing operate most centrally as themes. Viewed strictly as a story, the play is mainly about the origin, production, preservation, significance, and tradition of Galileo's *Discorsi e dimostrazioni matematiche*. I do not by any means claim that *Leben des Galilei* somehow escapes the condition of being written or literary. On the contrary, I contend that Brecht here exploits the literary quality of his work as a device for undermining the whole historical tradition of writing that he thematizes. And the result, I think, is that his work in the end constitutes at least as effective a challenge to its own condition of writtenness as does Artaud's.

Writing and Its Performance

In particular, by using the extreme case of scientific writing as a model, Brecht locates upon his stage the relation between writing as such (questionable as this concept may be) and its *performance* in the most comprehensive sense of the word. The statement "the earth moves," for example, is strictly meaningless in relation to any conception of direct or historically unmediated human experience; if the question of the earth's moving or not moving impinged on our immediate experience, it would be asked by every child. Both the prelates and the street singers make this point clear in their mocking, which is in each case *their historical performance* of the statement. What matters is the social performance of that statement, above all the exploitation of its inherently arbitrary or metaphorical relation to the idea of the papal seat at the center of a system of nested social spheres. The appropriateness of the notion of "performance" here follows from the clear analogy with the relation between the bare written history of Galileo (scraps of which appear before the audience as introductions to the various scenes) and the performance of that history, textual and vocal and gestural, that constitutes the play.

Even scientific writing—whose univocal semiotic identity seems guaranteed by its reference to observable facts and to natural mathematical "laws" presumed (for purposes of the specific semiosis in progress) to be both knowable and immutable—even scientific writing is exposed to performance. The exact referentiality of the writing turns out to be a kind of knife edge on which nothing that we might reasonably call "meaning" can be balanced. An assertion does not "mean" until it is located in a broad context of possibilities.[6] The statement "the earth moves" thus does not acquire meaning until it is performed: either as a potentially revolutionary awakening of "doubt" in socially subjugated classes (283) or else as a capitulation, an acceptance of the status of a mere "mathematical hypothesis" (239) that nevertheless provides the ruling classes with new machines (284) and more accurate star charts (269), hence economic advantages and a consolidation of political power. Moreover, as Galileo himself points out, writing not only needs to be developed by performance in order to receive meaning in history, but must also be anticipated by performance. Neither Galileo's writing nor, for example, Giordano Bruno's is possible except in a preexisting climate of social performance, which Galileo associates with the appearance of transoceanic navigation (190). And if Galileo escapes execution for the same utterances that had doomed Bruno, the reason is not, as Galileo imagines, that Bruno had lacked "proof" of his assertions (210); the reason, as we have learned in detail from the Kurator (197–200, 207), lies in performance conditions, in the preexisting political and commercial circumstances under which Galileo happens to be working—including his service to the Venetian republic as a maker of machines.

Another interesting question never becomes explicit in Brecht's text but is very strongly suggested. If scientific thought encounters substantially less political and ecclesiastical resistance in Holland than in Italy—as we are reminded on at least three separate occasions (195–96, 250, 278–79)— then why is the most important scientific work, Galileo's, done in Italy? An answer to this question is suggested by the idea of social performance in anticipation of writing. Precisely Italy, where the support of the Church lends a special traditional permanence to the society's structure of economic exploitation, is where Galileo's writing is *needed*, in the sense that it has an important and obvious role to play in the performance of latent social tensions. Precisely Italy, where economic misery is clearly recognizable as a performance of Church writing, of the metaphorical relation between imagined celestial conditions and actual social conditions, is where, on the level of performance (not on the level of a dispute concerning abstract truth), the countering force is likely to arise and insist on its own parallel metaphor. Indeed, we are shown an image of this dynamics in scene 14, where Galileo produces his last major scientific work under the greatest possible pressure from ecclesiastical authority. Even science never says simply, "the earth moves." It always says, in some form, "eppur si muove": it moves *nonetheless*; it moves in spite of what has been asserted to the contrary. Science does not arise and become articulate except in the dialectical dynamics of social and historical performance.

The Ambivalence of Performance

Writing, then, is exposed to performance. It achieves historical agency, even mere historical existence, only by way of a social performance to which its relation is never more than metaphorical, never escapes the ultimately uncontrollable arbitrariness of metaphor. But the exposure of writing to performance does not at all imply the overthrow of writing as an inherently conservative tradition. It also makes possible the co-option of the whole of written tradition by any social class or other political entity that happens to possess sufficient power to assert its own performance as definitive. And it is this process of co-option that first *gives* writing the character of a conservative tradition, for it makes possible a solidification (an authoritarian social performance) of the else fluid metaphorical relation between the permanent written object and what is now presumed (in the authorized form of the metaphor) to be a permanence of truth or value or social structure. ("But gentlemen," says Galileo, "surely human beings can misinterpret not only the movements of stars, but also the Bible!" And Bellarmin replies, "But how the Bible is to be interpreted is surely a matter for the theologians of the Holy Church to decide, no?" [238].) The survival of Galileo's *Discorsi* as a permanent physical object at the end of the play is therefore by no means an unambiguous image of political progress or enlightenment.

The exposure of writing to performance is not a solution to the problem of revolutionary writing but is itself a problem, and one that emerges with special clarity in scientific writing. For even if we agree that scientific writing cannot possibly escape the inherent metaphoricity of language, still there is in science a resistance to metaphor (we might say, a genre-conditioned resistance), an emphasis on the factual and the referential, which does have the effect of bringing to light the various levels of metaphoricity in other types of writing, including the metaphorical relation between writing and its performance. In this way, Galileo's writing brings to light the unstable metaphoricity of the relation between a hierarchical heaven and a hierarchical social order. *But scientific writing produces this effect only by itself implying an especially adamant truth claim (a denial of metaphoricity) for its own formulations.* And this truth claim in turn inevitably opens the way to a socially *conservative* performance of the writing, since it is already an instance of the type of metaphor that relates the supposed permanence of writing to a supposed permanence in empirical reality.

Brecht develops this form of the problem in Galileo's last speeches. On the one hand, Galileo attempts a radical modification of the truth claim of scientific writing: "A humankind that has been stumbling along in this thousand-year-old nacreous fog of superstition and antiquated words, too ignorant to unfold its own powers, will not be capable of unfolding the powers of nature that you scientists reveal" (284). Scientists, that is, must confront directly not only the question of scientific truth but also that of the possibilities for performance of their writing. And in response to the question of what scientists should aim for in their work, Galileo continues: "Ich halte dafür, daß das einzige Ziel der Wissenschaft darin besteht, die Mühseligkeit der menschlichen Existenz zu erleichtern." Here a problem begins to appear, because the criterion Galileo suggests for judging a science's goal—"to lighten the drudgery of human existence"—is exactly the criterion that had been employed in arguments *against* the social aspect of his teachings (243–45)—and employed not by his enemies but by the Small Monk, who admires and understands him. (Why not leave the comfort of religion intact, the Small Monk suggests, for people whose social condition offers them no immediate physical comfort?) If the scientist relaxes his strict focus upon truth and tries to give his work an ethical dimension, we conclude, does he not then enter a realm of slippery concepts and judgments where the advantage of scientific writing, its metaphor-breaking power, is lost? Galileo ignores this problem for the time being and presses on: "Wenn Wissenschaftler, eingeschüchtert durch selbstsüchtige Machthaber, sich damit begnügen, Wissen um des Wissens willen aufzuhäufen, kann die Wissenschaft zum Krüppel gemacht werden, und eure neuen Maschinen mögen nur neue Drangsale bedeuten" (284: If scientists, intimidated by self-seeking men of power, content themselves with accumulating knowledge for its own sake, then science itself can be made into a cripple, and your new machines may only signify new hardships). This whole passage of course belongs only to the last version of the play and presupposes the experience of World War II, but it contributes directly to the text's basic thought structure by permitting Galileo to adduce cogent reasons in support of his questioning of the scientific truth claim, a questioning he had earlier expressed only in general terms.

> DER KLEINE MÖNCH. Und Sie meinen nicht, daß die Wahrheit, wenn es Wahrheit ist, sich durchsetzt, auch ohne uns?
>
> GALILEI. Nein, nein, nein. Es setzt sich nur so viel Wahrheit durch, als wir durchsetzen; der Sieg der Vernunft kann nur der Sieg der Vernünftigen sein. (246; cf. first version, 67)
>
> THE SMALL MONK. And you don't believe that the truth, if it is truly truth, will prevail, even without us?
>
> GALILEO. No, no, no. Truth prevails only to the extent that we successfully assert it. The victory of reason can only be the victory of rational people.

Truth must never be regarded as an absolute content of writing but must always be treated as a function of the responsible social action of individuals here and now.

Yet neither science in general nor Galileo in particular can ever actually dispense with the radical scientific truth claim. In scene 14, Galileo mocks Andrea's willingness to forgive his recanting in view of the existence of the *Discorsi*: "O unwiderstehlicher Anblick des Buches, der geheiligten Ware! Das Wasser läuft im Mund zusammen und die Flüche ersaufen" (282–83: O irresistible sight of the book, the sanctified commodity! The mouth waters, and the curses drown in it.) The truth claim of science gives a special value to the *book*, which thus becomes a kind of commodity; and it appears that Galileo, by mocking it, is here again calling that truth claim into question. Only a few moments earlier, he had said, "Und es gibt kein wissenschaftliches Werk, das nur ein Mann schreiben kann" (282: And there is no scientific work that only one man can write), suggesting that his work would have been more valuable if it had been written by someone who had given a better example of resistance to authority.

But this last statement presupposes exactly the truth claim it questions. It does not matter *who* writes a "scientific work," except from an ethical or social point of view, because from a scientific point of view the work is fully determined by its referential adequacy with respect to facts and natural laws, by the strict truth of its content. In the very act of denying the truth claim of science, Galileo thus yet again—unwittingly?—affirms it. His parting words to Andrea are "Gib acht auf dich, wenn du durch Deutschland kommst, die Wahrheit unter dem Rock" (285: Be careful when you pass through Germany with truth under your coat). On the one hand, Galileo suggests that by exposing himself to danger, Andrea is performing a significant ethical act that will in a sense redeem the book from the ethical failure of its author. On the other hand, Andrea's act gains ethical significance only by virtue of the book's status as a bearer of *truth*. Again, in the very process of insisting on its ethical dimension, science inevitably involves itself in the truth claim that exposes its writing to a conservative or reactionary social performance.

The last scene of the play, in which it turns out that Andrea is in no real danger after all, echoes Galileo's recognition that the danger of his being burned at the stake had never really existed (284). But Galileo's belief that before recanting he had possessed actual political power ("Einige Jahre lang war ich ebenso stark wie die Obrigkeit") is mistaken. He had not been protected by his own political power any more than Andrea is protected by political power at the border station. In the final analysis, the scientist is protected by the simple fact that scientific writing *poses no threat to authority*. The unavoidable truth claim of science, which gives scientific writing its power to challenge accepted performative metaphors, also exposes that writing to the mechanism of authoritarian co-option. In the first place, that truth claim fixes scientific writing at a specific intellectual point that can easily be isolated from the sphere of social practice. "Don't throw the baby out with the bath water, friend Galileo," says Barberini (240); authority can always find a way to permit the practice of science without danger to itself. Or when Barberini later, as Pope, complains, "One can't condemn the theory and accept the star charts," the Inquisitor answers simply, "Why not?" (269). In the second place, the truth claim of science invites the use of the book, "the sanctified commodity," as a metaphor of permanence. Not only in Catholic Italy but also in reformed Germany, the land of Bible idolatry, Andrea will have to watch his step.

The Problem of Performance and Theory

The exposure of writing to performance thus opens both revolutionary and reactionary possibilities. In order to grasp how these possibilities may be manipulated in practice, however, we must refine the whole notion of performance, for there is danger of confusion if we do not distinguish carefully between performance and such concepts as "reception," in Hans Robert Jauss's sense, or the "shifting" or "fusion" of "horizons" in Gadamer's sense.[7] Both reception theory and philosophical hermeneutics modify the common and vague nineteenth-century view of literary tradition in such a way as to perfect its structure, to tighten it. They share with a great deal of literary thought in the twentieth century the initial radical move of abandoning the whole idea of the work, the opus, the idea that a text possesses its own basic meaning or even its own basic identity, an identity which is then responded to more or less directly in later literary history. And a principal consequence of this discrediting of the opus, especially in the more historically focused branches of literary thought, is practically to *define* the text as nothing but an aspect of the general historical weave of reception or interpretation. Thus literary history is imagined as itself wholly constituting the literary, as an ultimately only self-referred (if incomprehensibly huge) mechanism or system that enforces what I have called the tyranny of the tradition of writing. In chapter 2, I pointed out that a more extreme version of this thought is represented by the idea of literary hegemony *even in the domain of the real*, which is implied by the theoretical positions of de Man and Heidegger. But the notion of performance can be compromised, and stripped of its revolutionary dimension, even without going to that extreme.

The vision of a tyrannical tradition of writing is not a consequence of any particular version of reception theory or hermeneutics. It is inseparable from the historical-theoretical perspective *as such*. To theorize about history is inevitably to systematize history on some level, no matter how convincingly the individual theorist may deny our ability to know the historical system or even to ascertain its existence. And especially the quality of the *arbitrary*, which belongs indispensably to what I mean by "performance," is inaccessible from a theoretical perspective.

Neither reception nor interpretation (in the strict hermeneutic sense) can suffer the predicate "arbitrary." In the case of interpretation, this inability follows from the hermeneutic principle of strictly minimized category distinctions (discussed in detail in chapter 8). The absence of a category distinction between "interpretation" and "understanding," in philosophical hermeneutics, implies that the former can never be regarded as arbitrary— whereas what I have called the interpretivity of performance positively requires a category difference between performance and what it gestures at. And in the case of reception, the integrity of the theory requires that the only conceivable standpoint from which any form of reception might be regarded as arbitrary must be, in Jauss's words, "the apparently self-evident truth that in a literary text the essence of the poetic is timelessly present, and that its objective, unalterable meaning is at any time immediately accessible to the interpreter," a standpoint which the theory itself aggressively discredits.[8] But the relation between performance and its object, as I have said, is *metaphorical*, and metaphor involves by definition an arbitrary element. (If the relation between tenor and vehicle is either empirically or logically *necessary*, then it does not occur to us to speak of "metaphor" in the first place.) And in *Leben des Galilei*, it is clear that all the people who suggest or enact social performances of Galileo's science—with the possible exception of Galileo himself!—do so in full consciousness of acting arbitrarily. They interpret, but not in the sense of "understanding"; rather, they invent, they create.

But obviously there is a problem here, for historical literary theory and for my own argument as well. How can we even begin to talk about "performance" if the discussion must be based in part on an untheorizable concept? This is also a problem from Brecht's point of view. For if Brecht is concerned in *Leben des Galilei* with the question of writing and its performance, if this question is meant to be recognized by his audience, then how shall the audience for their part be prevented from theorizing it? This point is crucial, for it separates the reactionary possibilities of performance from the revolutionary possibilities and appears strongly to favor reaction or conservatism. A conservative performance metaphor will normally tend to hypostasize or solidify writing, to insist on the permanence and authority of writing, hence to deny the exposure of writing to performance (despite the conditions of its own genesis as a metaphor), whereas the revolutionary must affirm that exposure. Yet once we have begun theorizing performance, the idea of a strictly arbitrary performance of writing, one that does not simply lead back into the tradition of writing, becomes inaccessible. And how shall we affirm what we cannot even adequately conceive?

The Role of the Theater

The question thus becomes, how can the exposure of writing to performance be presented, publicized, propagated as a condition of our social existence without itself being exposed to the need for a theoretical resolution?
And the answer to this question, it seems to me, is contained *in the institution of the theater.* For theatrical performance is always arbitrary with respect
to the written text of the play. Performance is never definitive, never simply
a direct manifestation of the text, since different performances are always
known to be possible. Charles Laughton may play Brecht's Galileo; but not
only do we understand that other people can and do play the same role,
there is also a basic category difference between what Charles Laughton is
(an actual particular human being) and what Brecht's Galileo is (a complex
of signification in various Brechtian and also non-Brechtian texts). Indeed,
Charles Laughton cannot *play* Galileo, from our point of view, without our
understanding that he is *different* from Galileo, that his being coupled with
Galileo for a short space of time by some theatrical version of the verb "to
be" is at base an arbitrary coupling. This arbitrariness is a crucial part of
what Brecht expects to be laid bare by audience "alienation." It is of course
always possible to argue that this or that aspect of Laughton's person or of
his acting is "right" for Galileo, and hence not arbitrary. But in the first
place, such arguments are themselves arbitrary, leaping as they do the category difference between a structure of signifiers and a collection of "experienced" referents; and in the second place, there are always plenty of
elements in that collection of referents for which such arguments cannot
reasonably be made. In this respect, Brecht's theory of alienation simply
proposes that theater be honest about the irreducible arbitrariness of its
relation to what we regard traditionally as the organic integrity (the ability
to create "illusion") of literary signification.

But the relation of performance to text in drama is not merely arbitrary; in
a curious manner it is also *necessary.* For precisely literary tradition, the
domain of the tyranny of writing, insists on a clear generic distinction
between drama and other literary forms, which would be a meaningless distinction if it did not imply that theatrical performance is necessary for the
complete unfolding of the meaning (or indeed for the very existence) of a
dramatic work. This consideration does not deny the existence of dramatic
works that have never been performed. The point is that when a play *is* performed, we are predisposed by the whole weight of European literary tradition to recognize that the ceremony we are participating in is required by the
work's genre, that it is the necessary destiny of the text on which it is based.

Can the performance of a play be said to be "really" arbitrary or "really"
necessary? The question in this form is meaningless. The arbitrary, as I have
said, is inaccessible to theoretical discussion. To say "X *is* arbitrary" is to

couple the arbitrary with X in an order of thought that automatically reduces its arbitrariness. And the question of the necessity of performance raises the question of the necessity of the order of concepts in which necessity is defined (namely, the accepted traditional order of literary genres), and so on. My point, however, is that since our main concern is the possibility of a revolutionary move with respect to the tradition of writing, it is sufficient in the case of a literary form, like drama, if the arbitrary and the necessary are defined with reference to the specifically literary aspect of that tradition. And the very idea of drama as a distinguishable literary type involves in some sense the necessity of performance, whereas the very idea of performance, our sense of its being different from reading or from simply knowing about a text, implies a categorical difference, a relation of arbitrariness, between its torrential sensory immediacy (which confuses the distinction between signifiers and mere stimuli) and the presumably orderly operation of strictly textual signifiers. (This is the sense in which— as suggested in chapter 2—heteroglossia is actual in drama, merely theoretical in the novel.)

The relation of drama and its performance, then, in the context of literary tradition, is *both* arbitrary *and* necessary. This is not just a paradox; it is a contradiction. It cannot be resolved, for example, by the statement that it is necessary that there be *some* performance, whereas the choice of *which* performance is always arbitrary. For this statement presupposes a point of view from which it is possible to distinguish between possible performances and the drama "itself," and the existence of such a point of view would imply that performance is not strictly necessary after all, since the drama prior to performance is knowable. The only point of view from which the questions of necessity and arbitrariness make sense—in this conceptual context—is that of the spectator at an actual particular performance *in a real theater*, the spectator for whom that particular performance, given the assumptions dictated by literary tradition, shows itself both as necessary and as arbitrary. The work "itself" is not available as a standard. Only the performance is available and, in the light of literary tradition, exhibits strictly contradictory qualities.

The idea can therefore be restated: the theater, the real theater, is the point at which a contradiction appears within the tradition of writing, the point at which the relation of writing and its performance is not reduced by theory, not resolved into a mere structural peculiarity *of* writing, but rather remains open to question; the point, therefore, at which the exposure of writing to performance retains a revolutionary potential. Moreover, once this idea is grasped, it becomes a bit clearer how revolutionary drama must operate. Drama not only cannot but *need not* find a way somehow to avoid or reject or negate its status as writing. On the contrary, its position in the domain of writing is precisely the source of its revolutionary leverage.

To look at the matter differently, our situation as an audience in the theater is similar, up to a point, to our general situation as readers, as members of a culture of reading, as the audience of the tradition of writing. We
as readers understand that both writing and reading depend on context,
that we as readers never have any particular writing "itself" but rather
always receive it as a kind of performance. We recognize, in other words,
that performance is *necessary*. And only the opposed idea of the *arbitrariness* of performance can prevent our understanding that performance is
necessary from slipping easily into an acceptance of the particular performance we are faced with as *authoritative*, hence into the mechanism of
literary tradition in its narrowly conservative aspect. But how are we supposed to retain and develop the idea of arbitrariness in our reading? Even
literary critics and theorists, whose business is to dismantle the performances of literary writing that had earlier been considered authoritative,
would have no incentive to work in the first place if they did not think of
their own readings, their performances of the writing, as "better," which
only means more authoritative.

This is where the role of the theater begins. Our situation as spectators in
the theater is a scale model of our situation in literary tradition, except that
literary tradition itself creates for us in the theater the possibility—indeed,
the inevitability—of thinking the whole contradiction of necessity and arbitrariness. The theater becomes thus—whether or not this is the particular
practitioner's intention—a kind of training in revolutionary resistance to the
otherwise unchallengeable conservatism of writing. And this is of course
especially the case when a play like *Leben des Galilei* is performed, which
constantly directs our attention to questions of writing and its performance.
Theatrical drama—as Jennifer Wise shows—arises originally as an aspect of
the disruptive and radically innovative operation of the newborn art of writing in an else strongly conservative institutional reality. And now, in the age
of "literature," it is still the same conceptually refractory intrusion of writing
into the domain of the immediately real, it is still the theater, that preserves
the possibility of a progressive or revolutionary writing.

The Open Question

I think this conclusion is of great importance, but it does not remove the
problems in the argument, my argument, that leads to it. Some of these
problems seem easy enough to deal with. It might be objected, for example,
that even from the point of view of the audience in a theater, the idea of the
necessity of performance—the idea that the work is not yet fully itself
except in the process of performance—already inevitably implies our conception of the work prior to its performance, the work as that which is performed. But our conception of "that which" is performed need not

designate—and, I think, does not normally designate—the *work* we are confronted with; it is rather, by contrast with the immediacy of the performance, the conception of something relatively lifeless and *incomplete*, the conception, precisely, of something that was not until now the work of art it now fully is. In the opposed situation, where the text and the various possibilities of performing it are displayed before our intellect, the relation between text and performance is more like that between essence and manifestation: the essence may *need* to be manifested, but remains itself the basically complete heart of the matter.

This difference can perhaps be clarified by an analogy. From the point of view of an actual audience, the performed play is like a living human being, whereas "that which" is performed is that same human being minus only the breath of life—which is to say, a corpse, not a human being at all. From the intellectual perspective, "that which" is performed is like a musical instrument, its various possible performances like a collection of different players who will use it differently. In some sense the instrument *needs* to be played in order to be what it is; but even as it lies on the table, it is obviously much more fully itself than the corpse is a human being. And if it is remarked that these oppositions (and arguments by analogy, and appeals to experience) lack a certain conceptual integrity, then we must remind ourselves that the whole situation we are talking about is created and perpetuated precisely by a conceptual confusion, by the idea of drama as a literary type, which is unavoidable in literature's manufacture of a history for itself.

But there are problems that go deeper. In what sense, especially, can it be said that there "is" in literary tradition a contradiction between the necessary and the arbitrary marked by the form of drama? Any line of reasoning that pretends to demonstrate the existence of this contradiction will be theoretical in the sense in which theory cannot help but deny the possibility of the strictly arbitrary. Such a line of reasoning, therefore, in effect says no to its own conclusion. The situation here recalls the question of the possibility of a revolutionary move with respect to the whole tradition of writing. As soon as we embark upon any kind of theoretical discussion of this question, we find we have adopted a position (of dependence on the tradition) from which the answer can only be no. There is thus a kind of strict rhetorical consistency in Paul de Man's conclusion (discussed above) "that the bases for historical knowledge are not empirical facts but written texts, even if these texts masquerade in the guise of wars or revolutions."[9] If we ask whether dramatic performance escapes the condition of being a written text in disguise, the very form of the question dictates our answer: no.

But this "no," because it is already dictated by the form of the inquiry, has no claim to any degree of empirical validity and hence no claim whatever to operate as a guide for any of our actions, even our actions as writers. No matter how strongly my argument says no to its own conclusion, therefore, no matter how often *I* in effect say no to the point I myself am making, the question still remains open: the question of drama as a potentially revolutionary opening in the historical system of writing, the question of dramatic performance and of the performance of writing in general, which we now recognize must bear a relation of arbitrariness to its own asking—a relation wedged open by the inevitable answer: no.

The Extemporized or Ad Hoc Nature of Theater Itself

Finally, then, we must ask in what *manner* does the question of writing and its performance remain open? Is it kept open automatically by the existence of the form of drama? In what sense does *the* form of drama exist? These questions lead back to Artaud, for they define the arena—the theater, so to speak—in which both he and Brecht make their revolutionary moves.

The form of drama itself, first of all, is no less exposed to theoretical infection than my argument about that form. Both Brecht's and Artaud's projects and polemics are in fact directed against types of drama and theater that are infected in just this way. What both writers object to is the idea of a theater in which the bourgeois spectator experiences identification with the fiction. For Artaud, the medium of identification is a simplistic moral psychology anchored in the degenerate conventions of dramatic writing; for Brecht, it is a complex of textual and theatrical techniques calculated to produce the illusion of reality. Thus, both oppose not some natural emotional swamping of dramatic form but rather the imposition of *theoretical* ideas (mainly from the nineteenth century) upon a form that might otherwise have developed an important revolutionary function. (Brecht's notion of the "Aristotelian," of course, refers less to Aristotle than to the nineteenth-century version of a theoretical aesthetics that has been well established in Europe only since the seventeenth century.)

But the form of drama, considered as the insistent reopening of a fundamentally disruptive question in the bosom of literary tradition, is corrupted not only by particular kinds of theory but by theory as such. The more plausible and consistent a theory of drama appears, the more thoroughly does it thereby exclude the dimension of entirely uncontrollable arbitrariness upon which the revolutionary operation of drama depends. As a practical matter, therefore, given a historical situation (like that facing both Brecht and Artaud) in which the form of drama is already corrupted by theory, exactly how shall one proceed if one's project is to reform the theater in a revolutionary sense? It seems clear that innovations in playwriting, the production of new kinds of dramatic text, will not be sufficient. The theater, after all, exerts its revolutionary leverage within literature precisely by being something *other* than text, something not digestible in the process of conservative literary hermeneutics. When we imagine (like Brecht or

Artaud) a theater corrupted by theory, we mean a theater in which that con-dition of otherness has been collapsed or obscured, a theater now entirely suffused with the quality of interpretable text. And it does not seem that textual innovations alone can be expected to effect fundamental change in such a theater.

The reformer, therefore, in addition to whatever textual innovations seem appropriate, will have to aim for change in at least some nonliterary aspects of the theater: in the theater as a physical or social or legal institu-tion; in the character and organization of theatrical work and workers; in the expectations and attitudes of the actual theater audience. But in any of these cases the reformer will be working in close communication with other people, and how shall that communication be accomplished if not in some-thing approaching theoretical form, including a statement of goals and their justification, along with a description of means to achieve them? Of course, it does not follow from these considerations that theater reform is impossible. But it does follow that *permanent* reform is out of the question, that theater reform is always by nature temporary, provisional, always in the process of being undermined by its own procedure. Which means that *the form of drama itself*—considered as the insistent reopening of a funda-mentally disruptive question in the bosom of literary tradition—is always temporary, provisional, always the ad hoc solution to a problem that inevitably generates a new form of itself in the very process of being solved.

Both Artaud and Brecht, I contend, understand this state of affairs thor-oughly, and it is this understanding, principally, that they have in common. It is therefore always a mistake to try to pin either man down to his pro-grammatic statements, as if these represented a stable theoretical position with respect to a basically unchanging question of drama and theater. Artaud's insistence upon incantation, myth, quasi-magic in the theater, for example, is more than just the general advocacy of a turn away from writ-ing; it is an attempt to expose and so to liberate certain dynamic qualities of the theater that antedate its association with literature, in the hope that the-ater, thus renewed, will then assume its proper role as a fundamental dis-ruption or contradiction in the evolved literary system. And even if we had not already recognized that at least Western theater does *not*, in its basic components, antedate the tradition of writing, we would still have no trou-ble picking out the faults in this position. Artaud is, after all, himself a writer, and he cannot expect to write either himself or his theater out of the tradition that founds his own procedure. But to respond thus to Artaud would be to *mistake* his writing for the assertion, precisely, of a "position" with respect to the problem of drama and theater, which it is not. It is, rather, as it must be, text in the form of sheer temporizing, a systematically inconclusive assembling of critical, descriptive, technical, and imaginative material, not focused but aimed precisely at preventing focus or closure in any form, thus at opening yet again the question of drama, not once and for all but at least for as many pages or hours, maybe even years, as the situation permits.

The same, I think, is even more obviously true of Brecht's doctrine of alienation. A technique that was alienating in the theater last year, or for that matter last week, is no longer alienating today, for it has become accepted convention. The technique of alienation, therefore, to the extent that it reflects a clear understanding of the theater's historical situation—which is of course not an applicable criterion in practice—positively denies the possibility of any theory of the theater that is more than temporarily sustainable. If we agree, moreover, that theatrical alienation, in any form, tends to decrease the relative importance of immediate sensory stimuli for the alert spectator, then it follows that the theatrical experience as a whole is thereby intellectualized, or brought closer to the experience of writing and reading. Alienation thus insists on the situation of theater within the domain of writing—but it does so, paradoxically, with the same basic end in view as Artaud's. Brecht's procedure is riskier, more exposed to the danger of simple, unwitting capitulation, more easily theorizable. But it is also better able to exploit the disruptive operation of drama as a form *within* the system of writing than those theatrical techniques that attempt to dissociate drama from its written component. In any case, it is clear that both the risks and the advantages of alienation, with respect to the tradition of writing, are raised to a kind of maximum by being reflected upon in the content of *Leben des Galilei*.

Capitulation

Does Brecht's project succeed in being revolutionary, or is it a capitulation after all? In any event, the idea of capitulation figures very prominently in *Leben des Galilei*, and in view of the importance of the idea of writing and its performance in the play, it seems reasonable to see Galileo's recanting as an allegory of the sense in which Brechtian alienation in general is a capitulation of drama to the history of writing. Is Brecht's theatrical procedure really a capitulation, or is it a disguised revolutionary move? In the play (in the allegory) it is Andrea, and only Andrea, who insists that Galileo's capitulation had not really been a capitulation at all but a kind of "victory" (281–82). This is as it must be. Galileo himself cannot justify his recanting without—in the terms of the allegory—theorizing the revolutionary move (assuming that move exists) and so stripping it of its revolutionary force with respect to writing. As we have seen, it is not even clear in the play that the survival of the *Discorsi* should receive a positive social or historical valuation. But in the domain of writing, the revolutionary is not marked by any positive achievement or progress or any clarity of valuation; it is marked by an opening and a keeping open of the *question* of writing and its performance. And, paradoxically enough, that question is never more completely open than *at the point where one cannot tell the difference between a capitulation and a revolutionary move*, that point where the perilous exposure of drama to the tyranny of writing reaches a maximum, along with the possibility of a subversive operation within the domain of writing itself.

Thus it seems we have come within earshot, so to speak, of the conclusion that *Leben des Galilei* is an instance of drama as revolutionary as it gets. To be sure, it would in a strong sense be foolish actually to draw this conclusion. As always, we must remain aware of the limitations of our own procedure. Any critical account of what the play *is* or *does* must take the form of a "Protokoll," like the record written by the two secretaries in scene 7. And this type of document, by its nature, invites reactionary performance; it pins down to a doctrinal position even the dialectical attempt to escape doctrine. We can of course attenuate our formulation; we can speak of Brecht's play as opening the possibility of its own revolutionary character, or something of the sort. But there is no limit to the level of subtlety at which the obvious objections to our thought, the tendency of our argument to say no to itself, can pursue us. Perhaps we have no choice but to be foolish.

Leben des Galilei, then—let us take the chance and say it—is as close to a demonstrable instance of revolutionary drama as we are likely to find, and it is so mainly by grappling with the problem of writing and its performance on at least five different levels:

1. The title already presents a problem, since "Leben" means both real life ("le vécu," the immediacy of personal experience) and the written account of a person's life (the "vita," the "Protokoll" prepared by biographers and historians). This ambiguity emphasizes the fact that whatever vitality or immediacy the whole play (text and acting) might possess is based on a preexisting body of writing and is a performance of that writing.

2. The individual scene headings, read by the audience, are a selection of critical moments from Galileo's written "life" and thus in effect a performance of that writing (a series of decisions about what is important) while still themselves belonging to the domain of writing.

3. Given the setting of the play in Italy, the relation between the scene heading and the actual written dialogue of each scene reminds us strongly of the commedia dell'arte, of the relation between the *scenario* and the improvised dialogue in that form. Thus the dialogue is presented *both* as writing (we know that the text exists) *and* as if it were an improvised or arbitrary performance of the written scene headings.

4. The theatrical event itself (who the actors are and what they do on the stage) is a performance of the written dialogue; and of all the play's levels of performance, this one appears most clearly to support being characterized as arbitrary, since it involves all sorts of unforeseeable accidents. The possibility of the arbitrary, however, is also *problematized* by the implied parallel with the other levels of performance. On levels 1, 2 and 3, we recognize that the supposedly arbitrary performance of writing has a tendency itself to become writing in its turn; and this raises the question of whether even the theatrical event, with all its sensory immediacy, is not somehow reducible to writing.

5. Finally, on a thematic level, there is the relation between Galileo's own writings and their historical performance, which is now even more interesting, since it suggests that the play as a whole (as text *and* as performance) belongs to that continuing historical performance. The endless historical reperformance of Galileo's writing is a kind of "life of Galileo" after all, not in the sense of a written "vita" but in the sense that we speak of a text's "life" in history, a dynamic unfolding of assessment and debate constantly reopened to the possibility of the arbitrary, a life that is thus immediately continuous with the life of the actual audience (here in the theater) in history. If on level 4 we are worried by the tendency of performance to slip into writing, on level 5 we are encouraged by a sense of instability in the opposite direction.

The question of writing and its performance is thus repeatedly reopened in the play's structure. Especially important is the figure of an unending *string* of performances—in the progression from level 1 to level 4 and in the idea of a continuing reperformance of Galileo's writing in history. The performance of writing, we infer, is always itself reducible to writing but never in such a way that the domain of writing is finally closed, since further performance is always not only possible but inevitable.

This whole structure resonates significantly with its theatrical medium of presentation, with the dramatic theater considered as a locus of contradiction or disruption in the system of writing. The problem as such, the problem of writing and its performance, contains the possibility of revolution, the possibility of a radical reperformance of tradition or of social structures considered as a kind of writing. And the theater is that organ of society and literature whose function—when it is conceived so as to bring that function to the fore—is to expose and develop the problem of the performance of writing. By *not* trying to avoid its destiny as "literature," a work like *Leben des Galilei* becomes in the theater an inexhaustibly (circularly) provocative allegory or metaphor of the theatrical renewal required for the development of exactly that metaphorical function.

Should Galileo have resisted the Inquisition? This question has crucial allegorical significance. Galileo himself says that he had been wrong to recant, that he had missed the unique opportunity to establish a kind of Hippocratic oath for scientists (284). The whole play, correspondingly, is wrong to accept its situation in literary history, to conclude in fact by being the story of the adventures of a book. (Surely something more like a manifesto is required, a slap in the face of the culture and the classes whose existence is tied to the conservative operation of literature.) But this wrongness of the play, this incompleteness, this exposure to contradiction, refutation, co-option, is an instance of precisely the revolutionary historical leverage of drama and its theater. The fact that drama as a form is *never* "right," that it can never realize definitively its revolutionary or disruptive potential, that it is always radically open to question, always wrong *and hence never subject to theoretical closure, never fully digestible in literary tradition*: this state of affairs—upon which, it seems to me, *Leben des Galilei* is focused—is itself an instance of radical wrongness, a problem and a possibility of revolution, in the system of writing.

CHAPTER FOUR

Brecht, Artaud, Wedekind, Eliot: The Absence of the Subject

It is true in general, as I have said, or in the abstract, that theater reform cannot be effected by textual innovation alone. But these qualifications—"in general," "in the abstract"—have only a very limited applicability in the study of drama and theater, where *local* and *temporary* conditions tend to be of primary importance. I will argue now that for a definite period in nineteenth- and twentieth-century Europe, certain literary conditions obtain that in fact do make it possible for an appropriately conceived dramatic text alone—without assuming the use of any particular theatrical techniques— to assert the revolutionary function of drama. Indeed, if this were nowhere the case, in the whole history of European literature and drama, then since only text exegesis can anchor a critical argument, we would have nothing cogent to say about the *actual existence* of drama in the revolutionary sense. In the preceding chapter I suggested that *Leben des Galilei* is close to a demonstrable instance of revolutionary drama. Taken by itself, however, that argument is comparable to the assertion, say, that fascism is evil, which seems plausible enough but does not mean much if one has no basis for agreement that there is such a thing as evil to begin with.

Does Drama Exist?

Lessing, Goethe, Nietzsche, George Steiner, and plenty of other people have had opinions on the question of whether there is, or still is, or ever can be again, such a thing as tragedy. I have something of my own to say on this point further on, but first I want to open a simpler question. Is there, or has there ever been, such a thing as "drama," in a sense that would support the relation between theater and literature that I have sketched above?

I have already discussed, in connection with Aristotle, the general problem of the conceptual identity of drama. We can, if we like, call drama a literary or poetic genre. But as soon as we are asked to say exactly how it differs from other concepts in the same general category—say, epic, lyric, narrative—we find ourselves talking about ocular or material or social qualities that have nothing to do with literature *as* literature, as letters, writing, language, discourse. In order to distinguish drama, we must make reference to its theatrical performance. But how? Is a drama a drama because it *can* be performed? Plenty of nondramatic texts meet this condition. Is a drama a drama because it *is* customarily performed? This implies that a text receives its genre only after its composition, depending on what people decide to do with it. Is a drama a drama because it is written with a view to performance? There are plenty of obviously dramatic texts for which, as far as we can tell, this condition is not met. I have mentioned Northrop Frye's assertion that Shakespeare's plays are "radically acting scripts, and belong to the genre of drama."[1] "Radically" here asserts two things: (1) that *there exists* a clearly distinguishable class of literary works that it makes sense to call "acting scripts," and (2) that Shakespeare's plays belong to that class. But how do we know that statement (1) holds, that that class exists, except by first listing a number of texts that "radically" belong to it? Which produces a textbook instance of *petitio principii*.

I have also noted, however, that to say that drama is *not* a literary type or genre is to talk a kind of nonsense. Literature is not a natural phenomenon about which we might pretend to make scientifically objective statements. On the contrary, literature—the whole of literature, not merely every literary work—is an *artifact*, a thing consciously created, and consciously shaped, ordered, delimited, by human beings in history. Therefore, if we insist on recognizing drama as a basic literary type—"we" in the sense of a substantial number of competent individuals: say, you and I, and Goethe and Schiller, and Victor Hugo and Hegel and James Joyce, and Frye—if we are firm in this understanding of drama, then it follows that drama *is* in some sense a basic literary type after all. But surely not in anything like an absolute sense, since there is no sound theoretical basis for assigning to drama a place in the category of literary types. It must be true, rather, that if our intuition or conviction or dogmatic insistence on literary drama is valid, then it is valid only in a *historically relative* sense. What makes drama a literary type, in other words, is some *historically contingent* relation to other literary types and is bound to be a *different* relation in different ages or in different historical circumstances.

The general historical picture I am suggesting is this: in sixth-century Athens, for some reason—probably a political reason, but no one really knows—it became not only possible (with the spread of literacy) but also convenient to think of theatrical drama, in the form of tragedy and comedy, as a special domain (or group of genres) in poetry, with its identity as a domain marked by, among other things, what would elsewhere have been an inappropriate use of meter. Again, this is not something that happens "naturally" in literary history, and I do not think a parallel case can be demonstrated outside Greece. But in Athens, for whatever reasons, drama was installed as a type of poetry and in fact, in the fifth century and on into the fourth, became the city's dominant poetic form. Greek poetry, however, became in turn the principal model according to which, directly or indirectly, all the vernacular literatures of barbarian Europe were constructed, especially (but not exclusively) since the Renaissance. And the force of this tradition, I suggest, has been sufficient to persuade all Europe *that* drama should be regarded as a literary form but never sufficient to teach Europe *how* to regard drama in this manner. The problem thus created, the problem of how to fit drama into the scheme of literary types, which admits of no general solution, has in fact been solved only sporadically in European literature (not in the form of a continuous tradition) and solved *differently* each time.

Brecht and Artaud Once More

The view of the history of European drama that I am proposing obviously cannot be substantiated except one case at a time. Accordingly, I present here only one striking instance of a historically contingent generic definition of drama. I will argue that for a surprisingly diverse group of authors, the very identity of drama as a literary form is established in a manner that could not have been imagined before about 1850 and has probably been obsolete since about 1950.

The first two of the diverse group that I have in mind are, yet once more, Artaud and Brecht. I propose to show that both writers operate with exactly the same definition of drama *as a literary genre.* This does not by any means imply that drama, or theater, is the same thing for them. In fact, it is precisely the considerable difference between their ideas of the theater that lends special historical significance to the one question on which they are in perfect agreement, the question of the relation of drama to other literary types.

But "literature" itself is an idea on which Brecht and Artaud appear to hold diametrically opposed views. Artaud is implacably against what he calls the "Western" idea that "theater is a branch of literature."[2] Brecht, in his notes to the *Dreigroschenoper*, argues that the theater is *not "literary" enough,* that what we require is new "dramas" (in the sense of literary works that can be "read") which will break up and expose to change the established operation of "theatrical apparatus."[3] But is the notion of "literature" the same in these two contexts? Artaud qualifies his position by saying:

> It will be objected [to an argument against "speech" in the theater] that words have their own metaphysical properties, that it is not forbidden to conceive of speech as well as gesture on the universal level, and that it is on this level, moreover, that speech acquires its major power, as a dissociative force brought to bear on physical appearances, on all states in which the mind has become stabilized and tends to remain fixed. [Is this not almost the definition of a kind of metaphysical alienation effect?] It is clear, though, that this metaphysical way of regarding speech is not the way in which Western theater uses it. . . . Speech in Western theater is only used to express psychological conflicts peculiar to man and his situation in the daily reality of life. His conflicts lend themselves perfectly to the spoken word, and whether they remain in the psychological domain or pass over into the social domain, the moral interest of the drama will always depend on the way its conflicts attack and break down the characters. (Artaud, pp. 268–69)

What Artaud rejects, in other words, is literature considered mainly as a vehicle for *intuitive psychology*—which is what Brecht (p. 63) would call "Einfühlung" or empathy, precisely the tendency that must be *opposed* by a "Literarisierung des Theaters." By a "literary" theater, Brecht means not at all what Artaud means but something closer to what we might call a "readable" theater, which includes the equivalent of "footnotes, and the ability to page back and forth for comparisons" (Brecht, p. 31).

Of course, the opposition to intuitive or empathetic psychology leads Brecht and Artaud in different directions. Artaud, in keeping with his response to what he considers the callow political pretensions of the surrealists, is not interested in revolution. "The present state of society is unjust and should be destroyed," he says, but then continues, "If it is the business of the theater to be concerned about this, it is even more the business of the machine gun [we think of Genet's *Le Balcon*] . . . but even if [the theater] did raise the question, it would still be deviating from its purpose, which I consider higher and more mysterious" (p. 235). Brecht, by contrast, who *is* interested in revolution—and rather more so than the surrealists—moves away from empathy in the direction not of mystery but of science: for instance, in the posthumously published essay "Vergnügungstheater oder Lehrtheater?" he dismisses the idea that being a "poet" means having the intuitive ability to understand a murderer's mind from the inside out and insists instead that not only "modern psychology, from psychoanalysis to behaviorism," but also sociology, economics, and history must be drawn upon before one can claim any such understanding (p. 69).

And yet, if we turn to Brecht's and Artaud's essays on Oriental theater, we find that this divergence between mystery and science is not as deep-seated as it might appear. At least the two authors seem to agree about the *faces* of Oriental actors: about how the face becomes blank, illegible, *opaque*, no longer a kind of window into feeling or character; about what Artaud (p. 219) sees in Balinese theater as "these purely muscular facial movements that are superimposed on the features like masks"; or what Brecht (p. 76) sees as the Chinese actor's ability to "use his face as the empty page for the body's gesture to write upon." And although the mystery that Artaud speaks of elsewhere is certainly present in the Balinese theater, it is not present there in the sense of being penetrated or unveiled, in the sense that we might now decipher it; on the contrary, precisely the quality of clothing or covering is emphasized, in "these people who manage to give a mystical meaning to the mere shape of a robe and who, not content to place beside man his Double, attribute to each clothed man his double of clothing, who pierce these illusory or secondary [but never absent!] garments with a sword that makes them appear huge butterflies impaled on air" (p. 222). Brecht is less fanciful about his Chinese actors, but the substance of what he says (pp. 83, 84) is remarkably similar: "The Chinese artist, when he creates the impression of the mysterious, appears to have no interest in unveiling the mystery for us. He makes his mystery out of the mysteries of nature (especially human nature); he does not permit anyone to see how he brings forth the natural phenomenon, indeed nature does not yet grant even him such insight, despite its being he who has brought forth the phenomenon." And the connection with science is made by way of the idea that "the researcher, intent on making natural processes comprehensible, controllable, and mundane, will always first seek a point of view from which those processes appear mysterious, incomprehensible, and uncontrollable. He will assume the posture of astonishment and will apply the alienation effect."

What exactly is it that Brecht and Artaud agree about? What creates the occasional force of attraction between two thinkers who could hardly be more different in their temper and in their opinions? Clearly the idea of an opaque theater figures here, a theater that refuses to provide answers to the spectator's questions or mere echoes to the spectator's common personal concerns. Artaud, to be sure, tends to imagine this opacity as *material*, as a "poetry of space" (p. 232) which lacks the semiotic transparency of words—indeed, as the actor's actual "fluid materiality of the soul" (p. 261)—whereas for Brecht the theater must become, so to speak, *behaviorally* opaque, by encouraging alienation in the spectator. But the two theaters agree in what they are opaque or impervious *to*, what they repel, which is primarily *sympathy*, that comfortable feeling of human togetherness by which the theater (or literature, or art in general) supposedly reconciles us to the difficult external conditions of our existence. Brecht's theater, in this sense, is also a "theater of cruelty," a theater in which, as Artaud says (p. 256), "it is a question not of that cruelty which we can practice on each other by cutting up each other's bodies . . . but of that much more terrible and necessary cruelty which things can practice on us. We are not free. And the sky can still fall on our heads. And the theater has been erected to teach us, first of all, that."

Drama and Psychological Realism

What does the opacity of the theater have to do with the problem of drama as a literary type? Dorrit Cohn's book *Transparent Minds* suggests a very quick and efficient way of getting at this question. Cohn's subject matter is the novel of "psychological realism," a form of realism, paradoxically, that is defined by its claim to reveal to us something that is never directly revealed in reality itself: the inwardness, the subjectivity, the consciousness, of other people.[4] I contend, first, that psychological realism in this sense, understood as an invitation to perfected empathy, is the main tendency in *literary* history to which Artaud and Brecht are both opposed; it is mainly this form of transparency against which their theater's opacity is erected. As the first step toward a literary definition of the genre of drama, for Artaud and Brecht, we may say that drama is the antinovel; it is that literary form which specifically refuses to do what the novel (from about the mid-nineteenth to about the mid-twentieth century) takes as a principal task.

But is it only a matter of the novel here? Cohn adds to her final chapter, "Autonomous Monologue," an "Epilogue: The Relation to Drama and Lyric" (pp. 255–65), which includes a wonderful parallel of Joyce's "Penelope" monologue to Valéry's *La jeune Parque* (pp. 258–60). And of course both Artaud and Brecht detect a strong tendency toward psychological realism in the theater of their time. In fact, this questioning can be carried an important step further: is psychological realism a function more of the way texts are *written* (which is Cohn's concern) or of the way texts are *read*? I think it is obvious that the latter is the case—at least after psychological realism has been established as a convention. Any text that has a fiction and characters can be read as if it were a nineteenth-century novel. You can read the *Iliad* that way, or *Beowulf*, or (God help us) *Ubu Roi*. And people do in fact read *Waiting for Godot* as if the principal point of interest were the mode of subjectivity or experience of Vladimir and Estragon. This is why neither Brecht nor Artaud focuses on the novel as their theater's main adversary. It may be that literature has been "novelized," as Bakhtin puts it, that the dominant position of the novel among genres has infected (with psychological realism) our reading of all literary texts. But for practical purposes, what the theater of Artaud or Brecht is erected against is literature in general, in the sense of a nineteenth- and twentieth-century culture of empathetic reading. Railing specifically against the novel, for Artaud's purposes, is best left to people like André Breton, in the first Manifesto of Surrealism of 1924.[5] And when Brecht talks about the "bourgeois novel," as he does occasionally, it is usually with a kind of sadness, about the novel's failure to recognize that the "individual" it depicts no longer exists (p. 34), or about its failure to retain a genuinely "epic" structure (pp. 61–62).

But if psychological realism, once established in literary history, persists mainly as a culture of *reading*, then it follows that although techniques of text construction (as Cohn argues) may shape or channel the reader's apprehension of fictional subjectivities, no technique of writing can possibly *prevent* that receptive attitude. Not that writers have not tried to do this. In Robert Musil's *Die Verwirrungen des Zöglings Törless*, whenever the narrator sets about describing Törless's subjective state, the language has an unfailing tendency to become highly abstract and to fill itself with asides and allusions that quickly lose their connection with the boy's present thought or situation. Musil, it seems to me, is clearly *mocking* his reader for asserting the normal nineteenth-century novel-reader's prerogative of somehow managing to perceive an alien subjectivity. But what good is mocking if the reader does not know that he or she is being mocked? In fact, most readers of Musil—including most professional critics—simply plow ahead as if they were reading Henry James.

If we agree, therefore, that on the level of text alone, nothing can be done to block the transparency of mind in literature, to make literature opaque, to prevent the operation of psychological realism, then we are ready to state the generic definition of drama, for Brecht and Artaud, in its final form: drama, namely, is that unique literary type which *is* opaque to subjectivity after all, which *does* after all prevent psychological realism. This is, first, a strictly literary definition because it expresses nothing but a relation (in literary history) between drama and other literary genres. It is, second, a definition specifically of drama, since drama is the only literary type that is associated, by its very nature, with an expressive device or institution *other than text*—with the theater, which perhaps *can* after all be made strictly opaque or alienating to its audience. Third, of course, it is a historically contingent definition, since it is applicable only in a literary age dominated by psychological realism. And finally, it must be remarked that neither this nor any other literary definition of drama need be unique in its historical period. There is no reason why different literary definitions of drama should not be operating at the same time.

But what is wrong with psychological realism? Why is a literary form opaque to subjectivity desirable? For Brecht and Artaud, first of all, the main trouble with psychological realism is that when the reader makes a subjectivity-to-subjectivity connection with a text, what is in truth happening is that the text is pandering to, or being tailored to, the reader's subjectivity, which means that the text cannot possibly *change* the reader; and it is, above all, change that both Brecht and Artaud want from their theater. Thus we have here a particular version of the opposition between literary conservatism and revolutionary theater. Whether any particular type of theater actually *can* change its spectator is of course open to question, but doubts on this score do not affect the validity of the generic definition as a definition. Then, second, psychological realism is superseded *philosophically* even during the period of its literary ascendancy. Nietzsche, for example, in *Vom Nutzen und Nachteil der Historie für das Leben,* argues that "Innerlichkeit," or subjectivity, is in truth not a fact but a historically contingent *invention.* This insight cannot possibly be mastered by a literature of psychological realism. And third, finally, I will try to show here that *the absence of the subject in drama,* the psychological opacity that could conceivably be regarded as a defect in the form, in fact gives rise in particular works to unique and surprising expressive possibilities.

Does Drama Exist? If So, How?

Are the special theatrical techniques that Brecht and Artaud describe perhaps not very exactly, but at great length, strictly *necessary* in order to make the theater opaque to subjectivity? What kind of statement is the definition of drama I have suggested? Does it name only a *goal,* toward which playwrights and theater technicians must direct their innovative efforts? Or does it name a *fact*? Is it perhaps arguable that in the age of psychological realism, theater *automatically* evinces a subversive tendency, a tendency toward the kind of opacity advocated by Artaud and Brecht? In a climate of psychological realism, after all, literary language is understood to be a privileged semiotic medium in which distinct subjectivities may achieve direct sympathetic contact with one another. (If one wished to be unkind, one could say that the reader begins by saturating the literary text with subjectivity in the form of his or her cultivated imagination and then contrives to be astonished at how profoundly the text expresses subjective experience.) But in the theater, the visible reality of the stage (Aristotle's *opsis*), merely by being real and by making room for nonverbal semiotic initiatives, must surely at least threaten to disrupt the radically immaterial subject-to-subject intercourse that normally constitutes the reader's relation to literature. May we speak, then, of an *intrinsic* alienation effect in the theater, at least for audiences schooled in the conventions of psychological realism? Surely the focusing of our attention in the theater upon real people (the actors), whose consciousness or subjective experience is strictly inaccessible to us, must alienate us with respect to what would otherwise be the linguistically communicated subjectivity of the characters.

   Language, moreover, is not fundamentally a truthful medium. Umberto Eco argues that semiotics, in a sense that foregrounds theory of language, is basically a "theory of the lie."[6] Nietzsche, in "Über Wahrheit und Lüge im außermoralischen Sinne," questions whether there is any reasonable sense in which language can be reckoned suitable for containing or transmitting truth. And Percy Lubbock, one of the early theorists of psychological realism, makes an excellent perception about *The Ambassadors* when he points out that as long as the basic narrative voice is heard, the reader shares Strether's subjectivity, at least on its perceiving surface, but when Strether himself speaks, we find ourselves slipping out of him and are now confronted with him almost as "what he cannot be, an objective figure for the reader."[7] Our instinct, in other words, is to agree with Eco and Nietzsche and *not* to trust language as a window into the speaking subject; nonverbal signs, most of us would agree—or "body language," as we say—communicate subjectivity much more accurately. But in the literary theater, in the age of psychological realism, our instinctive response is turned on its head, for here the body language of the actors is mere acting, the mere *interpretation* of a subjectivity, a "character," that is transmitted mainly through the language of the underlying text. Surely this situation, to the extent that we are sensitive to it, is radically alienating and must eventually undermine our conventional acceptance of the subjective authenticity of the dramatic language itself (even in monologues). Precisely the depth to which our habits are shaped by the conventions of psychological realism must therefore measure the depth to which we are alienated (or the effort of self-delusion by which we overcome this alienation) in the theater as such, the depth at which we recognize, whether we admit it or not, that in the theater *the subjective experience of the fictional character is entirely inaccessible and therefore in effect simply absent.* Again, I think of Musil, who attempts to create this situation even in narrative and allegorizes his attempt in Törless's unexplained absence toward the end of the book.

There are, therefore, two paths by which the problem of drama in the age of psychological realism may be approached. One may, with Artaud and Brecht, insist on theatrical techniques that positively block the operation of a literary-sympathetic sensibility in the theater. Or one may choose to rely more upon the theater's *inherently* alienating quality, with respect to psychological realism, by selecting (or creating) for performance texts that are constructed so as to bring that quality to the fore. Even in the first case, however, the existence of an intrinsic opposition between the theater and literature in the historically limited sense of psychological realism must be postulated. Otherwise how would it ever occur to an Artaud or a Brecht to use the theater as they do—or, more especially, to an Artaud *and* a Brecht, given the distance between them? One can always find a way to shock or alienate one's audience. But how can one be sure of alienating the audience with respect, specifically, to their accustomed *literary* sensibilities, which is what both Brecht and Artaud require?

It may be that very few theatergoers—and probably, for that matter, very few playwrights—would agree with this argument on the inherent opposition between theater and psychological realism. But if at least some argument of the same general tenor as mine is not valid, if the theater is after all only another vehicle for the communication (illusory or otherwise) of subjective experience, if the body language of the actors in the end only perfects the transparency of mind that we seek in the literary language of the text, then it follows—to go back to the question I began with—that for us, at least, *there is no such thing as drama;* that our theaters, as both Artaud and Brecht complain, are nothing but platforms for the acting out of narratives in the manner of psychological realism. And yet I think I can show, after all, that there *is* such a thing as drama. Not, of course, as a matter of objective certainty. But also, not on the basis of patently unverifiable descriptions of "what happens" in the theater. What I can do is discuss two dramatic texts that fail to make any sense at all without the theorem of the strict inaccessibility or absence of the subject in the theater but, when interpreted in the light of that theorem—and I mean, interpreted *as texts,* with no specific theatrical assumptions—receive great historical significance as the achievement (despite George Steiner) of true modern tragedy. These two texts, moreover, are sufficiently different from one another to suggest an enormous range of possibilities.

Children

Let us begin with Frank Wedekind's *Frühlings Erwachen,* subtitled "Eine Kindertragödie," a children's tragedy, which most critics have read from the point of view of the children in it. A number of very intimate and powerful scenes involving only the children seduce us into this point of view: the opening conversations, circling around sex, between Moritz and Melchior (act 1, scene 2) and among the girls (1.3); Wendla's need to be beaten (1.5); Hänschen Rilow's ritual in the outhouse (2.3) and his love-scene with Ernst Röbel (3.6). But are we justified in adopting, or assuming we can adopt, the children's point of view? What is the difference between our perspective, relative to these children, and that of the adult characters in the play? If the conventions of psychological realism were in effect, the answer to this question would be that the children's minds are transparent to *us*—in our privileged situation as readers or spectators—but opaque, incomprehensible, to the adult inhabitants of the fiction. Plenty of readers and spectators adopt this assumption, but they do so, I contend, only by blinding themselves to its undeniable consequences. Given that the children in the play are typical—and what makes their scenes convincing, or seductive, if not this quality?—our ability to share in their subjectivity ought to imply, on our part, a deeper and more sympathetic knowledge of *children in general* than is shown by the adult characters in the play, which would imply in turn that our relations with our own children, in the privacy of the family and in educational practice, rest upon a firmer basis of communication than do those depicted in the play. It would follow, then, that what we see in the fiction is not strictly typical after all but characteristic of only a certain portion of our society, whom it becomes our task, and the play's, to enlighten.

What we are talking about here is, in effect, a limitation on the genre of satire. The object of satire can never be a strictly universal condition, since the perspective from which to observe and criticize that condition—or at least, to criticize it with the superior and confident gesture of satire—would be lacking. And in fact, *Frühlings Erwachen* is obviously not a satire. There is only one clearly satirical scene in the whole play, the conference of the teachers in act 3, scene 1. And why include this one scene, in which the lampooning atmosphere is so utterly different from anything in any other scene, if not to establish by contrast that the play as a whole is *not* satirical in character? Which means that our initial impression may have been correct after all, that the children in the play are, after all, strictly typical and that their relations with the adults represent a strictly universal condition in our own society. And this would imply in turn—since the existence of adequate communication between children and adults (like us) would contradict the universality of exclusion and suffering as undergone by the children in the play—that something is wrong with the customary literary assumption that the child characters' minds are transparent, that our inferences from their speeches constitute adequate knowledge of their subjective condition.

This suspicion—that for all the seeming intimacy of their speeches, the subjective point of view, the consciousness of the child characters is strictly inaccessible to us, strictly absent in the theater—is reinforced by the character of Frau Gabor, Melchior's mother, who is obviously the most enlightened of the adults in the play. Why is she as helpless and ineffectual as she proves to be in the end? She herself suggests an answer to this question. It is, she insists, only the inertia of habit and of ossified institutions that thwarts her good intentions: "Man muß ein vollständig entseelter Bureaukrat oder ganz nur Beschränktheit sein, um hier moralische Korruption zu wittern" (You have to be a completely soulless bureaucrat, or narrow-mindedness incarnate, to detect moral corruption here), she says to her husband in her son's defense.[8] But the ridiculous letter she writes to Moritz (pp. 508–9), which he at least has the sense to destroy before committing suicide (p. 517), and the equally ridiculous hyperbole in her defense of Melchior—"Gott, Gott, dieses frühlingsfrohes Herz—sein helles Lachen—alles, alles—seine kindliche Entschlossenheit, mutig zu kämpfen für Gut und Recht" (p. 530: his heart bursting with the joy of spring, his bright laughter, his childlike resolve to struggle courageously for goodness and justice)—all this not only reveals *her* thorough ignorance of the children's mentality, but challenges *us*, as well, to ask whether our recognition of her ignorance is translatable into a positive and useful knowledge, on our part, of the subjectivity in question. Could we write a better or more effective letter to a child in Moritz's situation? Can we be confident in our knowledge of children's subjective condition if that supposed knowledge does not enable us to communicate effectively? And even if some of us manage to raise children who neither commit suicide nor otherwise end badly, does this vindicate our claim to knowledge or understanding? In the world as Wedekind depicts it, is successful child rearing (i.e., making new adults) really an achievement at all—and not itself an act of ignorant cruelty?

Or perhaps the work is a kind of satire after all, in a sense that is established in the final scene, in Moritz's description of what it is like to be dead. "We smile at the tragedies [of living people]," he says, "each of us for himself, and we make our observations" (p. 542). Then he goes into detail:

> We can pity youth, for mistaking its timidity for idealism, and old age, brokenhearted over its own stoic superiority. . . . We ignore the mask of the actor, and observe the poet putting on his mask in the dark. . . . We watch lovers, and see them blush before each other in a foreboding of mutual deception. We see parents place children in the world in order to be able to tell them how lucky they are to have such parents, and we see the children go and do the same. We can eavesdrop on innocence in its lonely lover's pangs, and on the two-bit whore who is reading Schiller. (p. 543)

What is Moritz boasting of, if not his newfound ability to live life like a *reader*, to see into the secrets of subjectivity? What does this catalogue testify to, if not *the condition of being a reader under the assumptions of psychological realism*? By indulging ourselves in our supposed perception of a transparency of the subject that in the real world—and in the theater!—does not exist, we in effect remove ourselves from the world as if we were dead, as if we, like Moritz, could detach our heads, the centers of our percipient being, from the empirically limited condition of our bodies.

Tragedy

But to what positive end, beyond a satire directed at our literary sensibilities, does Wedekind exploit the absence of fictional subjectivity in the theater? It seems fairly clear, first, that the absence of the subject represents the inaccessibility *in general* of children's consciousness from an adult perspective, the phenomenon that we commonly trivialize by calling it the "generation gap." In truth, the external signs of generational miscommunication, especially the suffering we inflict on our children, are also symptoms of a profound internal problem, an inability on our part to communicate *with ourselves*, with the children we after all once were, hence symptoms of a rupture in the integrity of our own being. Somehow, at at least one point in our lives, we stop being one thing and start being another, and no effort of memory or self-knowledge can bridge that gap. And if it seems fanciful to ascribe this thinking to Wedekind, let me point out that the mysterious transition from child to adult, with respect to Melchior, *is actually represented in the play's last scene.* Of course, it is not represented "actually" in the sense of realistically, because it is not something that exists as an "actual" experience in anyone's memory. It is represented symbolically, with the aid of a muffled-up gentleman and a ghost. But there is no mistaking the process represented here, especially in Melchior's last words, which are a solemn promise that we know he cannot keep (if the mysterious gentleman is right, he will not even want to keep it, once he has a good meal in him): "I promise you, Moritz," he says, "no matter what happens, even if I become a different person ten times over, whether I succeed or fail, I will never forget you . . ." (p. 547). "Thank you my beloved friend" (Dank, dank, Geliebter), replies Moritz, thus betraying, in spite of himself, a sentimental streak. (Every psychological realist has one.) But Melchior continues, ". . . and when I am an old man with gray hair, it may be that you will then be nearer to me than any person still alive." Here, in the last instant of his childhood, and still on an empty stomach, Melchior is doing his best to hold his life together as a single unit, from childhood to old age. But it is hopeless. Whether he becomes a different person "ten times over" is not the issue. Once is enough, and that once is now, and any communication between the child of the past (who is Moritz's friend or beloved) and the man of the future, whoever he is, is out of the question.

But if the subjective condition of the children is strictly inaccessible from an adult perspective, then how does the author write the play? How do the actors act the parts? The answer, obviously, is that they do so not from the inside out but from the outside in, by imitating, as best they can, as many of the external gestures and attitudes and phrases of children as they can remember having observed. For like us, they too are excluded from the internal world of the children. And to the extent that we, in the audience, recognize this exclusion, we must also recognize that the acting here is not—as on many stages, in many theories and doctrines of acting—a kind of identification with fictional characters, a creation of subjectivities; it is, rather, something more like the *invocation* of absent spirits. By going through the ritual motions of childhood we summon those else inaccessible spirits, the true children, who are also in truth part of ourselves. And as I remarked at the outset, this summoning or conjuring of childhood, in the scenes where only children appear, is very earnest and powerful.

Indeed, to a certain degree, our summons is answered. For surely our feeling of exclusion from the child world resonates with the children's own sense of exclusion and abandonment (vis-à-vis the world as a whole), so that in a sense *they are there* for us in the shape of our feelings. Or it occurs to us that our failure to understand better than the blundering parents in the fiction makes us, in effect, not superior spectators but coparticipants in the fiction with the children, so that in a sense *they are there* for us after all, as if by blood. Or we recognize that by recognizing the actors' failure, we also at some level project onto the stage a kind of shadow of what they fail to grasp, so that in a sense *those children are there*—so that behind each hopelessly struggling actor stands the ghostly Double, the true child, the hopelessly struggling child, in much the same way that, for Nietzsche, the suffering god is detected behind the suffering victim of tragedy. And that true, truncated child, once again, is an intimation of our own truncated being, by being the other—missing—half of us. This may not be strictly tragedy in Steiner's neo-Hegelian definition, but it is, I think, if we follow out all its implications, tragedy enough. And it *is* this, once again, only by virtue of the strict absence of the subject in the theater.

Invocation

T. S. Eliot's *Murder in the Cathedral* is much more obviously an invocative tragedy. Indeed, if it is performed as a festival piece in Canterbury itself, its quality as an invocation of the spirit of Thomas is redoubled via the history and sanctity of the place. But on the other hand, it is also a play which in content, structure and style could hardly be more different from *Frühlings Erwachen*, which prompts us immediately to ask whether its invocative aspect can possibly be compared to that of the other play. On this point, I will argue that the absence of the subject in drama has almost exactly the same function for Eliot's play as for Wedekind's, and this argument completes what I offer as a significant quadruple structure in support of my suggestion for a definition of drama in relation to psychological realism.

For the purpose of understanding Thomas's mind—assuming this is part of our purpose in reading or hearing the play—the scene of the four Tempters is obviously crucial. Indeed, this scene, more than any other, awakens for us the *possibility* of knowing Thomas's mind, since it appears to dramatize that mind allegorically in a dialogue among internal tendencies. "Meanwhile the substance of our first act / Will be shadows, and the strife with shadows," says Thomas in introducing that scene; and the shadows in question are clearly his own thoughts and memories.[9] The first Tempter is dismissed with the words "So one thought goes whistling down the wind" (p. 185). The second Tempter, representing a better-founded thought, is banished with a statement of principle concerning "those who put their faith in worldly order" (p. 187). And the third Tempter, with his suggestion of a "new constellation" (p. 189), an alliance of Church and barons against the King, is dismissed with the recognition that "to make, then break" the King's power is an old "thought" that can be applied in various ways. "But if I break," Thomas concludes, "I must break myself alone" (p.190).

This thought, however, is the cue for the fourth Tempter, who is more exclusively than the others an aspect of Thomas's subjectivity—and in fact represents a kind of self-breaking on Thomas's part—in that he asks nothing but that Thomas follow his own desires. "You hold the keys of heaven and hell," he says, "Power to bind and loose: bind, Thomas, bind, / King and bishop under your heel." And when Thomas asks if, in using this power, he will be "Supreme, in this land?" the Tempter answers cryptically, "Supreme, but for one," meaning that Thomas will still be subject to Thomas, his actions still subject to his desires, to a particular view of himself, a satisfying and ultimately self-indulgent view of himself (p.191). This reflection (for it is a reflection, within Thomas's own mind) is then equally applicable to the dream of "glory after death," and even to Thomas's seeking of "the way of martyrdom" (p. 192). "Others offered real goods," cries Thomas, "worthless / But real. You only offer / Dreams to damnation." And the Tempter answers, "You have often dreamt them," to which Thomas can only say:

> Is there no way, in my soul's sickness,
> Does not lead to damnation in pride?
> I well know that these temptations
> Mean present vanity and future torment.
> Can sinful pride be driven out
> Only by more sinful? Can I neither act nor suffer
> Without perdition?
> (p.193)

And there is no solution to this problem. Thomas cannot deliberately offer himself for martyrdom—his doing which is the whole action of the play—without finding thereby some form of self-satisfaction. Past pride produces the need for martyrdom, which in turn is the source of a more insidious pride, and so on. The vicious circle is sealed when the Tempter now repeats, almost word for word, Thomas's first speech in the play (p.182).

Or at least this problem is insoluble, this "small circle of pain within the skull" (p. 220) is inescapable, when it is established *in a transparent mind*. For a transparent mind, in the literary sense, is by definition an *articulated* mind—which is not the same thing as being "articulate," able to express itself; rather, it means structured, organized as a system of related parts. (This meaning includes the meaning "spoken out.") If a mind is not articulated in this sense, how can it possibly be transparent in the medium of narrative discourse—indeed, in any grammatical medium? But Thomas himself, in his last speech to the fourth Tempter, articulates the problem of the recurrent sin of pride; and if that speech is understood as an adequate representation of his mind, if his mind is thus articulated and transparent, then it follows that the problem, for him, is strictly insoluble, and that his martyrdom is therefore invalid, inauthentic.

And yet it is obvious that on some level, at least, Thomas's martyrdom is meant to be understood as genuine, in the sense he himself articulates in his Christmas morning sermon, saying that "the true martyr is he who has become the instrument of God, who has lost his will in the will of God, not lost it but found it, for he has found freedom in submission to God. The martyr no longer desires anything for himself, not even the glory of martyrdom" (pp. 199–200). It is my contention that the genuineness of Thomas's martyrdom—to the extent that it is genuine—depends absolutely upon the operation of the genre of drama: namely, on the absence of the subject in the theater. For if Thomas were somehow all there in the play's discourse as a transparent, articulated mind, then his mind, ipso facto, would be irredeemably corrupt, and in judging him we would have no choice but to agree with the Fourth Knight Richard Brito's "verdict of Suicide while of Unsound Mind" (p. 219).

But Thomas himself claims to have surmounted the problem of recurrent pride. When he resumes speaking, after a kind of choral section that involves the Priests and the Tempters as well as the Chorus itself, he says:

> Now is my way clear, now is the meaning plain:
> Temptation shall not come in this kind again.
> The last temptation is the greatest treason:
> To do the right deed for the wrong reason.
> (p. 196)

And we cannot receive this speech as true, we cannot receive it as anything but a tissue of corruption if we imagine, or want to imagine, or force ourselves to imagine, that it is Thomas "himself" who is speaking. Its truth, if it has any, finds its way to us only through our understanding that the actor here—like the actors who play the children in *Frühlings Erwachen*—is invoking an absent spirit, an inaccessible subjectivity, an opaque mind. Later in the same speech, Thomas (or whoever it is) says:

> Servant of God has chance of greater sin
> And sorrow, than the man who serves a king.
> For those who serve the greater cause may make the cause serve them,
> Still doing right: and striving with political men
> May make that cause political, not by what they do
> But by what they are.

And this speech, I think, is one of the minor miracles in English dramatic poetry. For by what authority does the speaker here speak of what "they are," which of course means that "they are" impostors, not true saints? If he, the speaker on the stage, has that authority, if he "is" Thomas himself, if he represents an unfolding of Thomas's secret mind, then his speech, precisely by articulating and so rendering insoluble the problem of doing "the right deed for the wrong reason," condemns him for "being" exactly what he condemns. Only by *not* "being" Thomas, paradoxically, only by lacking authority, by being an actor, an impostor, an opaque mind, *is* that speaker Thomas after all, in the sense that is not condemned by his own words. And that these words are, after all, not strictly Thomas but an invocation of Thomas is then underscored by the swift modulation to an anachronistic audience address that follows:

> I know
> What yet remains to show you of my history
> Will seem to most of you at best futility,
> Senseless self-slaughter of a lunatic,
> Arrogant passion of a fanatic.
> (pp. 196–97)

Precisely these words, which *distance* the speaker from Thomas "himself," create the possibility that there is actual validity in Thomas's later assertion, "It is out of time that my decision is taken / If you call that decision / To which my whole being gives entire consent" (p. 212); the possibility (opened by the operation of drama as a genre) that Thomas's is *not*, after all, a mind that "decides" or, etymologically, cuts or articulates itself in a transparent display of itself to an audience of psychological realists.

The Truncated Audience

But what about the audience? In Wedekind's play, the connection with ourselves, the only conceivable basis for speaking of the play as tragic, is established by the idea of childhood in general, including *our* childhood, the irretrievably lost component of our very selves. But what about Eliot's play? Is the appreciation of *Murder in the Cathedral* as an invocation of Thomas restricted to faithful Christians? Is Christian faith—considered as a kind of blindness, as the ability to accept figures on the stage without speculating about their subjective state—is faith in this sense the only available alternative to simple psychological realism as a receptive attitude? If this were the case, then the play would certainly be Christian, but not a tragedy—the faithful would find in it a triumphant confirmation of their faith; we others would simply be confused in our literary sensibilities—and Lessing's doubts about the possibility of Christian tragedy would be sustained.[10]

In any case, the idea of two possible basic types of audience is written into the play itself. The fourth Tempter reminds Thomas of some visions of the future he has entertained, including that of "pilgrims, standing in line / Before the glittering jewelled shrine" (Eliot, pp. 191–92), which would clearly be the audience of the faithful. But there is another future, and another audience.

> And later is worse, when men will not hate you
> Enough to defame or to execrate you,
> But pondering the qualities that you lacked
> Will only try to find the historical fact.
> When men shall declare that there was no mystery
> About this man who played a certain part in history.
> (p. 192)

And this pair of audiences (religious and secular) is also represented in the pair of scenes that break the boundary between stage and auditorium and involve the audience in the action: Thomas's sermon, at which we the audience might as well be the assembled congregation of the faithful, and the mock-judicial public meeting conducted for our benefit (for us as a liberal secular audience) by the four murderers with a view to defending their action.

The two audiences, moreover, correspond to the two phases in Thomas's life that are separated by his "decision" that is not a decision, the cut that is not a cut, which occurs somewhere between his despairing reaction to the fourth Tempter ("Can I neither act nor suffer / Without perdition?") and his newfound resolution after the Chorus ("Now is my way clear, now is the meaning plain"). The secular Thomas—Thomas as a transparent mind, who is subject to the dilemma of the recurrent sin of pride—has been replaced by an opaque Thomas: Thomas as the fully committed martyr, a new Thomas whose words and deeds are indistinguishable in character from those of the old yet somehow have an entirely different meaning, an absent, opaque, unfathomable dimension in which, somehow, the problem of pride is simply forgotten. And just as the "decision" or cut between these two phases of Thomas is not really a cut at all, because the two Thomases are too utterly different, too perfectly incongruent, to be connected even by the notion of separation, so also the gulf between the two audiences is absolute. We of the secular audience cannot conceive what it is like to view the play from the perspective of faith, because faith has nothing to do with our powers of conception. And the faithful have forgotten, utterly and willingly, the discipline of delusion by which we read transparent minds and construct the relation between subjectivity and history.

The relation between the two audiences and the two Thomases, however, suggests a strong preference for the audience of the faithful. Indeed,
we of the secular audience are *mocked* in the public-meeting scene, in that
the self-justifying arguments of the four Knights reveal what our historically critical attitude boils down to in the end. We ourselves, or at least most
of us in this audience, are to an extent in sympathy with this attack upon us,
because we have recognized (as a *critical* conclusion) that the play is more
than merely a consideration of "historical fact," because we recognize
(again, as critics) that in order to complete our understanding of the play,
we require the perspective of the faithful, which is absolutely denied us. We
understand Thomas's absence, and its necessity in terms of the problem of
recurrent pride, but his corresponding *presence*, the manner in which the
play's invocation is successful, is not there for us.

And yet, let us look at the matter the other way round, to whatever
extent this is possible. If the public-meeting scene is a mocking of our situation as a secular audience, is it not equally true that Thomas's sermon (the
other scene that includes the audience in its action) is a mocking of the
audience of the faithful, a dramatization of the problem that by being too
simply and completely a faithful Christian, one reduces the whole play to a
mere sermon? For the faithful Christian, it is true, Thomas is present in the
play; but he is not meant to be present in the trivial sense that the preacher
of this Sunday's sermon is present. His presence, if he is present *as* Thomas,
has much more to teach the Christian than can be said in a sermon; it must
be achieved, by invocation, across the gulf of his absence, which the Christian Chorus imagines as "the Void" (p. 210), achieved by the decision that is
not a cut yet still somehow *is* the experience of decision. And in order to
achieve the experience of decision, in order to know Thomas's absence in
his presence, in order thus to complete their understanding of the play, the
audience of the faithful require (and know they require) *our* perspective,
the perspective of historical and literary criticism, which is absolutely
denied them. For us, as part of the operation of the genre of drama, Thomas
is *really* absent, in the very simple literary-critical sense of being opaque.
But we also recognize that his absence is *pointless* without his presence,
which is as simple and obvious to the faithful as his absence is to us, and as
unfathomable to us as his absence is to them, that absence without which,
they must recognize, his presence is *inauthentic*.

I contend, therefore, that *Murder in the Cathedral* is tragedy in almost
exactly the same sense as *Frühlings Erwachen*, tragedy presented to a truncated audience whose truncated condition *is* the tragedy—except that in
Eliot's case the audience is truncated by being split into two noncommuni-
cating parts, whereas Wedekind's audience is truncated by its separation
from a childhood that is not there. In both cases, the tragedy depends on a
sense of literature as characterized by psychological realism and on an

understanding of drama, with its institution of the absent subject, as literature's own internal self-subversive component—its conscience, so to speak. And in both cases, finally, the achievement of tragic meaning *profiles* for the audience, and for the culture at large, the generic distinctness of drama on which it depends, thus tends to break up the inherent conservative tendency of literature and to open, for the culture at large, revolutionary possibilities. Eliot can be as scrupulously conservative as he pleases in his political and religious opinions. His generically scrupulous use of the form of drama makes a revolutionary of him all the same.

The Theater That Never Was: Georg Büchner and Drama as a Philosophical Experiment

The previous chapter does all it can to avoid having its argument depend on a specific description of "what actually happens" in the theater. It proceeds by first establishing a strictly literary definition of drama, based on an admittedly narrow and timebound idea of the literary, and then argues critically (using basic exegetic methods) that certain texts do operate as dramas in the sense suggested by chapter 2. This chapter, by contrast, treats the work of an author for whom, as far as I can tell, no assumable definition of drama existed and who therefore had to invent his own rather complex idea of the theater and what actually happens in it. The case is instructive for a number of reasons, but especially in that it can only have been the pressure of his violent yet agonizingly self-critical revolutionary sentiments that drove Georg Büchner to experiment with the form of drama.

A Theory of Theater

There are several very long speeches in *Dantons Tod*, which fall into three basic categories: political speeches, especially by Robespierre (pp. 77–79, 201–3) and St. Just (pp. 103–5), which are based in part on actual historical material; meditative soliloquies by Robespierre (pp. 87–88) and Danton (pp. 97–98, 123–24); and in a class of it own, a long account by the prostitute Marion, spoken to Danton, of her own early life and character (pp. 80–82).[1] What is this last speech doing there? What is its function in the play's economy? Neither Danton's wife, Julie, in her dying monologue (p. 130) nor Camille's wife, Lucile, in either of her despairing fantasies (pp. 126–27, 132), is given even half as much room to express herself.

The most important thing about Marion's speech is its *falsity*. She begins by recounting her first sexual experience and how she had then quickly made herself available to "all men" (T16).[2] Her first lover, however, had taken her promiscuity as a betrayal and had committed suicide—which, she says, had been the only "break" in her life. And she continues: "Other people have Sundays and weekdays, they work six days and pray on the seventh; once every year on their birthdays they become sentimental and every year they think about the New Year. I don't understand that at all; I know nothing of such breaks in time, of change. I am always only one thing, an unbroken longing and grasping, a flame, a stream" (T16–17). This statement cannot be strictly true. Precisely Marion's ability to say what she says contradicts the content of her utterance. The "one thing" that she supposedly is has already undergone an internal division in speaking of itself, and the string of metaphors that follows—"an unbroken longing and grasping, a flame, a stream"—is nothing but a necessarily futile attempt to find its way back to itself again. "Your lips have eyes" (T17), she says to Danton; but this admonition against an excess of conscious detachment applies even more directly to herself. Marion, in other words, is an *impostor* in her own identity, which means that the difference between the "character" Marion and the actress who is "playing" her on the stage has *disappeared*. The actress, precisely by being an impostor, has become in a strong sense identical with the character whom she counterfeits. And this state of affairs is underscored by the fact that in "real" life, prostitutes are after all a special class of professional actresses.

Now I am going to jump to a conclusion. Why—I ask—is Marion's speech given such extension, and why is its significance profiled so clearly by the line "Your lips have eyes," if not to suggest that the coincidence of character and actor, the quality of being an impostor in one's own identity, *obtains in the play as a whole*? Are we not meant to infer, I ask—are we not meant at least to entertain the possibility—that even in the case of Danton and Robespierre and Camille Desmoulins and all the other historical personages, there is no fundamental difference between the "actual" person, who once "actually" lived, and the impostor on the stage before us now, that in effect, therefore, we in the theater find ourselves in the presence of the "real" Danton or Robespierre or Camille Desmoulins? Collot, in the Jacobin Club, screams, "It is time we tore off our masks!" (p. 77; T11), and Danton, when he hears of this demand, responds, "I'm afraid their faces would come with them" (p. 84; T19). The mask and the face are identical; there is no face that is not in truth a mask, no identity that is not in truth an imposture. Which means that in the theater, where the mask is frankly a mask, we see a truer "face" than we do in real life, a *realer* Danton than the Danton who, the play reminds us, died in April 1794.

I have, as I say, jumped to this conclusion. There is no way to get to it except by jumping, no gradual chain of argument by which to establish it as a plausible text interpretation. For it is not an interpretive conclusion, about the text of *Dantons Tod*, in the first place. It is the statement of a general philosophical theory of the theater, a theory that discards both the Platonic and the Aristotelian view of *mimesis*—of the theater as an imitation of the real—and insists instead that what we commonly think of as reality is really only a dim imitation and distortion of the truth that confronts us directly in the theater, the truth, again, that identity itself is always a form of imposture. The only way in which this theory of the theater could be conclusively linked to the play *Dantons Tod* would be by demonstrating that Büchner himself had worked out its details *as* theory. But he never did so, and I will show that he had good reasons for never doing so.

And yet, if I were inclined to defend the conclusion I have jumped to, I could find plenty in the text of *Dantons Tod* that would seem to support me. The idea of the theater, for instance, occurs repeatedly as a metaphor and always in a way that suggests the emptiness of what we regard as our identity. Danton remarks that it might be better to die by the guillotine than by fever or old age, because "there's still something to be said for leaving the stage with a good spring in your step and a fine gesture and hearing the applause of the spectators behind you. It's an agreeable way to go and it also suits us: we stand on the stage all our lives, even though in the end we are finally stabbed in earnest" (p. 92; T27–28). Why not die theatrically, since our whole lives are nothing but theater anyway? And it is nicely ironic that Lacroix says of Danton, immediately after that speech, "And [he] doesn't believe a word of what he said" (T28). For precisely such a lack of belief in his own words would prove the *truth* of what Danton says about our living (and speaking) as if "on the stage." A few pages later, Danton's "echo" (p. 91; T27), Camille, delivers his own diatribe on the theater (pp. 95–96), and on people's inability to imagine human character, human identity, human worth, except in a theatrically tarted-up form. Danton himself, to be sure, still doubts that there is any basic substance beneath that tarting-up. "What are we but puppets?" he says to Julie, "We are nothing, nothing in ourselves" (p. 100; T36). And finally even Camille, in the shadow of death, comes around more or less to this view: "We ought to tear the masks off for once and look around as if in a room of mirrors, and everywhere see nothing but the ancient, innumerable, and imperishable head of a fool.— Nothing more, nothing less" (p. 128; T66).

Or perhaps we might wish to see the matter not in its theatrical aspect but in its philosophical aspect. Our attention is then seized by the play's opening, where, after Danton's obscene remark about one of the ladies playing cards, Julie pleads, "Danton, do you believe in me?" (Glaubst du an mich? T3; p. 69). In its context, this question implies: do you trust me? But the words themselves, and Danton's complicated response to them, also suggest, do you believe in my existence, in my identity? Not only Julie but also Robespierre is compelled by Danton to confront the question of his identity. "Isn't there something inside you," Danton says to him, "that whispers sometimes, quietly, secretly, that you lie, Robespierre, you lie?" (p. 86; T21). And Robespierre, when he is alone, reformulates this idea even more powerfully: "Ich weiß nicht, was in mir das Andere belügt" (I don't know which part of me is lying to the other: p. 87; T23). The quality of untruth pervades the self to such a depth that even the agent or agency of untruth is unidentifiable. But the most powerful formulations of this questioning of personal identity are still Danton's own. Especially important is his first speech in act 2, which develops the ideas suggested by Marion's monologue. "How tedious it is," he says, that we always get dressed in the same way and do the same things day after day. "It's very sad," he continues, "millions have already done so and millions more are destined to do so; and besides that we consist of two halves, each doing the same thing, so everything happens twice—it's very sad" (p. 90; T26). The "two halves" he speaks of clearly represent the internal division of consciousness that keeps us from being the "one thing" Marion claims to be. But it is not as if these "halves" produced an internal *difference* by which we might gain that (however illusory) leverage or control over our existence that is presupposed by the idea of an identity. On the contrary, those halves simply repeat each other and so do nothing whatever except deny the possibility of unity in our lives; they leave us in the condition of being insincere, being impostors, yet with no conception at all of what we are being insincere *about*.

Textual Incongruity and the Psychology of Compensation

Again, however, this type of interpretive argument from the text does not support the conclusion I have suggested concerning a theory of the theater. For interpretive arguments, by definition, have *meaning* as their object, and meaning—however we imagine it—presupposes on some level a communication uncorrupted by imposture. What we must ask, I think, is what is *wrong* with the text, what glaring instances of disproportion or incongruity it presents. This is what attracts our attention to Marion's monologue, the question of why a relatively inconsequential speech should be given so much time.

Especially with respect to the play's historical material, glaring incongruities are easy to spot. Why, for instance, is Thomas Paine made into a pedantic atheist when, precisely in *The Age of Reason*, the book he had in progress when he was imprisoned in France, he takes a position strongly opposed to atheism? Büchner knew full well from his sources that the resident doctrinaire atheist in the Luxembourg prison was Baron von Cloots, known as Anacharsis Cloots. Unfortunately, Cloots was executed on 24 March 1794, a week before Danton's imprisonment. But surely a week's fudging of dates would have been preferable to the complete misrepresentation of Paine's views. And why does Büchner give the name "Julie" to Danton's second wife, Louise *née* Gély, who remarried after Danton's death and was in fact still living when Büchner died in 1837? Why is Lucile Desmoulins permitted to end her life romantically, when in reality it took a denunciation by Laflotte to get her imprisoned? What are those two insufferably sentimental subplots doing there in the first place, the suicides of the two wives who cannot live without their husbands? Have the husbands deserved it of them, especially Danton with his whores? And above all, why is Danton's character made so inconsistent? In his last speech in the last philosophical discussion among the prisoners, he says, "The world is chaos. Nothingness is the world-god yet to be born" (p. 129; T67). There are some indications in Büchner's sources that Danton showed cynical tendencies toward the end, and some suggestion of sexual excesses. But why does Büchner insist on creating a full-fledged philosophical nihilist, while in the same play he reproduces and develops the speeches of impassioned self-defense delivered by this same supposedly uncaring philosopher?

One might say, and people have said, that Büchner is simply portraying life, in all its illogical unaccountability. One might, in other words, deny that there is a question here. But there is a question. Why, for example, insist *both* upon Danton's insufficiently documented sexual self-indulgence *and* upon the inherently undocumentable intellectualized sentimentality of his attachment to Julie? Büchner is forcing contradictions into the foreground here, and we must ask why.

Let us begin with Thomas Paine, and with the assumption that Büchner is neither stupid nor ignorant nor careless in the use of his sources—the assumption, in other words, that "Payne" is here created with a view not only to the interlingual pun formed by his name with the German word "Schmerz" (p. 107) but also to the flat contradiction between the views he expresses on stage and the doctrine of his book *The Age of Reason*. Let us note, moreover, that the scene Payne dominates is given great weight in the play's structure, as the first scene of act 3, thus the opening of the play's second, despairing half. (Scenes dominated by Danton—for whom there had still been some hope—had opened acts 1 and 2, and Julie's decision to die opens act 4.) Can we explain the contradictoriness of Payne's with Paine's own views in terms of the hypothesis I have suggested concerning the theater?

In fact, we can. If we start with the assumption that Payne, as he appears on stage, is a realer or truer version of himself than the "actual" Thomas Paine of *The Age of Reason* (is this why Büchner uses the common French misspelling of his name?), then the whole picture presented to us is an instance of what we might call *psychology of compensation*. Payne knows that there is no God. But for all the confidence and eloquence with which he defends it, this knowledge, considered as feeling, has the quality of an abysmal dread:

> Merke dir es, Anaxagoras, warum leide ich? Das ist der Fels des Atheismus. Das leiseste Zucken des Schmerzes und rege es sich nur in einem Atom, macht einen Riß in der Schöpfung von oben bis unten. (p. 107)

> Pay attention, Anaxagoras: Why do I suffer? That is the very bedrock of atheism. The least quiver of pain, in even the smallest of atoms, makes a rent in creation from top to bottom. (T44, modified)

Payne's rhetoric carries him a step too far when he says not merely that pain disproves the existence of God but that it tears the whole world apart. What experience of agonized rending can really be on his mind here if not that it is *his own* world that is torn apart, revealed as vacuous by his own feelings and arguments? And it is this strictly unbearable revelation of nothingness that the "actual" Thomas Paine (whom we do not see on stage but only know of from his work) compensates for in the Deistic piety of his writing. The actual Thomas Paine, whom we know from history and books, is only a mask by which the *real* Payne, whom we see on the stage, compensates for the anguish of his atheist's knowledge.[3]

Is it far-fetched to suggest that Büchner conceived his Payne in this way? Not at all. Because it is *exactly* the way he conceives, in full detail, the figure of Robespierre. We have already remarked that under pressure from Danton—though only after Danton leaves—Robespierre virtually admits that his practical and theoretical insistence on morality and virtue is nothing but compensation for his deep and terrifying knowledge of the emptiness of these qualities. And as with Robespierre, so also with Danton, who presents himself in his philosophical speeches as a strict nihilist. That he does not *act* like a nihilist, that he indulges a desperately sentimental attachment to his wife, that he defends himself passionately before the Revolutionary Tribunal, these are precisely the compensatory moves we are taught, by the play, to expect from a strict nihilist. If Danton did not make such a move, if he thought and acted in strict consistent accord with his knowledge of emptiness, this would only show that he had transformed that knowledge *itself* into the vessel of some sort of pleasure, into something *positive*, which would mean in turn that he had violated that knowledge (how can nothingness be positive?) and could not be a strict nihilist after all.

Thus, moreover, we are also able to account for the play's sentimental subplots. If we are right about Payne and Robespierre and Danton, then it follows that the message of the play is basically nihilistic. But are we, the audience in the theater, any better able to face such a message, to accept it, than Payne or Robespierre or Danton? Of course not. Precisely our under-standing of the play's message must be measured by the incongruous arbi-trariness of the compensatory move by which we veil or avoid or postpone that understanding. The play's ridiculous sentimental subplots thus oper-ate as a *test* for the audience. If we merely dismiss that sentimentality as irrelevant or incongruous, then we merely show thereby that we have missed the point of the play, that we have failed to engage its nothingness *as* nothingness, on a level deep enough to force a compensatory move on our part. Somehow, in order to be an adequate audience, we must find our-selves in full participation with *both* the play's utterly impermeable hope-lessness *and* its equally indigestible coating of emotional fluff.

The Full Theory and Its Problems

And if that little word "somehow" seems evasive, then it is only because we have lost sight, for the moment, of the *theatrical* aspect of this argument. For the psychology of compensation clearly implies that all human charac-ter and conviction, anything positive about us, anything that can be reck-oned our identity, has the quality of *imposture,* an ultimately arbitrary compensatory move with respect to our underlying knowledge of empti-ness. We are, again, all of us, impostors in our own identity; and again, this truth is bodied forth as meaning in every instant of every dramatic per-formance—as we learn from Danton and Marion—by the mere fact of the difference between actor and role. (Consider even the point where Payne says, "we know quite certainly that the world, or at least our ego, exists" [p. 105; T42], or the point where Danton says, "The pitiable fact is that *I am something!*" [p. 119; T56]. Is the integral being of the self affirmed here after all? Not a bit. Even these speeches—in being spoken by real actors, to whom the word "ego" or "I" can obviously be referred, so that on stage the reference of these words is *split* between actor and character—actually only intensify the focus on imposture, on the emptiness between the self and itself.) In the theater, therefore, we are always inescapably engaged with the truth of nothingness. And yet, as Camille points out, it is empirically indis-putable that we also always use the theater as an emotional *escape* from reality, nature, the world—from truth. Therefore, both components of the seemingly impossible attitude Büchner requires of an audience are *inher-ently* given in our condition as we sit in the theater.

The cohesion of this argument is reinforced by a recognition of how clearly Büchner's work is structured with respect to the central notion of compensatory psychology. The structure is one of gradation. At the first step, in Robespierre, we have a figure who carries out the compensatory move without being fully aware of the abyss of knowledge behind it. Then, in Danton, the figure is still entirely contained within the fiction but has achieved something comparable to an audience's full engagement with nihilistic truth, although this does not exempt him from his necessary compensatory blindness. At the third step, in Payne, the abyss of knowledge is represented in the fiction, but the compensatory move is found only *outside* the fiction, in *our* historical knowledge and reading. And at step four—for us, in the auditorium, as spectators of both the main action and the subplots—both knowledge and compensation are established outside the fiction, in our own experience, in the two contradictory ways we must receive the play. Thus our understanding of the play's fiction is transmuted, step by step, into an understanding—however contradictory—of ourselves. And I think it is evident that the correspondence of those four main steps to the play's four acts can be argued convincingly.

But why, finally, for the purpose of illuminating this quality of the theater, write a play about the French Revolution? I think the answer is fairly clear. The French Revolution, for Büchner and his contemporaries, marks the advent of modernity, and for Büchner himself, I contend, modernity is constituted primarily by a growing manifestness of *the substantiality of discourse*. Over and over in *Dantons Tod* we hear that mere words have somehow acquired presence and power, especially destructive power, in the brute physical world. Every grammatical component of the "theorem" of human equality, says St. Just, has killed people (p. 104); and Barère later mutedly reproaches St. Just for his "sentences, with every comma the stroke of a sword, and every period a chopped-off head" (p. 116; T54). "Look around you," says Mercier to his fellow prisoners: everything you see, all the Revolution's butchery, is what you have spoken; it is "the pantomime version of your words" (p. 110). The Revolution, that is, as a radical retheorizing of society and government, had entailed the complete demolition and rebuilding of human community in the medium of discourse and had thus revealed that human community, human existence, had never really had any substance *except* discourse. And this understanding, in turn, is logically equivalent to the psychology of compensation. For where, but in discourse, does that doubling or repetition of ourselves happen, by which our identity is undermined in the very process of grasping itself? In what medium, if not in discourse, is the inevitable futile move of compensation, which *constitutes* our positive existence, carried out?

These truths, of course, if true at all, had been as true before the French Revolution as after. But in Büchner's view, I am suggesting, the French Revolution had brought this despairing abyss of truth to a new level of manifestness in our public life, endowing it almost with institutional character. Public life in post-Revolutionary Europe, in other words, has taken on something very like the philosophical transparency of the theater, whence it follows—to bring the argument full circle—that the performance of *Dantons*

Tod is indeed, in effect, an immediate enactment of the French Revolution here and now.

This is, to put it mildly, an ambitious theory of the theater, extravagant in its claims and, for all its pessimism, intriguing in its ramifications. But it also raises problems, inasmuch as it seems to imply for the theater a philosophical transparency that ought to be rendered impossible by its own doctrine of compensation. Would there not have to be, somehow, a compensatory *obscuring* of that transparency? We can of course insist on the contradictoriness of the attitude that is required of us in the theater. But are we imagining that this contradictory attitude is somehow magically engendered in us when we take our seats? Does it not remain true that in the structure of *Dantons Tod,* that contradictoriness, in Robespierre, in Tom Paine, especially in Danton, is also exhibited to us as in a mirror, thus placed within our knowledge and power in a manner that the theory cannot permit? Perhaps the idea of a fundamental questioning of identity in the institution of the theater need not be thrown out. But it does require a more cogent formulation—which brings us to Büchner's *Woyzeck.*

Theater within Theater

There are at least three scenes in *Woyzeck* that show the structure of play within play, or theater within theater: first, the scene "Fair booths. Lights. People," along with "Interior of the brightly lighted booth"; second, the scene at the inn, in which Woyzeck observes Marie and the Drum Major through an open window as they dance; and third, "The Doctor's courtyard," where Woyzeck is exhibited to an audience of medical students. The last of these scenes is perhaps the most immediately significant, and the most uncomfortable for us because of the parallel that is established with *our* quasi-experimental use of Woyzeck as we sit in the theater. Woyzeck is being exhibited to us as well, and we, like the medical students, are expected to draw general conclusions from what we see, conclusions having to do, perhaps, more with society than with medicine, but conclusions—scientific conclusions in a broad sense—nonetheless.

Therefore, the obvious questions that arise concerning the Doctor's procedure are also questions that must be asked about what we are doing in the theater. Do we have the right to observe human suffering, even the mere fictionalized image of human suffering, in a scientifically or aesthetically detached manner? Indeed—given that we recognize differences between the real and the theatrical Woyzeck—is it not precisely the communal mechanism of aesthetic detachment (in which we participate, along with the performers and the author) that *causes* those differences and thus in the end actually *conceals* from us the real suffering of a real person? Do we not, precisely by observing Woyzeck, thus also turn our back on him, just as the Doctor does? May it not even be inferred that our attitude as a theater audience (however sympathetic or socially conscious we may be) is itself a symptom of the social causes of Woyzeck's condition? Within the fiction, the Doctor, with his diet of peas, *creates* the condition in Woyzeck which he then observes. Are we too—by our participation in the fictionalizing, the aestheticizing of Woyzeck—not in at least a roughly comparable manner responsible for what we see?

In the process of asking these questions, we find that we have become not only the observers but also the *object* of the experiment that is underway in the theater—just as the Doctor, precisely by being a mere observer, has become the object of our socially critical scrutiny in the auditorium. The parallel here is quite exact. Just as the Doctor creates the morbid physiological condition that he observes, so we, by going to the theater, create a morbid social condition—or at least contribute to the maintenance of such a condition, by aestheticizing urgent social questions—which is then represented to us in the play's fiction. And if it perhaps seems extreme to speak of the theater as a contributing cause of morbid social conditions, we need only recall *Dantons Tod,* where the morbidity of the social situation depicted (in the wake of the French Revolution) is exactly equivalent to its pervasive *theatricality,* where the public figures, the people who attempt to rescue or heal their society in the medium of discourse—Robespierre and St. Just, Danton and his associates—can never escape the theatrical structure, the equivalence of success and applause, that governs and perverts their efforts. Or we think of the many letters in which Büchner, explicitly or by implication, disparages as "Komödie" the ineffectual activities of precisely those liberals and radicals whose actual principles he *shares.*[4] The theater may not be a root cause of social injustice; but theatricality, it appears, is a characteristic perversion of the attempt to remedy social injustice. And we, by going to the theater precisely in order to develop or exercise a socially critical attitude, thus inevitably reinforce the association of ideas and activities that produces that perversion.

Camille's long speech about the theater in the second act of *Dantons Tod,* therefore, takes on a new dimension in the context of *Woyzeck.* It is now revealed as the indictment, the entirely futile indictment, of an actual social evil. In order to become the object of that focused general consciousness which is needed as a first step toward reform, social injustice *must* be displayed, thus theatricalized, whereupon the world in which social injustice and human suffering actually happen, by comparison with its theatricalized version, is reduced to "miserable reality" (p. 96) about which nothing ever gets done. We, in the theater, thus find ourselves at the *actual* center (not merely the imitated center) of an infernal machine in which social reform is incessantly thwarted by precisely the mechanism that is employed to achieve it.[5] What is new in *Woyzeck,* however, is the association of this quality of the theater with the idea of a scientific experiment, an experiment in which the observer becomes part of the object. It is this association that needs to be gone into now.

Drama as Experiment

What *question*, first of all, is the experimental procedure in the theater meant to throw light on? "Gentlemen," says the Doctor, introducing his experiment in feline defenestration, "we are concerned with the weighty question of the relationship of the subject to the object" (p. 250; T128). There is of course a humorous disproportion between what he says and what he is about to do, but I do not think we can simply dismiss the idea of the relation between subject and object. For that relation, in at least one important sense, is mediated by *the body*, which can be regarded as the subject's organ in the realm of the object. When the body is healthy, however, when it mediates successfully and produces a relation of harmony, the distinguishable effects of subject and object, hence the details of their relation, become difficult to pin down. Therefore a condition of disorientation or morbidity in the body is required—the cat thrown out of the window, the Captain's foreseeable apoplexy, Woyzeck's nutritional deficiency—in order to disrupt the relation of subject and object and open it to investigation. The Doctor's ultimate interest, in other words, is exactly what he claims it is.

But the question of the relation of subject and object is the question of the basic structure of human existence, the question, What is man? What is human nature? And it is this question, accordingly, that we see travestied in the other two theater-within-theater scenes I have mentioned. At the inn, after Woyzeck has seen Marie with the Drum Major, the Apprentice delivers a "sermon" on the question:

> Why is there Man? Why is there Man? Yea, verily I say unto you: How should the farmer, the cooper, the shoemaker, the doctor, live, had not God created Man for their use? (p. 247; T125)

This is a *reductio ad absurdum* of what Büchner, in his lecture on the cranial nerves, calls the "teleological standpoint" (p. 259), as applied to humanity. And in the sideshow booth we are asked to speculate: suppose the outward effects of rational reflection can be demonstrated in the behavior of a horse; suppose even the horse's defecating can be interpreted as evidence of "double reason" (p. 238; T115), of self-conscious rationality. Does this not mean that the horse is a human being?

What is man? Is there even a reasonable *approach* to this question? Obviously, no list of observable outward effects can ever produce an adequate definition; and obviously, the teleological approach, the asking of why or for what purpose man is, leads nowhere. But what about the Doctor's experimental method, the attempt to unravel the relation of subject and object by disrupting its bodily vessel? There are two things wrong with the Doctor's method, two unjustifiable presuppositions. In the first place, if I am willing to torture a person's body for scientific purposes, then I have thereby already denied out of hand the existence of a basic *moral* component in human nature. (We think here of the Captain's clumsy struggle with the idea of morality.) And in the second place, Woyzeck as an experimental object is, for the Doctor's purposes, *contaminated* by his social situation. For the relation of subject and object is mediated not only by the individual's body but also, no less directly, by the particular social structure that obtains. The articulation of experience into subjective and objective components, the very idea of what subjects and objects *are*, itself always presupposes a social or communal act of valuation. And if the condition of society, for the Doctor and Woyzeck, were not *already* morbid—if, in other words, the relation of subject and object were not *already* disrupted in an uncontrollable manner—Woyzeck would not be desperately poor and would not be available as an experimental object to begin with.

This criticism of the Doctor's procedure, however, allows us finally to say something specific about the nature of the experiment that is in progress *in the theater*. For if it is true that the social is a principal mediating vehicle between subject and object; and if it is true, as I have suggested, that the audience, by being in the theater, are in a sense responsible for the corrupt social situation shown them; and if it is true that we nevertheless come to the theater in order to learn, to gain knowledge or useful experience; then it follows that the theater may be regarded as *the ultimately deliberate creation of a morbid social condition for the sake of studying the question "What is man?" by way of the disrupted relation between subject and object.* Now this statement, clearly, is not yet a conclusion, for it invites exactly those criticisms that I applied to the Doctor in order to arrive at it. The theatrical production of social disharmony is still uncontrollable, because the sense in which we, as an audience, are responsible for what we see can never be sufficiently narrowed down; theatergoing, after all, is as much a result as a cause of social conditions. And the ethical issue is also still unsettled. Do we have the right to carry out this theatrical experiment? Indeed, the issue can now be broadened. Do we have the right to ask, "What is man?" in the first place? Is that question, "What is man?" not perhaps itself *already* corrupt? Does the attempt to answer it not perhaps *of necessity* involve ethically unjustifiable actions? And yet, on the other hand, how shall we *be* human without asking, "What is man?"

The question "What is man?" has thus apparently become not merely unanswerable, but unaskable. For as soon as we ask it, and oblige ourselves thereby at least to attempt an answer, we find ourselves in the ethically untenable situation of an audience in the theater of *Woyzeck*—unless we beg the question by responding to it with something like the grandmother's nihilistic fable: the story of the poor child who is all alone and goes searching, and then returns to the earth and is now more alone than ever (p. 252; T133). And *Woyzeck* itself, accordingly—which does ask the question "What is man?"—also appears to answer it with a fable of despair. There is a quasi-narrative focus in the play upon Marie and Woyzeck, who are the only three-dimensionally *human* figures, the only figures with a personal past and more than one level of operation, the others being mere sketches or caricatures. Marie and Woyzeck are thus evidently *the site of the human* in the play—except that Woyzeck, in consequence of a deliberate interference with his alimentary processes (which, again, corresponds to the aesthetic operation of representing him fictionally), is distinctly less human, has had his humanity impaired, and is struggling to retrieve it. Whereas Marie's thoughts and fears, her memories and inner conflicts, appear naturally, in monologues directed at her baby and in confrontations with others, Woyzeck must cling to his human identity (as opposed to the broodings of his induced mental disturbance) by recording its particulars on paper (p. 250; T132). But Woyzeck does in the end reachieve his humanity, does arrive at the uniquely human state of despair, and does perform a uniquely human act, in his murder of Marie; and it is here that the structure of the philosophical fable emerges. We cannot—this fable suggests—lay hold of the human, the human cannot be represented adequately, except in the form of its destruction, the destruction of Marie, who is the single most completely and integrally human figure on the stage. It follows that we are utterly alone after all, utterly exposed as individuals. The attempt to grasp our humanity, to retrieve our origin, our knowledge of what we are in a larger sense, is hopeless. The earth, so to speak, is an overturned pot, emptied of whatever value it might once have held for us (p. 252; T133).

Human Nature as Experiment

Can this interpretation of the plot, which clearly has some justification, be settled upon as representing the play's meaning? In the final analysis, I think not. Not only does it fail to account for the idea of experiment as a means of understanding the human, but it also contains a logical difficulty: namely, in order to interpret the plot as a fable of despair, focused upon the impossibility of knowing what "man" is, we must first *agree* upon what we mean by "the human" in the figures of Marie and Woyzeck. And on the deeper level of signification thrown open by this inconsistency, I suggest that the following formulation applies: that "man" is *nothing but* the endlessly repeated and varied experiment carried out by humans upon themselves—in science, philosophy, society, government, indeed in art, in drama and theater. I do not mean that man is first a particular kind of creature which then experiments upon itself. I mean that *the process of experimenting, the condition of being always both experimenter and object, is man, is human nature*—however much that process, from a more rigid perspective, may appear to violate whatever we have already hastily defined as "the human." This formulation does not pretend to answer the question "What is man?" It says, rather, that the answer to that question is never anything but the question itself all over again, ad infinitum. And it should also be noted that this type of thinking corresponds nicely to what Büchner calls the "philosophical" outlook in science (p. 260), as opposed to the "teleological." Just as the plant is a development of the theme "leaf," and just as the theme "vertebra" is developed in the skeleton (p. 261), so the human, in its entirety, is nothing but an endless variation on the theme "experiment."

Perhaps more important for our purposes, however, is that the dramatic theater, from this point of view, no longer is merely a means of *representing* human nature (the representational being, we recall, a main source of its ethical questionability) but has become, rather, an authentic instance of that experimentation which *is* human nature, indeed a very highly developed instance (as the skull is to the spinal column, the brain to the spinal cord). For the theater is an experiment which—unlike, say, the practice of government—is fully transparent not only to its quality as experiment but also to both the ethical danger and the philosophical significance of that quality; the theater is an experiment that experiments precisely with the idea of humanity as the happening of self-experiment. However distorted, grotesque, problematic, perverted the representation of humans on the stage may seem, still human nature *happens* in the theater with an intensity and completeness that can hardly be matched in any other human institution.

And this point, finally, brings us back to *Dantons Tod* and the question of the symbolism of actor and role. If we agree about the earlier play, about stage-acting as a sign of the compensatory imposture in our own identity that is necessitated by a modern confrontation with nothingness in the political arena, then we shall probably also agree that identity is equally questionable in *Woyzeck*, that its questionability continues to be represented by the disproportion between actor and role, but that that disproportion is now understood not in terms of compensation or imposture so much as in terms of *experiment*, as an instance of the experimentation that is human nature on every level. The idea of identity as experiment is made fully explicit in Büchner's other play, the little comedy *Leonce und Lena*, in which Valerio and the Prince joke their way through a regular menu of possible identities before deciding to become *lazzaroni* (pp. 171–72, T87–88). And in *Woyzeck* itself, the idea of identity as experiment is arrived at by little more than a terminological adjustment to the argument above concerning subject and object. Experiment, we saw, creates the very separation of subject and object (which is what we understand as identity) that it studies.

But the mood of *Woyzeck* seems infinitely bleaker than that of *Leonce und Lena,* more grim even than the mood of *Dantons Tod,* whereas the idea of identity as experiment—by comparison with the idea of identity as a desperate compensatory move in the face of nothingness—suggests a friendlier and even potentially joyful view of the human condition. In fact I am suggesting that there is something fundamentally joyful or at least conciliatory about *Woyzeck.* We do not ordinarily recognize this, because we encounter *Woyzeck* primarily as readers. Even when we see the play performed in the theater, we and the performers all bring our readerly sensibilities and prejudices with us. But in the theater *as Büchner imagined it,* I contend, the grimness of the fictional world is counterbalanced by the mere fact of theatrical performance, by our understanding that inside the figure of Woyzeck—or Marie, or the Doctor, or the Drum Major—is a mind for whom that identity is a matter of choice and artful construction, an experiment. And if we agree with the logical conclusion toward which every aspect of the play impels us, if we agree that every actual human identity is in truth a kind of histrionic experiment in identity, then it follows that in a strong sense the actor on the stage—the actor as experimenter—*is* Woyzeck (we have come full circle, to the condition of Marion and the actress) and that Woyzeck himself is therefore on some level active and enterprising after all, that he is perhaps even joyful, or "gay"—as Yeats says of Hamlet and Lear, using the older sense of the word. Nihilism and despair are still possibilities here; they are given a place in the play's landscape, so to speak, in the grandmother's fable about the child who is all alone in the world. But we have also, so to speak, outgrown this fable in the sense that we understand now (after *Dantons Tod*) that the theater cannot support philosophical nihilism as a meaning, that its transparency to that meaning would violate the meaning itself. Now, when we hear the Policeman say, as he observes Marie's corpse, "What a murder! A good, genuine, beautiful murder! Beautiful a murder as you could hope for! It's been a long time since we had one like this!" (p. 255; T137–38), now, for all the irony here, we are also secretly inclined to agree that the theatrical proceeding is in fact good and genuine and beautiful. It may be, for all we know, that this joyful or beautiful aspect of *Woyzeck* is only a compensatory move that veils the abyss of truth. But since we have learned that the matter is undecidable anyway, we are invited to accept this joy or beauty for what it is worth to us.

Even in social thought, it seems to me that *Woyzeck* is less pessimistic than *Dantons Tod.* It is true that the experimentation that produces social injustice and human misery is now recognized as unavoidable not only in the theater but everywhere in life. But on the other hand, any positive concept of the "human"—hence any standard against which to measure a *causal* relation between the experimentation which we *are* (experimentation in the most general possible sense) and specific features of our individual or social condition—has been discredited. The causal relation has been replaced by an identical relation, and there is now no longer any basis for an ethical argument against experiment as such—although there certainly will be against particular kinds of experiment. The Doctor's experiments on Woyzeck, if imagined as real, remain impermissible. But the French Revolution, and the revolutionary sentiments of "Der hessische Landbote," may once again be considered as at least possible avenues for productive human effort. All politics and diplomacy, as Leonce suggests, are "infusorial" (p. 189; T105), a kind of microbiological experiment, but this fact is no longer available as a reason for rejecting politics and diplomacy altogether—perhaps not even as a reason against war or the guillotine. Our dramatic exploration of the idea of human nature as constituted by the quality of experiment has not produced any specific responses to social injustice or individual suffering, and it *has* exercised our sense for the treacherous complexity of the ethical considerations that bear upon our every activity, even upon something as harmless as sitting in the theater. But that exploration has not turned "philosophical" in the sense of simply denying on principle the efficacy of all social or political or direct humanitarian action.

The Question of the Theater

This leaves, for the time being, only one question, which may be the most interesting, and most vexing, of all. Büchner never saw any of his own plays performed; he never attempted to get them performed; and he had no significant contacts in professional or even amateur theatrical circles that might have bridged the gap between his manuscripts and the actual stage. How, under these circumstances, can it have occurred to him to write his plays in such a way that we cannot understand them except by imagining their actual performance and, in fact, imagining it under the guidance of a highly specific philosophical theory of the theater? Does Büchner ascribe *validity* to that theory of the theater? If so, in what sense? Surely he does not suppose that theater in general, or any particular theater, was ever founded in the spirit of his theory, or that theater is anywhere actually practiced or enjoyed in that spirit. His theater, as I have suggested in my chapter title, is a theater that never was. And yet, its nonexistence somehow does not prevent this theater from operating, from acquiring potency and significance, in relation to at least the three texts I have spoken of. And if these texts, in turn, have become part of actual theatrical repertoire, does it follow that that nonexistent theater has also, to an extent, acquired *reality*?

These questions, clearly, are less about Büchner than about theater. I ask you, the reader, to think back over the interpretation I have offered of

Büchner's work, and I ask you to concede that even if you disagree with my conclusions, you were *not* inclined to dismiss, as methodologically illegitimate, my procedure for arriving at them. It seems perfectly natural, even in the literary discussion of plays, to include an idea of the actual theatrical event in one's evidence. In the case of Büchner, it is not until we understand that we have been talking about a theater that never was, and perhaps never will be, that we begin to worry about the logical and critical situation we have gotten ourselves into.

What is there about the theater that attracts—or at least appears to permit—the kind of theorizing I have attributed to Büchner and have invited the reader to engage in? If we had been talking only about theories of human nature, there would be no difficulty. We expect a literary or poetic work to produce and express for us the theory of human nature in terms of which it wants to be understood. And human nature itself, in the most general possible sense, is after all nothing but an open space for humans to theorize in. The theater, however, is a real institution with a well-documented history and established practices. And even if it is true that critics, and people in general, like to think of the theater as an open space to be filled by our imagination, we must still ask *why* we think thus, or *how we have come* to think thus of the theater. For the theater, in reality, is precisely not an open space; it is filled with people and objects which, being real, are *categorically* different from the creatures of imagination and cannot possibly be mistaken for them. Indeed, this categorical difference (the relation between actor and role) happens to be an integral element of Büchner's theorizing, in both its early and its late forms. But if we recognize the brute reality of the theater—if indeed, like Büchner, we insist theoretically upon this quality—how can it possibly occur to us to fill the theater with our highly rarefied theoretical speculations in the first place?

Perhaps it will be suggested that Büchner is not really theorizing about the theater; he is simply using it as a poetic symbol. But again I would have to ask, is there not a category difference between a real thing (a real situation, here and now, for the spectator) and a poetic symbol? And when Büchner suggests (or when the structure of his dramatic texts suggests) that the theater is a prime instance of the experimentation that defines humanity, is it really only a question of poetic symbolism? The whole idea of human nature as constituted by experiment would be pointless, would lose its quality as a kind of intellectual Thermopylae, a last stand against utter nihilism, if Büchner were not showing the truth about what the theater is— *and in fact about what it always has been*, without our knowing it till now. Where does a medical graduate with some philosophical training, but no knowledge of the theater, get the nerve to suggest such an assertion? Or rather, what is there about the theater's actual and historical mode of being that prevents us from dismissing such a suggestion as the mere raving of a lunatic? At least we can now understand why Büchner himself never attempted to set forth his idea of the theater in detail.

These questions about the theater are answerable, if at all, only to a limited depth. But their very existence as questions is already itself a kind of answer, for the theater has the curious property of *being an entirely different thing* (not merely showing a different aspect of itself) depending on the point of view from which one looks at it. Measured against literature or the poetic imagination, as I have said, the theater is an assemblage of real physical objects (including people) embedded in the reality of social and economic institutions. But from the point of view of our everyday existence in brute reality, and precisely in relation to our dealings with real social and economic institutions, the theater shows itself as a tissue of fantasy, an open space in which, from time to time, the otherwise merely individual literary imagination generates sharp and uniquely accessible representations of itself.

The same basic doubleness, it is true, already characterizes literature, but here it is really only a question of aspects. On the one hand, literature has a concrete institutional aspect and is associated with certain physical objects, especially books; on the other hand, its history is built mainly of intellectual relations and developments, and the true content of each work is understood to reside in the domain of the imagining mind. By comparison with philosophy or science, literature favors sensory immediacy, the particular, the individual, whereas by comparison with our daily experience, literature is more illuminated, idealized, generalized. But the theater surpasses literature in both directions. In the theater, where everything that makes up a literary fiction—the people, their voices, the sights, the sounds—is actually, immediately present, we are confronted with *nothing but reality*. And yet at the same time, this reality—in its order, its purpose, its effect—is also *nothing but fantasy*, and is indeed more fantastic, more adventurously imaginative, than anything we ever encounter as readers, for its range is not limited by our personal experience, by the inventory of stored sensory data that we draw upon to clothe, in our mind, the words of a fictional text. It is, so to speak, a fantasy grown too large and powerful to be contained any longer in any one individual mind. Again, as I have suggested in other connections, it is as if the business of theater were to exaggerate literature's doubleness of aspect, to sharpen it into a contradiction, and so to explode the integrity of literature (and of itself, of theater) as a concept.

Having said this, finally, I hasten to add that these ideas are not conclusions from evidence and can claim no form of general validity. They are an elaboration upon certain unanswerable questions that appear to be provoked by a single and (in his time) solitary dramatist. They are, by their nature, not conclusive but suggestive and perhaps most directly useful here as a corrective to the attempt, in the two preceding chapters, to

approach as closely as possible a positive conception of revolutionary theater—without any particular revolutionary program to link it to. For the
last of the questions suggested by Büchner's struggle with his form is the
question of whether perhaps the theater itself, the real theater, even in its
reality (or precisely in its reality), is not also somehow a theater that never
was, or, what comes to the same thing, an excuse, a stopgap, the vision or
promise of a theater that has yet to be. In connection with Brecht, after all,
we have already had to recognize the provisional or ad hoc quality of theater in general.

CHAPTER SIX

Hofmannsthal's Theater of Adaptation

As I suggested in chapter 2, the idea of meaning—especially in the form of a postulate of communication—becomes questionable, becomes an issue, in the course of any serious theoretical discussion of drama and theater. This issue has emerged peripherally in the three preceding chapters. Here I attempt to develop it and deal with it in relation to the possibility of intransitive or absolute performance.

Adaptation, Interpretation, Performance

Hugo von Hofmannsthal's plays can be divided into several broad categories. The early "lyrical" plays belong together in a fairly obvious way, as do the opera libretti. The series of comedies, despite some overlap with the first two classes, gradually develops its own unique manner of representing the social, culminating in *Der Schwierige* and *Der Unbestechliche*. And if we look at the major works that fall outside these categories—*Elektra*, *Das gerettete Venedig*, *Ödipus und die Sphinx*, *König Ödipus*, *Jedermann*, *Das Salzburger Große Welttheater* and *Der Turm*—we find that they too form a class, united by the idea of *dramatic adaptation*. The range covered by this idea is considerable. *König Ödipus* is close to a simple translation of Sophocles, albeit with much of the choral material omitted; the connection of *Der Turm* to Calderón's *La vida es sueño* has become extremely tenuous; and *Ödipus und die Sphinx* fits the pattern only by suggesting interpretive perspectives upon Sophocles. But still, the class is extensive and cohesive enough to justify the question, precisely how, and with precisely what end in view, does Hofmannsthal adapt dramatic works of the past for the modern theater?

"Tradition" is not the issue here. Like any writer, Hofmannsthal both receives and develops tradition with every stroke of his pen. But in the short essay "Das Spiel vor der Menge," which is meant mainly to justify his and Max Reinhardt's *Jedermann*, he himself indicates clearly that at least one main concern, in dealing with his adaptations, must be the question of the theater or of theatricality. And the idea of theatricality I propose—in the process of ascribing it to Hofmannsthal—is radically structural, practically geometric in nature, and meant to avoid entirely the emotional-ideological slipperiness of such phrases as "das Geheimnis deutschen Wesens" (the mystery of German-ness),[1] which seem to me more a response to Reinhardt than an expression of Hofmannsthal's own professional thinking. In the case of adaptations, I contend, the interpretive relation of theatrical performance to its text is repeated in the relation of the text itself to the earlier dramatic text it supposedly represents. As spectators in the theater, we are thus presented with the interpretation of an interpretation; and the question of where the poetic *meaning* of the work resides now becomes difficult. We are compelled to ask ourselves where the *original* is to be found upon which these layers of interpretation are constructed.

It is not sufficient to say that the original is the earlier dramatic work of which the present text is an adaptation, and that the meaning conveyed by the performance is the meaning of that original work in a form adapted to our present cultural situation. For the obvious structural parallel connecting interpretation in the forms of adaptation and performance foregrounds the quality of *unreliability*. Theatrical performance considered as interpretation is not only empirically but also inherently questionable, imprecise, groping, because it is, above all, mute. It has no words of its own, no rational-verbal leverage upon its object; the only words available to it are exactly the words of the text it is supposed to interpret. The structural parallel in the theater we are talking about therefore calls our attention strongly to the corresponding unreliability of adaptation considered as interpretation. The mere existence of an adaptation, assuming such a thing is needed, presupposes the *inaccessibility* of the work being adapted, at least from the point of view of the present reader or audience. (If it *were* accessible to this reader, why would he or she use an adaptation?) And just this reader or audience can have no basis on which to judge the adequacy of the adapter's work. The problem here is repeated at the level of the adaptation's writing. If the adapter is attempting to do nothing but translate the language, then it follows that he or she is deliberately concealing any interpretive bias in the process; if the adapter makes substantial changes, then we must ask how an "interpretation" that alters its object can be trusted. In every possible case, we are faced with a complete lack of certainty or reliability in the interpretive process.

There are logical difficulties in the very idea of adaptation. Adaptation would not be undertaken without the belief that a work of literature, or drama, must be suited to its audience, shaped by its audience's needs. But if this is true, then it is also true of the original work being adapted. That work must have been uniquely suited to *its* original audience, which raises the question of why it should be adapted in the first place, why we would not do better simply to write a new work for the new audience. If I "see" in the original something that makes it suitable for adapting and useful for my contemporary audience, then precisely the cultural assumptions that my activity rests on imply that that "seeing" is almost certainly a misinterpretation of the original, which means that in effect I *have* written a new work. Again, therefore, why make adaptations in the first place? Is it merely a question of "tradition"? Is it an attempt to have one's audience occupy two different historical situations at the same time, in order to teach them about the immanence of the past in the present? (One might conceivably ascribe this intention to *Jedermann*.) But this formulation does not eliminate the basic problem, for the *differentness* of that other historical situation would still, somehow, have to be conveyed. Otherwise our own situation would not be enriched.

What we find ourselves involved in, therefore, in the theater of adaptation, is a complicatedly self-questioning interpretive and performative procedure that has no semiotic center, no original source of meaning—or at least no such source that is in any way accessible to us. Of course, the text of the adaptation can be interpreted more or less strictly on its own terms and can thus have a meaning ascribed to it. But precisely by being an adaptation, that text itself constantly undermines any such interpretation by deferring to its absent original; and we are left in the end with a work that *has no meaning*, strictly speaking, a work in relation to which the hermeneutic process can form not even a provisional or heuristic idea of itself as goal-directed. (If we ask for the meaning of the adaptation, our attention is directed to the original, as the object of its interpretive work. But for the reasons noted above, the original must be assumed inaccessible, at least for this purpose.) Or, to put the matter in different terms, we find ourselves involved in a theatrical event which, since it cannot be reduced to the expression of a meaning, assumes the character of absolute or radical or intransitive performance, performance subordinated to no higher category, performance that is not a "performance of" anything else. The theater of adaptation, in this sense, would be something approaching the strictly nonliterary theater imagined by Artaud, who of course was also a theatrical adapter.

Hofmannsthal and the Poet's Meaning

But what justifies specifically our application of these ideas to Hofmannsthal? One of Karl Pestalozzi's many contributions to Hofmannsthal studies was his recognition of the importance of the "Vorspiel für ein Puppentheater" of 1906 (DIII:485–90), which apparently was not written for an actual puppet theater (it was published in the *Neue Rund-schau*) and can therefore be taken as a general comment on drama and the-ater.[2] The first figure who appears in this little text, "Der Dichter," the Poet, begins by imagining that he is on the verge of experiencing an ecstatic union with nature itself, with nature as a "goddess" whom he will "kiss into life." But then the bushes part, and out of the forest emerges a comic but ugly old woman with a bundle of dried twigs and an urban Viennese accent. After a quickly abandoned attempt to unveil the supposed "angel" hidden in this mask, the Poet resigns himself to "reality" and to the recog-nition that "I am meant to embrace my own kind," that his is a fundamen-tally human world, that nature as such is beyond his reach. Thus, it appears, the transition from lyrical mysticism to the more social and realis-tic art of theatrical drama is being negotiated, and the Poet accordingly becomes aware of specific human "forms and figures" taking shape in his imagination—as it were, in his blood—while he also willingly abandons his current sylvan "dream" in favor of that "other dream" called "the world of life and humanity."

At this point, however, the text becomes problematic. The Poet now turns and speaks "Ad spectatores"; and if we are following a supposed transition from the lyrical to the dramatic, we expect him to promise that the human figures in his imagination, perhaps somehow combined with the real people he is now determined to live among, will soon appear on the stage before us. But what he actually promises is completely different: neither newly imagined characters nor "real" characters but rather those *stock* figures ("Kaspar Hauser . . . die Pfalzgräfin Genofeva . . . Leda . . . mit ihrem Schwan . . . Doktor Faust mit dem Gespenste Helena") that are required by the genre of the theater in question, here the puppet theater. The secret of theatrical drama, in other words, is that whereas from the point of view of the dramatic author himself, his work may have meaning, may be the product of strong personal vision, still, what actually appears on the stage, what is actually made available to the audience, *has no manifest connection with that meaning.* This is the condition, the old hag of "reality," that every dramatic author must come to terms with: that the knowledge and vision that have driven him to write do not survive as communicable meaning in the theater; that whatever is understood publicly as the "mean-ing" of drama is as arbitrary, as inherently questionable, as the theatrical performance that supposedly interprets it; that in effect, theatrical drama has no meaning (unless one is willing to admit the possibility of noncom-municable meaning, which seems to me a contradiction in terms). And I contend that Hofmannsthal's way of accommodating this condition, or one of his ways of doing so, is to anticipate it by the structural attenuation of meaning in dramatic adaptation.

The author of drama, like the Poet of the "Vorspiel für ein Puppenthe-ater," is always in the situation of speaking with two voices: a personal voice that arises, so to speak, in his blood and is never available for us to hear directly; and a public voice whose whole sound and content is deter-mined by circumstances. But if we can only really hear the second of these two voices—as we have heard Hofmannsthal himself, in Reinhardt's vicin-ity, speaking of "das Geheimnis deutschen Wesens"—then how can we have any knowledge whatever of this dichotomy or disjunction of voices, this absence of meaning in theatrical drama?

Contingency, Disorder, Performance

It must be understood, first, that if this argument has any claim to validity, then its range cannot be restricted to the field of drama. It must be true that the content of personal poetic vision is never, in any genre, successfully transformed into communicable meaning. (I have made exactly this argu-ment elsewhere, based on an interpretation of Hofmannsthal's poem "Die Beiden.")[3] And the uniqueness of drama, then, is that it offers special possi-bilities for disrupting the otherwise practically unavoidable *illusion* of com-municated meaning, the possibility, in particular, of representing structurally the inherent radical unreliability of its own communicative procedure. It is only in this way, only indirectly, only negatively, that the operation of an absent voice can be suggested.

But if the business of drama for Hofmannsthal—or at least a major part of the business of drama—is to bring to light in the theater an otherwise automatically self-obscured linguistic or communicative problematics, then exactly what type of drama will we expect to find him cultivating? I have already begun to answer this question in discussing certain general fea-tures of the theater of adaptation, especially the tendency of that theater in the direction of pure performance, ungoverned by any original source of meaning. On the same basis, we can also account in part for Hof-mannsthal's choice of texts for that theater. At least in the case of Sophocles' *Electra*, Thomas Otway's *Venice Preserved*, and Calderón's *La vida es sueño*, we recognize plots and motifs that serve as *allegories* of the theatrical situa-tion by foregrounding the qualities of disorder, disconnection, contingency, lack of satisfying resolution—qualities that resonate with the general unregulated centerlessness of the theater of adaptation.

Already in the original Greek *Electra* there is a definite sense of imbal-ance, incompleteness, loose ends. Orestes does finally return and complete the needful act of revenge. But if it is really Electra who is meant to stand in the work's focus, then that act has also in large measure become pointless, since it arrives too late to make any difference in her existence, too late to restore to her the possibility of marriage and children. Nowhere, moreover, are we offered any explanation of why it has taken Orestes so long to embark upon his mission, even though there are clear suggestions in the text that he and Electra had long been in contact, that he had already promised a number of times that he would soon return (lines 164–73, 303–306, 319). And to this unsettled situation Hofmannsthal adds not only the vertiginous and lacerating psychological depths for which his text is famous but also the motif of Electra's failure to provide Orestes with the fatal weapon she has saved for him, and the unfulfilment of her prophetic dream of being present at Clytemnestra's death.

The same sort of fundamental disorder obviously characterizes Otway's play, whose plot—about a conspiracy that is both formed and then betrayed for trivial reasons—is focused less upon action or conviction than upon vacillation and uncertainty. And again, as with Sophocles, Hofmannsthal outdoes this model in any number of ways, most strikingly by eliminating the final heroic reconciliation between Jaffier and Pierre. Even *La vida es sueño* fits this pattern in that its main action is the *failure* of a prophetically established structure of fate to be realized. To be sure, Hofmannsthal's relation to his model here becomes thoroughly problematic. For when the final version of this project, *Der Turm*, is at last completed in 1925, the Calderonian emphasis on a successful ethical avoidance of fate has been almost entirely lost. But *Der Turm* is a problem for any number of other reasons as well—especially in its apparent attempt to give direct expression to the same type of philosophical truth that the "Puppentheater" Poet cannot communicate—and I will come back to it below.

Are there similar grounds for arguing that the Oedipus plays or *Jedermann* or the *Großes Welttheater* can be regarded as fundamentally disordered? For the time being, let us go back over our main concepts and note that it is theoretically all but impossible, in any literary form, to convey a genuine sense of chance, disorder, contingency, negativity. Hofmannsthal's Oedipus, after defeating the Sphinx, can say to Kreon, "auf mir liegt das Chaos und / zernagt mich" (DII:476: chaos is upon me and chews me to pieces). But no sooner do we read or hear that word "chaos" than we attempt to interpret it, to make sense of it, to submit it to a larger order; and chaos itself (whatever that might be) is therefore no longer strictly what we understand. Hence, again, the importance of the theater of adaptation. For the automatic ordering process that informs our reception of poetry, or of literature in general, presupposes as its object a coherent ordering impulse behind the text it is confronted with: the impulse, precisely, that makes it this particular text. And in the case of an adaptation—if we have thought the matter through far enough to recognize the necessary inaccessibility of any "original"—the dependent or contingent quality of what is actually presented us is sufficient to disrupt that presupposition and perhaps, so to speak, permit "chaos" to mean something a bit closer to chaos after all.

Only in the theater of adaptation, therefore, if anywhere, can the disorderly elements of plays like *Elektra* and *Das gerettete Venedig* actually *be* disorderly or discontinuous enough to function as allegorical reflections of their larger rhetorical situation.

The theater of adaptation, then, is important to Hofmannsthal as a theater in which something like *actual* accidentalness or contingency operates, not merely the regulated fictional image of these qualities. And why should this be important, in turn, if not as a guiding image of what *theater in general* should become? Of course it is impossible—even in the case of improvisational theater (recall Hofmannsthal's often attested interest in the commedia dell' arte)—for theater ever to become in the strictest sense what I have called "absolute or radical performance," with no regulating or ordering framework whatever. But Hofmannsthal, in his dramatic adaptations, appears to be suggesting the possibility of a theater in which the semiotic organizing power of the literary text is at least strongly reduced vis-à-vis the contingency, the arbitrariness, the unpredictability of performance. And, recalling the "Vorspiel für ein Puppentheater," we can make reasonably good sense of this suggestion. For if poetic vision as such (assuming it exists) can never survive as communicable meaning, then it follows that what is imposed upon us (or what we are in the habit of expecting) as the focused or unitary meaning of a poetic work, in particular of a drama, is always some form of delusion or deception or, at best, confusion. In the theater as Hofmannsthal imagines it, therefore, to the extent that the imposition or expectation of poetic meaning is reduced in relative importance, the truthfulness or honesty of the institution (in a sense yet to be specified) will be increased.

What is at stake here, to be precise, is not the theater in any of what we would normally regard as its objective aspects: not the shape of the stage, not the way sets are constructed, not methods or conventions of acting. (The quality of contingency, or its opposite, is not a function of these objective details. Everything that happens in the real theater, by comparison with what happens entirely within our imagination, is strictly contingent simply by virtue of being real; and at the same time, if what happens in the theater is regarded—with perfect legitimacy—as the product of either a poetic or a public imagination, its accidentalness evaporates.)[4] What matters here is the institution of the theater as a whole, including its actual and potential audiences, and the manner in which this institution (in all the individuals composing it) regards itself. And what Hofmannsthal envisages, what is implied by his theater of adaptation, is a theater characterized (in its own view of itself) not by the authoritative organization of realities into a system of meaning but by the unceasing *tension* between an unavoidable systematic tendency and the unbroken uncontrollability and contingency of its material elements.

Negativity and the World Theater

Still, if this is Hofmannsthal's view of the theater, why did he not himself produce a theoretical exposition of it? In fact he did, except that the work in question does not look exactly like what we expect in a theoretical work. I am referring to *Das Salzburger Große Welttheater*, where the relation between the authority of "Der Meister" and the strict freedom of his creatures is a clear and precise allegory of the theater Hofmannsthal has in mind—and an allegory, of course, that even calls itself a "theater," thus making no secret of its representative function. Normally, critics treat Hofmannsthal's "world theater" play exactly as they treat Calderón's: they read the given structure of the theater as a metaphor for the true character of the world. I am not suggesting that this reading is invalid. But at the same time, I think we have understood enough about Hofmannsthal's practice of dramatic adaptation to recognize that we must also read the *Großes Welttheater* the other way round, that the given structure of a Christian idea of the human world as at once both determined and free, both systematic and contingent, here operates as a metaphor for the true character of the theater—of a theater, perhaps, which in its modern version has been corrupted by an excessively literary quality and must now be restored with the aid of the theater of adaptation.

Once we have accepted the possibility of viewing Hofmannsthal's text in this way, a number of its features make rather more sense than they would have otherwise. For example, when the play is performed, it turns out that the actors and actresses assigned to the inner play (the human figures whose lives unfold) are not playing "parts" at all, in the sense that the part is distinct from the playing of it. The actor who plays the Beggar, for instance, is not simply playing a beggar; rather, he is playing the playing of a beggar. He is playing someone playing a beggar, but that "someone" has no identity, not even that of an "actor," outside of the beggar's own, so that the distinction between the role he is playing and what he is simply actually doing vanishes. (The one character in Calderón for whom a formulation of this type would have been questionable, the *Niño* or stillborn child, is omitted by Hofmannsthal.) To look at it differently, the actor playing the Beggar cannot possibly get his part wrong, since no matter how incompetently he speaks or gestures, he is still exactly representing an otherwise nonidentified individual playing a beggar; by the same token, of course, he cannot get his part significantly right either. His "part," as an element of meaning, a literary or imaginary object against which his acting might be measured, is in effect simply not there. And what we have in the inner play, therefore, is something very like a concrete instance of the notion of absolute performance that we have seen to be associated with the theater of adaptation.[5]

As with contingency, moreover, there is no place within the thoroughly intentional structure of poetic vision or meaning for *negativity* in anything like a strict sense of the term. There may be oppositions or tensions or conflicts, but to the extent that these things have meaning, they contribute positively to an encompassing order. The only way to subject some element of a literary text to strict negation would be to convey to us (somehow) the instruction not to read it. And yet, in the case of the *Großes Welttheater*, negation is an unavoidable issue. One of the characters Hofmannsthal adds is precisely the Negator, the "Widersacher," who says: "Erlaub der Herr die eine Frage: wie kann ein Schauspiel den ergetzen, der es vorbestimmt, Eingang und Ausgang, bis aufs I-Tüpfel?" (DIII:112) How can God be entertained by a play he himself has predetermined? Or to shift the question slightly: how can this play lay claim to theological accuracy when, by its very nature as poetry, it must resolve even the radical negativity of sin into a positive element of meaning and so cannot possibly include the whole range of what God calls humanity's "highest freedom" (113)? That this is a matter of real concern to Hofmannsthal is clear in, for example, his treatment of the Rich Man, whose abrupt dismissal at the end, with the two words "Nicht ihm!" (163: not him!) stands in stark, maximally negative contrast to the scene (absent in Calderón) of brotherly affection between him and the Beggar (160–61).

But more important is the scene in which the Beggar refrains from striking, with the Peasant's axe, a blow that the text suggests would destroy the very fabric of the world: "Schlag zu und bring mit eins die ganze Welt zu Falle!" (DIII:144). This motif, which parallels the Kaiserin's "Ich—will—nicht!" (DV:374) in *Die Frau ohne Schatten*, sidesteps the inherent opposition between poetic vision and negativity by positing an act of negation that is necessary to *uphold* the poetically imagined "world." Left to itself, the world, or the orderly poetic vision, provides material for reasonable trains of thought that will lead ultimately to its own destruction, especially in the Beggar's argument that the very notion of "order" favors the oppressing classes in society. "REICHER: Ordnung ist's, die ihr braucht! BETTLER: Mit dem verfluchten Wort / Kommst du mir nicht. So nennt ihr die Gewalt, / Die uns in Boden druckt" (DIII:135). Therefore an act of simple radical negation is required in order to preserve the very existence of that orderly vision—to negate its tendency toward self-destruction—and negativity has thus established itself even in the apparent domain of poetry, in the literary theater, after all.

This argument perhaps appears to be mainly a play with words, but only until we recognize that it reflects an entirely palpable state of affairs in the theater. For as we sit in the theater we are presented with two different objects whose modes of existence are entirely incommensurable: first, the poetic work as such, the system of signs, considered purely as a mental or intentional or imaginative entity; and second, the vehicle, the accidental collection of physical objects (including people) by which, tonight, that system happens to be represented. And the system, the work as such, the "world" as the work imagines it, cannot be said to attain its own coherent existence except by virtue, somewhere, of a move of strict negation with respect to the arbitrary physical vehicle that has brought it to us, which move is then itself represented quite transparently in the scene where the Beggar refrains from striking. Indeed, if we recall what was said above about the peculiar situation of some of the actors in this play, if we recall that the Beggar's own acting is in the strict sense not regulated by a distinct "part" belonging to the work as system—so that his speeches turn out to be characterized by an arbitrariness not fundamentally different from that of the performance's physical vehicle—then it might even be said that his refusal to strike, his rescue of the poetic order, constitutes a kind of uniquely concentrated *self*-negation.

Two points must be borne in mind here. First, arguments like this one on the *Großes Welttheater* cannot possibly become interpretively complete with respect to their texts, because they turn on the uncompletable notions of contingency and negativity. They are oriented, rather, toward this chapter's main argument about the theater of adaptation, which they support by showing how works that Hofmannsthal chooses for this theater resonate with its tendency to suggest and foreshadow a renewal of theater in general, a readjustment of the balance of its systematic and contingent elements. And second, this main argument in turn concerns not the theater in a strictly practical sense—where categories like contingency, and communicative adequacy, or its lack, could not be applied anyway—but rather the manner in which the theater, by way of its audience, understands itself. By saying this, of course, I do not mean to diminish the matter. The nature of theater or of a particular theater—to the extent that such a "nature" can be spoken of—certainly has more to do with how that theater is regarded than with any catalogue of objective features. But it remains true nonetheless that the ground of the present inquiry (and of Hofmannsthal's project) tends to shift, and that our concepts and arguments therefore require constant reinspection.

Jedermann, in fact, seems to me a fairly clear instance of the kind of danger or difficulty that besets my own endeavor and Hofmannsthal's. The theater of adaptation, I have said, brings to light a failure of communication. But is this bringing to light not itself a *form* of communication? And if so, then communication on what level, by way of what medium—assuming that what has been brought to light is the inevitable failure of communication among individuals, communication of anything like the "Puppentheater" Poet's vision of natural truth? From here it is not very far to the idea of some type of slumbering collectivity within which the failure

of individual communication assumes positive value as a raising and articulating of collective consciousness. Ideas like "das Volk" or "das Geheimnis deutschen Wesens" begin to suggest themselves; and if we can believe
"Das Spiel vor der Menge," it is in the spirit of this sort of thinking that
Hofmannsthal prepares *Jedermann* for the theater of adaptation. But as I
have suggested, this grasping for the positive is in truth a perversion of
that theater, a danger to be avoided. Not only the quality of negativity in
its structure but the irreducibly negative operation of that theater as a
whole must be maintained, reinspected, reaffirmed, at every step. Exactly
how this process works can be made clearer by a discussion of the question of *acting*.

The Paradox of the Actor

In the *Buch der Freunde*, Hofmannsthal—relying, as usual, on his memory
rather than his library—misquotes Diderot's *Paradoxe sur le comédien* as
follows:

> Die meisten Menschen fühlen nicht, sie glauben zu fühlen; sie glauben
> nicht, sie glauben, daß sie glauben. (RIII:236)

> [Most people do not feel, they believe they feel; they do not believe, they
> believe they believe.]

Actually, Diderot distinguishes between most mediocre actors, who would
simply reject the proposition that their art has nothing to do with genuine
passion, and "some others" of whom it could be said "qu'ils croient sentir,
comme on a dit du superstitieux, qu'il croit croire" (that they believe they
feel, just as it has been said of superstitious people that they believe they
believe)—actors, in other words, who are less certain about their genuine
passion but whose art still depends on their believing in its existence.[6] But
Hofmannsthal's misquoting itself ought to provide an insight into his own
thought on the question of acting and feeling.

It is evident that Hofmannsthal means to contrast the deludedness of
"most people" with the relatively clear self-knowledge of a small group;
and since he associates his thinking with Diderot's *Paradoxe*, it seems fair to
infer that that small group is constituted by those theatrical actors who are
fully in command of their craft. But does the implied contrast then have the
form, "Whereas most people only believe that they feel or believe, competent actors *actually* feel, *actually* believe"? No one with even the most perfunctory knowledge of Diderot—and Hofmannsthal is by no means
normally satisfied with a perfunctory knowledge of the texts he reads—
could draw this conclusion. What Hofmannsthal means to suggest can in

fact only be that whereas most people believe that they feel or believe, competent actors understand clearly that they do *not* genuinely feel or believe (this being Diderot's main point) and restrict themselves accordingly to a mastery of the supposed outward signs of feeling or belief.

The consequences of this idea are considerable. For if "most people" plus the elite group with whom they are contrasted add up to *all* people, then it follows that "genuine" feeling or belief simply does not operate in life. Or perhaps we might wish to say—with an eye to the discussion above of the "Vorspiel für ein Puppentheater"—that genuine feeling or belief, for all we know, may in some sense exist but, if so, then in a way that is entirely disconnected from any form of communicable meaning. The main implication for our purposes, however, remains the same in both formulations: that the theatrical actor, merely by competently executing his or her craft, by being precisely a "mere" actor and not a "natural" person, offers a more accurate and complete representation of truth than could possibly characterize the supposedly communicated meaning of any poetic text. By imitating feelings and beliefs that we know are not his own, not anchored in his natural being, the actor represents for us the truth about *our* feelings and beliefs, however deeply these may seem to affect us. Thus, again, the importance of the theater of adaptation emerges, since any undermining or suppression of the category of meaning in the theater will tend to bring acting as such, with its cargo of truth, more clearly into focus. And in the special case of the *Großes Welttheater,* we can now form a more complete idea of why it is important that the acting of the inner play approach the condition of absolute or intransitive acting, acting regulated by a strict minimum of the ultimately only distracting operation of "role."

Of course, the *Buch der Freunde* comes fairly late in Hofmannsthal's career (1921), and a single misquotation of Diderot does not seem like much on which to build a philosophical theory of acting. But the whole of the argument so far on theater of adaptation favors that theory. And the very character of the theory makes it unreasonable to expect from Hofmannsthal a systematic exposition of it; such an exposition would necessarily presuppose the direct communicability of a belief about inner human existence, a belief according to which precisely that form of communicability is excluded. Again, the closest one can come to an adequate exposition is in the theater itself, especially in the performance of plays like the *Großes Welttheater,* or perhaps plays modeled on *La vida es sueño,* where the idea of treating one's own life as a dream suggests the possibility of living without the aid of convictions concerning one's "genuine" thoughts or feelings.

And yet there are after all other texts in which we can follow the development of Hofmannsthal's idea of acting. Claudio's final speech in *Der Tor und der Tod* (1893) begins:

Wie auf der Bühn ein schlechter Komödiant—
Aufs Stichwort kommt er, redt sein Teil und geht
Gleichgültig gegen alles andre, stumpf,
Vom Klang der eignen Stimme ungerührt
Und hohlen Tones andre rührend nicht:
So über diese Lebensbühne hin
Bin ich gegangen ohne Kraft und Wert. (DI:296)

[Like a bad actor on the stage—he appears on cue, speaks his part and
goes, indifferent to everything else, unmoved by the sound of his own
voice and in his hollowness leaving others unmoved as well: so, across this
stage of life, I have gone without strength or value.]

And the opposite of a "bad actor" is of course not a somehow genuine or
complete or natural human being but rather a *good* actor, who takes his craft
("the sound of his own voice," as it were) seriously enough to make it operate among other people in the service of what we are now in a position to
call truth. Hofmannsthal's little play is not about a decadent aesthete who
has missed natural human life; it is about an aesthete who, for all his depth
of artistic sensibility, has failed to grasp the fundamentally *histrionic* quality
of human life.[7]

Or, to jump to much later in Hofmannsthal's career, recall the dialogue
"Das Theater des Neuen," in which Homolka seeks to win over his Josef-
stadt colleagues for Brecht's *Baal,* and with Friedell's assistance arrives at
the idea that the task of a truly "new" theater must be to rescue its time
from enslavement to the concept of the *individual,* "this monstrosity,
whelped in the sixteenth century and fattened up in the nineteenth"
(DIII:510), as Friedell puts it. "Individuality is one of the arabesques that
we have cast off," says Homolka. For reasons we have already noted (in
discussing the difficulty of a systematic exposition of Hofmannsthal's theory of acting), the ideas here edge toward the ridiculous, the tone toward
the satirical. But Waldau, who begins by finding himself entirely baffled
by this type of thought—"I can't pretend to get a joke when I don't really
get it" (511)—then saves the day when it occurs to him that precisely
actors, by their profession, have *already* abandoned any belief in their natural individuality.

WALDAU. . . . . Nun allerdings, für die Schranken des Individuums in die
    Schranken zu treten, dürften wir, wie wir da sind, jedenfalls die
    Ungeeignetsten sein.
Einer reicht ihm eine Zigarette, die er anzündet.
THIMIG. Inwiefern wir?
WALDAU. Wir Schauspieler.
THIMIG. Ach so!

WALDAU. Denn wenn man schließlich das Schicksal hat, nur man selbst zu sein, indem man immer ein anderer wird . . .

THIMIG. *lächelt* Ach so!

Homolka tritt näher.

WALDAU. Ich meine, wenn man sozusagen nur durch neue Situationen und Begebenheiten erfährt, ob man eigentlich eng oder weit, energisch oder energielos, ein Mörder oder ein Träumer ist . . .

THIMIG. *völlig entspannt* Na ja, natürlich.

WALDAU. Ich weiß nicht, ob einer von Ihnen sich so ganz im klaren ist, wo er anfängt und wo er aufhört . . . ich bin es nicht (512)

[WALDAU. In any case, we, as we stand here, are probably the people least suited to defend the idea of limited individuality. (*Someone hands him a cigarette, which he lights.*) THIMIG: Why "we"? W: We actors. T: Aha. W: For if one is fated to be oneself only by always being someone different . . . T (*smiling*): Aha. (*Homolka comes closer.*) W: I mean, if one, so to speak, only discovers in new situations and events whether one is really narrow or open, energetic or lifeless, a murderer or a dreamer . . . T (*completely relieved*): Yes, of course. W: I don't know if any of you is entirely sure about where "he" starts and where "he" leaves off . . . I'm not.]

The idea that the natural or genuine individual does not exist, which is clearly an absurd idea when individuals discuss it seriously, becomes by contrast perfectly obvious and convincing when regarded as a description of the craft of acting. This "new" theater, then, for all its revolutionary pretensions, will in the end be merely a reaffirmation of what has always been the theater's philosophical burden, as theater, and the single basic "meaning" of every play performed: the idea that the natural or genuine or sincere individual does not in truth exist.

To complete the picture, we might turn finally to Hofmannsthal's short prose pieces on Eleonora Duse. In 1892 he emphasizes Duse's ability to convey "the philosophy of her role" (RI:476), which still seems to imply that acting transmits poetic meaning. But in "Die Duse im Jahre 1903," he writes:

Mehr als jemals ging diesmal, während sie auf der Bühne stand und spielte, etwas Größeres vor als das Schicksal dieser Figuren [her roles], etwas Allgemeineres, etwas von so hoher Allgemeinheit, daß es dem tragischen Leben erhabener Musik sehr nahe verwandt war. . . . Es lebt in dieser Schauspielerin eine solche Seele, daß vor der Erhabenheit ihrer Gebärden jedes Stück, in welchem sie spielt, aus seinen Fugen geht und nur mehr sie da ist, ihre Natur, die unfähig ist, sich zu verbergen. (RI:484–85)

[This time more than ever, while she stood on the stage and acted, something much greater than the mere fate of her characters was happening, something more general, something of such lofty generality that it was very closely related to the tragic life of sublime music. . . . There lives in this actress such a powerful soul that every piece she acts in is broken apart at its joints by the sublimity of her gestures, and only she, she alone, remains before us, her nature, which is incapable of concealing itself.]

Here the idea of absolute or intransitive acting is quite fully developed. Neither the character nor the play is of any further consequence; only the acting, as acting, matters now. We must not be confused by the terms "soul" and "nature." Hofmannsthal is talking not about the qualities of a particular person but rather about a maximum of "generality," which in this context can only mean sheer acting as *itself* the vehicle of truth, of the inherently untheorizable, indeed indiscussible truth concerning the radically histrionic nature of human identity.

Oedipus and the Allegory of Acting

Once this theory of acting is understood, and its relation to the theater of adaptation, it becomes possible to account for Hofmannsthal's interest in the Oedipus material as a vehicle for that theater. As with the texts discussed above, it is a question here of allegorical reflections, in the myth, of the essential but historically obscured theatrical situation. For the actor, like Oedipus, is from the outset saddled with a fate. He or she is doomed, in pursuing the theatrical craft, to pass beyond the limits of normal "individual" existence and to become something more "general"—an icon, a symbol, a vessel of truth. And he or she, like Oedipus, fulfills this doom *precisely by striving to avoid it*, by striving repeatedly to be fully contained within the circumscribed individuality of each dramatic role. ("And Duse wishes to be a mere actress, and she strives to cover herself, and she summons up the whole demonic force of her body in an attempt to refract the pure ray of her being in a thousand metamorphoses" [RI:485].) In *Ödipus und die Sphinx*, when Oedipus is first told of the heroic deed the Thebans require of him, he says to himself:

> Ihr guten Götter!
> Welch eine Tat, ihr Seligen! Baut ihr
> dem Heimatlosen solche Taten auf,
> so funkelnde Paläste, drin zu hausen
> für eine Nacht und wiederum für eine,
> wohin sein Fuß ihn trägt? So habt ihr mich
> mit eurem Fluch gesegnet?
> (DII:462)

[Good gods! What a deed, you blessed ones! Do you erect such deeds for
the Homeless One, such gleaming palaces to be lived in for a night or two,
wherever his path leads him? Is your curse thus a blessing to me?]

Like the actor, he imagines himself as a kind of anonymous nomad who
repeatedly receives the opportunity to define himself individually as the
doer of a particular deed (as the actor of a particular role, in the allegory)
and then always leaves that deed (or role) behind him for the next. And like
the actor, he never manages actually to realize this vision of himself, this
anonymity, his costume never fully conceals him, and wherever he goes he
is inevitably recognized for who he truly is—first unconsciously by Jokaste,
then explicitly by the Sphinx—always inevitably recognized as the doomed
vessel of truth. ("But in all these metamorphoses, Duse still belongs too
completely to herself. . . . The curtain falls and she stands there, alone, and
shakes off the remnants of those things, her roles, like mere dust" [RI:486].)

Thus not only the Oedipus myth in general but also Hofmannsthal's
Ödipus und die Sphinx makes sense in relation to the theater of adaptation.
In response to Phönix's insistence that, after receiving at Delphi the
prophecy of his parricide and incest, he should have pressed the original
question of who his real parents are, Oedipus says: "Nicht zweimal redet /
der Gott. Den er sich wählt, von dem wird er / begriffen" (DII:398: The
god does not repeat himself. Whom he chooses, by that person is he understood). The idea that he has been "chosen" by fate, in other words, for all
its horror, still awakens in Oedipus a kind of pride that prevents him from
asking the question that would have prevented his fate. His perverse pride
in his vocation is the vehicle by which his vocation is realized, but realized
in a sense that he must necessarily strive to avoid. Or, in the allegory, it is
the actor's following of his vocation as an actor, as one who acts—not a
speculator, not an asker of questions, not a person who ever fails to focus
on the particular—that proves the vehicle by which his vocation is realized, but on a level of "generality" entirely different from the level on
which he follows it.

Even the figure of Kreon, as Hofmannsthal sees him, assumes allegorical
significance here. It is Kreon whose use of theater terminology in the
phrase, "sich . . . mit Taten schminken" (DII:429: to put on deeds like
makeup), establishes clearly the connection between acting in the sense of
doing deeds and acting in the sense of playing roles. And precisely in using
this phrase, Kreon marks himself as the man who wishes at all costs to *avoid*
becoming an actor. He goes through the motions of maneuvering politically
for the throne of Thebes, and indeed his very name means "ruler." But
when the time comes for taking the final step that will secure him the king-
ship, he refuses. He wishes to *be* king, but somehow without ever *becoming*
king ("ich läg und schliefe jetzt, und aus dem Schlaf / mich wecken kämen

sie und legten mir / die Krone auf mein Bett" [432]), without ever passing through a moment of clear focus upon the goal, without ever "putting on the makeup" of a king. In this respect, Hofmannsthal takes his cue (cf. DVI:353) from the speech in Sophocles' *Oedipus the King* (lines 582–615) where Kreon states his natural preference for royal privileges without royal responsibilities.

Kreon, in Hofmannsthal, is thus the diametrical opposite of Oedipus, and between them the two figures allegorize the truth that there is no alternative in human existence to the condition of being an actor, that even the most determined resistance to this condition, the most consistent refusal to "put on makeup," is itself a form of acting, a deliberate shaping and focusing and particularizing of one's existence. Kreon in the end becomes king of Thebes after all, and king in exactly the sense he had wanted to avoid, faced with decisions that are too much for his vacillating temperament—should Oedipus be granted his wish for exile? (Sophocles, lines 1515–20; DVI:379–82)—and faced, if we look ahead to *Oedipus at Colonus*, with complete civic disaster. The lesson of the theater, *as* theater, remains what it had been in *Der Tor und der Tod*: that the substance of human life is not feeling or passion or conviction but only *choice*, and that the only true choice is between being a good actor (Oedipus) and being a bad one (Kreon).

The Paradox of the Author

Several problems remain. Especially (1) if the renewal of the theater Hofmannsthal envisages is really only a renewal of how the theater regards itself; and (2) if this renewal requires a reduction in the relative importance of poetic meaning in drama, so that the truth-bearing quality of absolute performance can come into focus; and (3) if Hofmannsthal therefore constructs a theater of adaptation and, in order to ensure that the character of this theater is properly understood (see condition 1), selects texts for it in which various significant aspects of the theater itself are allegorized, then how are these allegories, these uses of text to influence spectators' view of their theater, at all *different* from exactly that literary "meaning" against which they are employed? Is there, in other words, any actual hope for a renewal of the theater in Hofmannsthal's sense, or does the theater always automatically repoeticize itself in the process of renewal? And does it really matter if there is no hope? What is the use of truth as I have suggested it is conveyed by absolute performance? Why should we not be content with our belief in "individuality," in our genuine convictions and passions, however delusive this belief might be?

I think all these questions point toward *Der Turm*, but not by any means in the sense that the play provides answers to them. On the contrary, the single most striking thing about *Der Turm*—especially in the original long version published in *Neue deutsche Beiträge* (1923, 1925)—is that for all its enormous rhetorical weight and density, it cannot be regarded as an "answer," in any respect, to anything whatever but is constituted entirely by ambiguity, indecision, equivocation, inconclusiveness, rhetorical *emptiness*. In act 5, now that Sigismund has survived years of solitary philosophical training, the debacle at court, the collapse of his father's regime, Julian's huge ambitions and tragedy, and his own capture by Olivier, we expect that the play will finally shape itself into some form of relatively coherent philo-sophical-political vision. Sigismund himself seems to expect this when his consciousness of having now learned "die Sprache der Welt" (the world's language) is balanced by a philosophical remark to the Doctor, that "nichts ist da oder nicht da: alles, indem es ist, war schon da" (DIII:360: nothing is there or not there: everything, by being, was already there). But the gypsy woman is already present on stage when he says this; and Graf Adam soon appears with news of "die Grünen" (361: the Greens), who turn out to be the troops of the Kinderkönig (Children's King). Sigismund does his best, even in the scene with the gypsy, to maintain a practical, political-military focus, but of course he cannot. The real gypsy is replaced by her spectral double (366–68); the whole character of the stage thus changes from reality to sym-bolic vision; Sigismund then receives his death, which on this stage, how-ever, is not even an unequivocally real death; and the play is then closed by the Kinderkönig, whose appearance simply begs any serious political (or philosophical) questions we might have wished to consider.

And yet, the play is anything but perfunctory. It moves, in fact, with a cer-emonial deliberateness that apparently seemed excessive even to Hof-mannsthal, when he produced a shorter version for the first book publication at the Bremer Presse. Brother Ignatius, at one point, has occasion to say:

> In Rom hab ich Theaterspielen sehen, in einem grossen Saale, aber schlecht. Was sie nicht anging agierten sie mit gespreizten Leibern und schleppten gebauschtes Zeug hinter sich drein, wie Schlangenschweife. (DIII:296)
>
> [In Rome I saw theater acting, in a great hall, but bad. Things that were of no concern to them they acted with inflated bodies, and dragged in puffed-up cloth behind them, like snake-tails.]

He could almost be talking here about the play in which his own scene takes up much more time than is justified by its contribution to the central action. The "puffed-up cloth" that those Roman actors supposedly drag around might even suggest inordinately long speeches; for it is certainly true that all the major characters in *Der Turm* are given more than enough room to develop their positions and feelings in language. Julian, in fact, is not finally silenced even by death.

Why, we must ask, does this play *talk* so much, yet in the end not arrive an anything resembling a meaning? Or does this question perhaps contain its own answer? Here, perhaps, the theater of adaptation approaches its audience with an unprecedented directness, unmediated by the complications of allegory. The naked confrontation between ego and universe (recall the "Puppentheater" Poet) is enacted over and over again, not only by Sigismund but by Basilius, Brother Ignatius, Julian, even Olivier; the stage does not represent a world (how can it be a world, with practically no women?) but is exclusively the locus of this confrontation. Poetic vision is not avoided or suppressed or attenuated but rather—in its very kernel, as the collision of ego and universe—is the only thing that actually happens in this play. And yet this happening, this staging of pure poetic vision, even for Sigismund, is ultimately *empty.* "Gebet Zeugnis: ich war da. Wenngleich mich niemand gekannt hat" (381: Bear witness: I was there, even if no one knew me), says Sigismund—looking at the Doctor! thus including him in the "no one." What communicative value will such "witness" or testimony have, if its object is strictly unknown even to the witness himself, if there is "no place in historical time" for it? Sigismund's demeanor may be joyful, but when he dies on the words, "Hier bin ich, Julian!" (Here I am, Julian), he still thus associates his death with Julian's descent into "Nichts!" (351), into sheer, simple nothingness.

The whole substance of the play is poetic vision, which, however, repeatedly proves ineffectual, noncommunicable, and so in effect repeatedly evaporates, leaving in the theater nothing but performance. Here is theater of adaptation reduced to absolute simplicity. *Der Turm* is not even really any longer, at this stage of development, an adaptation of *La vida es sueño*. It merely makes the *gesture* of being an adaptation, and in this case the gesture is better than the reality, since the actual "original" is thus placed at too great a distance to be effective as a counterforce to its own undermining of the new text's meaning. In the same way, moreover, *Der Turm* makes merely a *gesture* at the theme of living one's life as if it were a dream; thus it mobilizes the association of this idea with the actor's detachment, but without embarking on a necessarily obscure allegorical elaboration of it.

And yet, even without the specific complications of allegory, all these ideas can still be regarded as aspects of the text's or, more important, the author's meaning, of what the author wishes to accomplish with his work. How do we get around this objection? How does Hofmannsthal? To the extent that this question can be answered, an answer is suggested by the discussion above of Hofmannsthal's response to Eleonora Duse. Like the actress, every author begins by submerging himself entirely in each particular work; and like the actress, every author finds over time, in spite of himself, that this submergence becomes less and less complete, that he tends to become something "more," and "more general," than his works in the very act of continuing to produce them. Hofmannsthal grows especially conscious of this process around the time of *Der Turm*.[8] In the sketch of a letter to an older man like himself, he says, "Unser eigentliches Geheimnis war unsere Haltung im Leben, die Perspektive unserer Äußerungen,— damit waren wir Vorläufer, Vorfühler" (E:584: Our true secret was our posture in life, the perspective of our utterances—in this respect we moved, or groped, ahead of our time). Not the utterances themselves but the perspective from which they emerge now becomes crucial. And in order for *Der Turm* to be effective in the manner I have suggested, this authorial perspective—in relation to which the play itself (the text, the structure of meaning) crumbles into nonessentialness—must be present and operative even for an audience in the theater. "Bear witness: I was there." [Gebet Zeugnis: ich war da. Wenngleich mich niemand gekannt hat.] These words are spoken not only *in* the play—where they do not signify much—but also, as it were, from *behind* it, by an author who thus insists on his separation from the knowable text, an author whose role is completed by simply "being there," not by saying anything specific.

Hofmannsthal's Retreat

But how can we be sure this actually happens? What evidence have we? Obviously, we cannot be sure; there can be no conclusive evidence. We can understand that the theatrical situation required by *Der Turm* is more easily imaginable in the case of an older author with a long public career behind him, an author who is more likely to be preknown, preunderstood, prejudged by tonight's audience and thus more likely to "be there" *for* that audience. But there is no place in the logic of textual or cultural criticism for anything like certainty in this matter. What I have described is the situation that *must* obtain if *Der Turm* is to have a culminating function in the theater of adaptation, but with nothing like a guarantee that it *does* obtain.

Hofmannsthal himself, of course, can be no surer of his ground here than we are, which is why he is willing (under Reinhardt's influence) to revise *Der Turm* and to give the new version a fairly clear philosophical and political message after all. In the end, that is, Hofmannsthal turns his back on the theater of adaptation and on his years of struggle with its complexities. But in doing so, he also at last provides—as it were inadvertently—a justification of that theater, an answer to our final question concerning the *importance* of truth as it is conveyed by the possibility of absolute or intransitive performance.

The most significant change in the last version of *Der Turm* is the development of the figure of Olivier, who is permitted to give expression to what Hofmannsthal evidently considers the main political danger of his time. In the last scene, for instance, when the Doctor approaches him in a posture of supplication, pleading for Sigismund's life, Olivier responds: "Gebärdet Euch nicht. Die Pfaffen- und Komödiantensprache ist abgeschafft. Es ist ein nüchterner Tag über der Welt angebrochen" (DIII:467: Don't make a fuss. The language of priests and actors is abolished. A sober day has dawned on the world). In this new atmosphere of sobriety, he implies, serious things will at last be taken seriously; people will be taken at their word and held to their word. What matters now is the "utterance" itself, not the "*Haltung*," the attitude, the theatrical pose behind it; what matters now is the utterance as *meaning*, as doctrine or, ultimately, dogma. Society will be constituted no longer by the fluid interaction of actorly types and moves, but by the clash of meanings, of uncompromising positions or formulations, and ultimately therefore by the hegemony of one such position, one established order. "Denn ich und einige, wir haben uns aufgeopfert und nehmen dem Volk die Last des Regimentes ab, damit es nicht schwindlich werde" (468), says Olivier (For I and others like me, we have sacrificed ourselves and we relieve the people of the burden of government, that they might not grow dizzy). The dizzying, disorderly quality of human existence (as represented, for example, in the uncenteredness of the theater of adaptation) will finally be brought under control; and control in this sense is by definition radically impersonal, hence a violation of the single actual form (that of the experiencing person) in which humanity is manifest.[9]

Or to put it differently, Hofmannsthal imagines a coming hegemony of the *nameless*. In his last speech, Olivier says:

Jawohl! man sollte nach Recht vor uns liegen, für das, was wir auf uns genommen haben, aber wir verschmähen es, und auch mit unseren Namen soll kein Götzendienst getrieben werden, darum halten wir sie geheim.

[Yes! It is right that people lie prostrate before us, considering the burden we have assumed, but we scorn such homage, nor do we wish that idolatry be practiced with our names, and therefore we keep them secret.]

And it is against the threat of the nameless that the theater of adaptation, by way of its inevitable arrival at the idea of absolute or intransitive authorship, is erected. For the work or product of absolute authorship—if there is such a thing, which cannot be decided—can be, precisely, nothing but name, not even a particular name, but the quality of name as such, as an instance of language entirely dissociated from meaning, language as sheer performance ("Komödiantensprache" in the strictest conceivable sense), which does nothing but bear witness: "ich war da."

CHAPTER SEVEN

Diderot, Shaw, Beckett,
and the Meaning of Plays

This chapter, like the previous one, is focused ultimately on the question of *meaning* in drama. But the extended discussion of Diderot has the effect here not only of enlarging that question's historical range but also of exhibiting a more theoretical or systematic approach to it. In the end, Diderot never actually formulates a theory of theatrical meaning; but his reasons for not doing so belong—transparently, it seems to me—to the theory itself.

Where Is the Paradox?

One of the many curious features of Diderot's *Paradoxe sur le comédien* is that it contains no statement or proposition that is actually paradoxical.[1] The opinions of the "first speaker," who is later called "l'homme au paradoxe" (374, 376) and "l'homme paradoxal" (377), are perhaps unusual, and sometimes confusingly expressed—he claims not yet to have had time to link his arguments together (306/103)—but on the whole, they seem derived from sound common sense and do not contradict one another. His principal point, in fact, seems thoroughly convincing the very first time he states it:

> If the actor actually felt what he was doing [*Si le comédien était sensible*], would it honestly be possible for him to play a part twice running with the same warmth and the same success? He would be full of warmth for the first performance and exhausted and cold as stone at the third. Whereas if he's a close imitator and thoughtful disciple of nature, the first time he appears on stage as Augustus, Cinna, Orosmane, Agamemnon, or Mahomet, being a strict copyist of his own acting or the part he has studied,

and a constant observer of our sensations, his performance, far from falling off, will benefit from the new ideas he's gathered. . . . What confirms me in my opinion is the unevenness of actors who play from the heart. Don't expect any kind of consistency from them; their performance is alternately strong and weak, hot and cold, dull and brilliant. . . . Whereas the actor who acts from the head, from studying human nature, from constantly imitating some ideal model, using his imagination and his memory, will always be the same, unchanged from one performance to the next, always with the same degree of perfection: everything has been measured, thought out, learnt and organized in his head; there's no monotony, nothing out of place in his delivery. . . . He won't vary from day to day: he's a mirror, always ready to picture things and to picture them with the same accuracy, the same power and the same truth. Like the poet, he's ceaselessly delving into the inexhaustible wealth of nature, whereas he would soon have come to the end of his own potential. (306–7/103–4)

One can of course disagree with this view; but it is hard to see how one's disagreement could take the form of logical argument, for one would be arguing in favor of the irrational, the purely emotional. And where, then, shall we expect to find "paradox," which requires a particular structure in logic?

At least somewhat akin to paradox, perhaps, is a quickly emerging tendency in this text to strain the limits of language. The first speaker, at the very beginning, disparages the art of the "imitative actor," the "comédien imitateur," whose performance is characterized by "sustained mediocrity" (303–4). But then, only a couple of pages later, it is precisely "the art of imitating," "l'art de tout imiter," that he claims to prefer, and it is the actor as "close imitator," "imitateur attentif," whom he now praises (306). Of course, the idea of imitation operates differently in the different places he uses it. But why make a point of the ease with which the text's central terminology loses focus? Or if the terminology is unavoidably precarious, why not take special care to use it consistently?

Another instance of terminological incongruity, less obvious but more significant, involves the verb "sentir." The paradoxical man says, early on, that after the performance is over, "l'acteur est las, et vous triste; c'est qu'il s'est démené sans rien sentir, et que vous avez senti sans vous démener" (The actor is weary, and you are sad, because he has exerted himself without feeling anything, and you have had the feeling without the exertion: 313/108). Leaving aside, for the time being, the question of why it should make us *sad* to undergo feeling without exertion, it is clear that "sentir," in this passage, means "to feel emotion," and in plenty of other passages (310, 312, 326, 336, 342, 346) the same meaning is equally clear. But then, toward the end, we read: "C'est qu'être sensible est une chose, et sentir est une autre. L'une est une affaire d'âme, l'autre une affaire de judgement" (You see, having sensibility is one thing, and feeling is another. One is a matter for the heart and the other a matter for the judgment: 372/150). In what sense can it possibly be meant that "sentir" is a matter for the judgment? And why *oppose* "être sensible" and "sentir," as if, now, the latter were meant to characterize the true actor, by contrast with the "sensibilité" of the bungler? (Compare the earlier opposition of "jugement" and "sensibilité" [306].) The passage continues as follows:

> C'est qu'on sent avec force et qu'on ne saurait rendre; c'est qu'on rend, seul, en société, au coin d'un foyer, en lisant, en jouant, pour quelques auditeurs, et qu'on ne rend rien qui vaille au théâtre; c'est qu'au théâtre, avec ce qu'on appelle de la sensibilité, de l'âme, des entrailles, on rend bien une ou deux tirades et qu'on manque le reste; c'est qu'embrasser toute l'étendue d'un grand rôle ... c'est l'ouvrage d'une tête froide, d'un profond jugement, d'un goût exquis, d'une étude pénible.

> [You can feel deeply and you can't convey it; you can convey something sitting alone, in private, by the fireside, reading a part aloud for a few listeners, but you can't convey anything that would work in the theater; in the theater, with what's called sensibility, heart, inner depth, you can carry off one or two big speeches and muff the rest; to embrace the whole range of a great part ... this needs a cool head, profound judgment, sophisticated taste, laborious preparation. (modified translation)]

Is "sentir" thus left behind, as having nothing to do with competent theatrical acting? Actually, the only reasonable way to read the last long sentence quoted is this: it is possible to feel and be unable to convey, or to feel and convey, but not theatrically, or to feel and be able to deliver in the theater certain types of speech; but in order to master a whole theatrical role, one's feeling must be tempered by (among other things) judgment.

Does this statement contradict those other passages, where all connection between "sentir" and acting is denied? Not if one reads "sentir," here (and here alone!), in the entirely normal meaning of "to sense, to perceive, to be aware of," with the suggestion of perceiving by a kind of sympathy the emotional condition of another (fictional) person whose part one must play. This reading, I think, clarifies the present passage and explains well enough how "sentir" can be connected with "jugement." But it does not even begin to explain why the verb "sentir," which is crucial in the dialogue's terminology, is allowed to undergo such a huge slippage, one that places it on both sides of the division between actor and bungler. It is as if the paradoxical man were admitting that language itself is unable to represent his thinking, that the reader must make his or her own independent choice among multiple word meanings in order to reconstitute and so comprehend the argument.

This impression is reinforced, in turn, by the presence of the idea of multiple word meanings—the idea that language cannot determine, by itself, a single clear meaning—in the *content* of the dialogue. The paradoxical man says:

> And how could a part be played in the same way by two different actors, since even with the most clear, precise and positive writer the words are never, can never be, anything but signs approximating to a thought, a feeling, or an idea, signs whose value is completed by movement, gesture, tone, the eyes and the particular situation. (304/101)

Then, after illustrating this proposition with an exchange from *Tartuffe,* he offers, as a second example, not a passage *from* drama, but a work *about* drama, the book *Garrick ou les acteurs anglais,* which the two interlocutors had been discussing at the dialogue's opening.[2] And it is only with reference to this second example that he goes into full detail:

> Ask a French actor what he thinks of [the book] and he'll agree that it's all true. Put the same question to an English actor and he'll swear, *by God,* that there's not a sentence to be changed and it's the true gospel of the stage. Yet as there's hardly anything in common between the English way of writing comedy and tragedy and the way it's done in France . . . it follows clearly that the French actor and the English actor, who fully agree on the truth of your author's principles, don't understand each other, and that there is in the technical language of the theatre such looseness, such vagueness, that sensible men with diametrically opposed views can both think they're seeing the light of truth in it. (304–5/102)

What is being discussed here, it seems, is a form of representational inadequacy which, while it appears with special clarity in dramatic language (by way, more or less, of heteroglossia), actually characterizes language as such, including the arguments of the text before us.

Thus, although we are probably not yet in a position to formulate or circumscribe the paradox of Diderot's text, we can at least make a reasonable supposition about where it is located. We shall look for it between the lines, among the unspoken consequences and premises of the arguments that are actually made, especially when the silence of these consequences and premises appears to mark a limit of the representational capability of language. We will of course keep in mind, as a point of departure, the words of the paradoxical man:

> I want him [the actor] to have a lot of judgment, for me there needs to be a cool, calm spectator inside this man, so I demand sagacity and no feeling, the power to imitate anything, or, what amounts to the same thing, an equal aptitude for all characters and parts. (306/102–3)

But we will also keep in mind that this statement occurs at the end of his discussion of English and French actors, which means, presumably, that the imitative versatility of the competent actor does *not* extend to the ability to move between languages or national cultures. (The theaters of ancient Greece and Rome are later included in the picture.) What exactly is the difference between types of difference here?

Sentir/Sentir

Of all Diderot's other writings, the one closest to the *Paradoxe* in spirit and content is *Le Rêve de d'Alembert*. Both texts deal, in the main, with questions related to the notion of "sensibilité," and both contain almost exactly the same argument for considering the "great man" as the man who either lacks sensibility altogether or succeeds in suppressing it in himself (309–311/105–6).[3] But for the purpose of understanding better the apparent double meaning of the verb "sentir" in the *Paradoxe*, our attention is drawn, in the *Rêve*, to the prefatory conversation between d'Alembert and Diderot.

Diderot's basic position in this little debate is that "sensibilité" must be regarded as a universal attribute of matter (1:619). But sensibility, as it characterizes matter in general, is not the same thing as the feeling that we human beings know from experience. For as d'Alembert is compelled to admit, a being that feels ("un être sentant") cannot exist without the faculty of *memory*; otherwise, its life would be "an interrupted set of sensations with nothing to connect them." We humans, therefore, must be thought of as "instruments endowed with sensibility and memory" (1:616–17). And I contend that what Diderot here calls "memory," "mémoire," is basically the same thing that is referred to by the *second* meaning of "sentir" in the *Paradoxe*—"sentir" as it must characterize even the actor—which is not feeling "itself" so much as the perception of feeling. What Diderot and d'Alembert come to agree on, namely, is that we never really have a feeling or emotion in the first place until we are conscious of having it, which means, until we also have a relatively distanced perception of it.

If this parallel holds, however, then it seems to imply a refutation of the central argument of the *Paradoxe*, not to mention Bordeu's argument in the *Rêve* about great men's lack of feeling. For the two meanings of "sentir," in the *Paradoxe*, need to be *separable* in order to be applied, as they apparently are, to two different groups of people. "In the great comedy, the comedy of the world, the one to which I always return, all the hot-blooded people are on the stage; all the men of genius are in the pit" (311/106). But in the *Rêve*, it is shown clearly that these two ideas—*having* sensibility and *perceiving* sensibility—both belong to the single process that constitutes human feeling, a process that does not happen without the operation of both elements. Thus, in order to rescue the paradoxical man's idea of the competent actor—or Bordeu's idea of the great man—we must show (it seems) that although it is not possible to have feeling without the perception of feeling, it is still possible to have the latter (a distanced understanding of feeling) without the experience of feeling itself. But is this really possible, in Diderot's own terms, or not?

Terminology suggests clearly a denial of this possibility. In the *Paradoxe*, where the two basic elements of feeling are named "être sensible" and "sentir," the latter, even in the meaning of "to *perceive* sensibility," cannot escape being the same verb that had earlier meant "to *have* sensibility." In the *Rêve*, where the two elements are named "sensibilité" and "mémoire" (1:617), the latter clearly means "memory of *oneself*" and so indicates that the perceiving of sensibility is not detachable from the fact, or the (at least remembered) experience, of sensibility. And as in terminology, so also in logic—even if the logical argument is not carried out in either text. The paradoxical man asserts glibly that the actor's "talent consists not in feeling . . . but in giving such a scrupulous rendering of the outward signs of the feeling that you're taken in" (312/107). But how can I, as an actor, even begin to learn my craft, how can I make even the first connection between a particular "outward sign" and a particular "feeling," if I have no unmediated knowledge of the feeling itself? The number of "outward signs" exhibited by any human body in any instant is in effect infinite, since it depends on definitions, on which qualities of which bodily members are grouped together as a "sign," and how shall I, the aspiring actor, correctly analyze this infinitude of material without the aid of self-memory (*mémoire*), the memory of how *my* feeling had affected *my* body? Or even if I do correctly identify a particular "sign," how shall I know what it is a sign *of*? If the actor's business is to enable us "to appreciate . . . what goes on inside us" (apprécier . . . ce qui se passe au dedans de nous: 358/140), how can he even begin his task without his own direct appreciation of that "dedans"?

(Toward the very end of the *Paradoxe*, in the coda that follows the dialogue proper, Diderot finally takes up this question explicitly: the paradoxical man suggests that "of all qualities of character sensibility is the easiest to mimic, since there's perhaps not a single man who's so cruel and inhuman that the germ of it is not present in his heart, that he's never felt it; something you couldn't say about all the other passions, such as avarice or distrust" [375/153]. The actor, it seems, could therefore be copying from memory after all. But then Diderot and his paradoxical man quickly turn the tables on us by insisting that even if his memory contains a "model" of sensibility, the great actor imitates precisely by *ignoring* this model, by insisting that "never being brought down to the level of the little model inside him, he'll be as great, as amazing, as perfect an imitator of sensibility as of avarice, hypocrisy, duplicity, and any other characteristic which is not his own, any other passion which he does not feel." And the proof of this proposition is precisely that the exact artistic "imitation" of those other, less universal passions—as the second speaker has admitted [374–75/152]—is possible.)[4]

We thus arrive at what we might call the paradox of the great man, the extraordinary individual of whom Bordeu says:

> At age forty-five he will be a great king, a great minister, a great politician, a great artist, especially a great actor, a great philosopher, a great poet, a great musician, a great doctor. He will rule over himself and over everything around him. . . . People of sensibility and madmen are on the stage; he is in the pit watching, and it is he who is wise. (1:660–61)

The great man, that is, exercises control over himself and others, whereas it is the nature of the person of feeling (the "être sensible") to *submit* to control, to be governed, as Bordeu says, by his or her own diaphragm (1:660). And the image of the world theater, where the great man observes his mediocre fellows, makes clear that his control over others is based on his *knowledge* of their emotional susceptibility. But again, where does this knowledge come from? The observation of "outward signs," for the reasons I have given, cannot alone suffice.[5]

This is the paradox—or, perhaps we should say, the problem—of the great man. If we admit that great men, in Diderot's or Bordeu's sense, exist, then the question of *how* they exist turns out not to be an easy one. Or at least it turns out so when we are moved to ask that question, which is why the special case of the actor is important. For the great politician, or the great physician, does not advertise the fact that his power in human affairs is based on his knowledge and manipulation of others' emotional submissiveness. Only great actors permit us to grasp this fact; indeed, they positively flaunt it, in that they exercise power over us precisely by imitating our feelings, thus constantly revealing the deep expert knowledge on which their power is based. *As* a problem, therefore, as an askable question, the paradox of the great man is manifest primarily as the "paradox of the actor."

Diderot's Theater and Hofmannsthal's

The underlying premise of the paradox of the great man, without which it would not be a paradox or problem, is that the inner world of our feelings can be strictly distinguished from the outer world in which the signs of our feeling become visible. As Hamlet says, referring to the signs of grief in his demeanor: "These indeed seem, / For they are actions that a man might play; / But I have that within which passeth show— / These but the trappings and the suits of woe" (1.2.83–86). It has to be true that the individual is a fully integrated unit, having its own inviolable space "within" itself, and that the feelings located "within" exist in an entirely different way from the outward signs by which we think we recognize them. In particular, it must be true that feelings themselves can be known directly only by the pérson whose feelings they are, that only I have direct access to my own inner life. Feelings of others are known only indirectly, by inference from outward signs. When I feel a particular emotion, my body tends to react in a specific way, and when I observe the same bodily actions in others, I infer that they feel the same emotion. Hence the paradox of the great man. For if he himself *never* feels that particular emotion to begin with, then on what does he base his inference of feeling in others?

Or is this really the question? Perhaps we have got things backward. Perhaps what is being called into question here is the *premise* of the paradox, the assumption of a substantial emotional life, a real and natural "within," in human individuals. Perhaps Hofmannsthal's use of Diderot (discussed in the preceding chapter), is also a correct reading of the *Paradoxe* itself. With reference to the passage in which he describes the man of genius as a cool spectator at the comedy of life, the paradoxical man says, "Even if these truths were proved, the great actors would never admit them; it's their secret" (311/106–7). But what precisely is "their secret"? Is it merely that they do not actually undergo all the emotion they feign on the stage? In itself, that is not much of a secret, and for the reader of *this* text it is no secret at all. Hofmannsthal's reading at least envisages a significant secret knowledge for the actor: the knowledge that genuine feeling or belief, true sincerity, a substantial or natural inner emotional life, either does not exist at all or may as well not exist, since it would in any case be strictly incommunicable; and that the supposed "outward signs" of that inner life are therefore always histrionically contaminated, always feigned, exaggerated, delusive. This reading of course implies that the paradoxical man himself is being secretive, not saying all he knows, which seems to conflict with his warning at the beginning: "Il me serait plus aisé de me taire que de déguiser ma pensée" (I should find it easier not to say anything than to disguise my thoughts: 303/101). But the paradoxical man chooses his words very carefully here, and does not in fact say that he is *not* going to disguise his thoughts.

Immediately after the sentence quoted above, concerning great actors and the "truths" that they keep "secret," comes the passage Hofmannsthal misquotes in the *Buch der Freunde*:

> Les acteurs médiocres ou novices sont faits pour les [ces vérités] rejeter, et l'on pourrait dire de quelques autres qu'ils croient sentir, comme on a dit du superstitieux, qu'il croit croire; et que sans la foi pour celui-ci, et sans la sensibilité pour celui-là, il n'y a point de salut.

[Indifferent actors and novices are the type to reject them [those truths], and it could be said of a few others that they believe they're feeling, just as it's said of superstitious people that they believe they're believing, and that there's no hope [better: no security] for the second without faith, nor for the first without sensibility.] (311/107)

We can see, now, why this passage stuck in Hofmannsthal's mind. For if the inner life is really autonomous and substantial, and truly *inner*—that is, directly accessible only to the one person whose inner life it is—then how could it ever be asserted that this or that individual merely believes in his belief or feeling, without "really" believing or feeling? In order for a judgment of this kind to make any sense, there has to be something fundamentally wrong with the idea of a strictly inner life (with the idea that my feelings are mine alone, not available to be judged), hence also with the idea of a fully integrated human individuality. This idea of the integrated individual with its own inner space—as Diderot clearly suggests in the passage above—represents not a fact or a truth but merely a *refuge,* the illusory vision of a place of safety ("salut") for the individual whose integrity as a coherent being is otherwise called radically into question.

And the place where this calling into question of substantial individuality occurs, for Diderot as for Hofmannsthal, is the theater. As I noted in connection with Hofmannsthal, *only* the theater—only the symbolism of the actor *as* actor, as shape-changer, as counterfeiter—provides an adequate vehicle for this questioning, because doctrine or argument would inevitably presuppose, as both its origin and its recipient, exactly the sort of integrated, intellectually independent individuality whose very existence was meant to be questioned. In Diderot as in Hofmannsthal, this questioning function of the theater is only hinted at—to do more would be to make the illegitimate move into doctrine or argument—but hinted at pretty strongly. When talking about the real theater, Diderot quite consistently suggests that the role of the audience is to be moved emotionally, to be deceived and subjected to illusion: "The illusion is only for you, the spectator" (313). But when he uses the theater as a *metaphor*—for the "comedy of the world" (311/106)—he situates all the raging emotion on the stage, while calm, observant rationality prevails in the audience. And this metaphor, in this text, cannot possibly be innocent; it must draw our attention covertly to an *actual* property of the theater. (Otherwise, Diderot would be using a metaphor of the type "as blue as a tomato.") On its surface, the theater appears made to engage us (the audience) emotionally. But for those of us with a sense for its "secret," the theater becomes a place of serious philosophical contemplation, an opportunity to observe and to think and so to participate in the symbolic thinking of thoughts that are beyond the conceptual range of the strictly individual mind, as well as beyond the expressive range of a language assumed to have meaning in the form of system or doctrine.

Once we start to read the *Paradoxe* in this spirit, I venture to say that it makes a great deal more sense than when we read it as literally as possible. Only a few pages into the dialogue, for example, we are brought up short by the point that "imitation" in the theater is not really imitation at all but an enormous exaggeration of the supposed outward signs of emotion.

> FIRST SPEAKER. And the Cleopatra, the Merope, the Agrippina, the Cinna of the stage, are they even historical figures? No. They're figments of the poetic imagination; I'm going too far: they're specters created in the particular manner of various poets. Let these monstrous creatures stay on the stage with their gesturing, their strutting and their shouting: they'd draw shouts of laughter in a literary circle or any other social gathering. . . .
>
> SECOND. But why don't they put you off in the theatre?
>
> FIRST. Because it's a convention. It's a recipe from old Aeschylus; it's a system that goes back three thousand years. (315/110)

The signs by which emotion is indicated in the theater, it turns out, are not natural but *conventional* signs. This explains how the actor can have "an equal aptitude for all characters and parts" (306/103) and yet be utterly unable to play a part written by someone on the other side of the English Channel. "All characters and parts"—for English actors or French actors— must be understood to mean all parts conceived in the convention in which they have grown up and been trained.

But if, as Diderot repeatedly asserts, we are emotionally engaged, moved to tears, by theatrical playacting, then it follows that we recognize something of our own intimate selves in that acting. And if—as we must now concede—we thus recognize our very selves by way of convention, does it not follow in turn that the self itself *is* a convention?

"au dedans de nous"

The paradox of the actor, in the sense of the paradox of the great man, is thus resolved, for the premise on which it depends has been discredited. We are no longer puzzled by the question of how the great man gains his knowledge of natural inner feelings that he has never experienced. It now turns out that those feelings are not natural at all but the products of convention, and we now understand that the great man is simply he who grasps this truth most firmly, who most consistently resists the temptation to indulge that convention of inner feeling, to seek refuge in it, as if it were his very nature. We also no longer have difficulty with the paradoxical man's remark that after the performance is over, we the audience are "sad" because we have had "the feeling without the exertion" (c'est . . . que vous avez senti sans vous démener: 313/108). In the theater, where we receive feeling in something like a pure state, unmixed with any effortful activity on our part, we are by consequence especially likely to have a melancholy intimation of the *emptiness* of precisely that "feeling" which we otherwise imagine is the very substance of our individual being.

But even if some questions are answered by the idea of feeling or passion as a conventional construction in history, the new questions that are raised are more profound. The true climax of the dialogue, I think, approaches when the paradoxical man says:

> Do you not categorically declare that true feeling and acted feeling are two very different things? You were laughing at what you would have admired on the stage? And why, pray? . . . The images of passions on the stage are not the true images, they're only exaggerated portraits, great caricatures subject to conventional rules. Well then . . . which artist will be better able to confine himself within these given rules? Which actor will better understand this prescribed puffing up, the man who is dominated by his own character, or the man born without character, or the man who divests himself of it to assume another which is greater, nobler, more violent and more elevated? (357–58/140)

At first, it appears that the argument is falling apart. If the actor must imitate all the nuances of a true natural character (as had been implied at the beginning of the dialogue), then it seems likely that his own character would get in the way. But if it is merely a matter of following "given rules," or executing a "prescribed puffing up," what is there for one's own character to get in the way of?

Actually, the argument still does make sense, *but it now makes sense in a different way*! The same argument has changed its meaning in the course of the dialogue, and so we find ourselves again on the slippery ground of multiple meanings. What the argument means now is roughly this: acting can never be "merely" a matter of following rules, for those rules are of the same type as the conventional elements that constitute what we experience as our own immediate self, our individual sense of identity, our very being; if we take them as "mere" rules, therefore, then we have not understood what kind of rules they are, and so we cannot properly follow them; and it is precisely the man who "has" a character, in the sense of believing himself to have a naturally shaped identity, who *will* understand the rules of a theatrical role as "mere" rules (by contrast with his own supposed naturalness), so it still remains true that the man with a minimum of character is the best actor. The argument in this new form is then restated elliptically in the very next sentence: "On est soi de nature; on est un autre d'imitation"

(One is oneself by nature; one is another by imitation: 358/140). In its context, the full meaning of this sentence is that the very notion of being "oneself" presupposes the idea of nature, therefore fails to grasp the cultural constructedness of identity, and so interferes with the actor's indispensable knowledge that one in truth always *is* an "other" (since there is no natural "self") by imitation, by conformity to rules.

But that last sentence is not quite finished. It continues: "le cœur qu'on se suppose n'est pas le cœur qu'on a" (the heart you imagine for yourself is not the heart you have). Here the multiplicity of meaning is concentrated in one word, the verb "supposer." In order to connect the sentence with its context, where the topic is playacting, one has to read etymologically, taking that verb in the sense of its Latin ancestor *supponere*, which gives the meaning "the heart that one takes over (places in one's bosom as a substitute) is not the heart one really has." But the more usual meaning of French "supposer" produces a reading that has nothing to do with playacting: "the heart that one supposes in oneself (the heart one thinks one has) is not the heart one really has." This reading states the simple psychological fact that self-awareness is always delusive. And it is hard to see why these two readings should be compressed into a single sentence if there is not a substantive relation between them—if, in particular, the figure of the actor *as* actor, in adopting a "heart" that is not his own, is not a *symbolic enactment* of the inevitable deludedness of self-knowledge and hence, again, for practical purposes, an enactment of the nonexistence of the supposed object of such knowledge. "On est un autre"; one is always "other," because being integratedly "oneself" cannot happen. This, it seems, is in Diderot's view the message of the medium, the message of the dramatic theater *as such*. And it is, again, a message that violates the limits of language. For if it is true, then its truth denies the existence of a stable vantage point (a stable individual mind) from which precisely that truth, that valid piece of self-knowledge, could be asserted or understood.

Does this conclusion settle the matter? Do we now have a complete structure of paradox, of aporia, of articulative impossibility? The passage we are looking at continues as follows:

> What then is true talent? Being familiar with the outward signs of the nature one has assumed [*l'âme d'emprunt*], directing one's performance at the sensations of those who hear and see us and deceiving them by the imitation of these signs, an imitation which enlarges everything in their minds and becomes the standard for their judgment; because it is impossible to appreciate what goes on inside us in any other way. (358/140)

There seems to be an inconsistency here. The actions that had been called, only a few lines earlier, "conventional rules" and a "prescribed puffing up" are now again accorded the status of "outward signs," "symptômes extérieurs," by which an "âme," a coherent identity, is revealed. But this is not an inconsistency. It is a *vacillation* in terminology and, as we have seen, a necessary vacillation. For to call these signs mere "given rules" is to claim a perspective we cannot occupy, since exactly such "rules" constitute our own inescapable sense of a natural identity: "On est soi de nature." But to call those signs the "exterior symptoms" of a natural self is to make an equally unfounded claim, since our only warrant for the possible existence of such a self is a self-knowledge in ourselves that we know to be delusive. Each manner of speaking needs to be countered by the other; no single terminology suffices.

Therefore it should not surprise us that the terminology now once more veers in the opposite direction, practically in midsentence. The actor's imitation, we hear, should "deceive" the audience, but not by its similarity to their idea of nature; rather, it should overpower their minds by sheer magnitude and *become* their standard of judgment, "la règle de leur jugement"—meaning, presumably, their judgment of naturalness.

And then follows a short clause in which practically all the dialogue's complicated development is distilled: "car il est impossible d'apprécier autrement ce qui se passe au dedans de nous" (because it is impossible to appreciate what goes on inside us in any other way). We "appreciate" what goes on inside us, we ascertain its value (*pretium*), not by looking into ourselves but by accepting as nature a public, historically conditioned standard of judgment that is offered us in the theater. What one experiences as a unique identity, one's inner self, in other words, is in truth a historical construct. This idea is condensed still further in the phrase "au dedans de nous," for we normally assume that the "inside," the "dedans," in human experience is a quality of the individual: the "moi," not the "nous." On the contrary, the paradoxical man implies, human interiority is a *collective* phenomenon, of the same type as, say, convention. And then, in the final sentence of this long paragraph, he cuts out from under this idea the heuristic question that had led to it, the question of whether the actor feels the emotions he plays: "And what does it matter anyway whether they feel what they're doing or not, as long as we don't know about it?" Whether the actor (or any individual) feels what he is doing is a misguided question and inherently unanswerable. What the actor does, merely by being an actor, is enact for us our understanding that the integrated self of "genuine" feeling— hence the very idea of such feeling—is an illusion, that our "inner" experience is fundamentally collective, that always, even in real life, "on est un autre." (Or "JE est un autre," as Rimbaud writes to Izambard in May 1871.)

The consequences of this thinking for the theory of drama and theater are considerable. For it follows now that neither the quality of the text nor the quality of the acting has any substantial influence on the philosophical meaning of any performed play, or even on the effectiveness with which that meaning is expressed. As also in Hofmannsthal's view of the theater, the whole philosophical burden of the event is always already there in the structure of the institution, in the process—as such—of playacting. The second speaker in the *Paradoxe*, as the dialogue approaches its end, says he has only one more question for the paradoxical man. "Have you ever," he asks, "seen a play absolutely perfectly performed?" And the paradoxical man, for once taken aback, responds, "Ma foi, je ne m'en souviens pas . . . Mais attendez . . . Oui, quelquefois une pièce médiocre, par des acteurs médiocres . . ." (My goodness, I don't remember . . . Wait though . . . Yes, occasionally an indifferent play, performed by indifferent actors . . ." 373/151). And this is exactly as it must be. For if either the play or the acting is too *good*, then that quality—paradoxically enough—will inevitably distract the spectator from what really matters in the performance, from the sheer fact of its happening.[6]

True Tragedy

Two major questions remain. First, as in the case of Hofmannsthal, one must ask why Diderot bothers with the difficult and thankless task of giving expression to a view of human nature that cannot be grasped in the form of system or doctrine or argument—and, as with Hofmannsthal, one expects to find a political answer to this question. The second question is more immediate. If what we experience as natural feeling is in truth theatrical convention, then how does it happen—as Diderot insists it does—that theatrical emotion appears ridiculously exaggerated when it is expressed, as if it were real emotion, in any normal social situation?

With respect to the second question, the only way to avoid convicting Diderot of a ruinous inconsistency is to see the discrepancy between "real" and acted feeling as the reflection of a defect in our *manner* of feeling. We are confused and ignorant with regard to "our" own feelings; "le cœur qu'on se suppose n'est pas le cœur qu'on a." A few pages earlier, this inner self-division had been described in different terms:

> A citizen who goes to the Comédie leaves all his vices at the door and picks them up again as he goes out. Once inside, he is just, impartial, a good father, a good friend, a lover of virtue; and I've often seen, sitting next to me, rogues who get deeply indignant at actions they would certainly have committed if they'd been in the same position as that in which the poet placed the character they detested. (354/138)

The gap between stage feeling and ordinary feeling, it appears, may be regarded as the symptom or correlative of a form of deep hypocrisy in our personal and social life.[7]

Nor is it difficult to see how this state of affairs is related to the delusive belief in "natural" feelings and in their unmistakable "outward signs." For in order to sustain this delusion, we must have confidence in our ability to make clear judgments about other people's feelings; and since no standard for such judgments really exists in nature, the standard we use ("la règle de [notre] jugement") must be supplied by culture, especially (if perhaps not uniquely) by the theater, where the largest and most extravagant effects will of course stamp our judgment most deeply. But in the world outside the theater, where we expect not to receive our judgment but to exercise it, where we expect our judgment to be challenged, exactly the same large and extravagant effects must strike us as oversimple, as caricatures. Thus the real world and the "world" as seen in the theater tend inevitably to diverge, which makes it possible for us, as Diderot complains, to be fully receptive to the moral content of the latter without its having any effect on our conduct in the former.[8]

I think this is what the second speaker means by his objection to the paradoxical man's "cruel commentary . . . on actors and authors" (358/141). When the paradoxical man asks him to be more specific, he continues: "It is, I imagine, permissible for anyone to have a great and strong character; it is, I imagine, permissible to have the bearing, the speech and the actions which go with that character, and I think that the image of true greatness can never be ridiculous" (359/141). The whole theatrical calculus of "feeling," in other words, has co-opted (as the "outward signs" of feeling), and thus corrupted, what we might otherwise have recognized as evidence of true human greatness. Our deeply habituated hypocrisy has cost us the ability to take even the most precious things at face value in intercourse with our fellow humans.

And this is also what the second speaker means when, on being pressed further, he is compelled to state as a final consequence of his reasoning "that true tragedy is still to be discovered, and that for all their faults, the Ancients were probably nearer to it than we are" (359/141). True tragedy, we infer, will be achieved only when the gap between reality and the theater is closed, when theatrical heroism at last actually is what the paradoxical man has called it, an "imitation," and as such would not be out of place in the society it imitates. And the precondition for this new (or old) relation between theater and society—if our reading so far is correct—must be the elimination of our deluded belief that the substance of inner individual existence consists of natural feeling. Again, it is this deluded belief that causes the divergence between reality and its theatrical imitation. Somehow we must learn to accept our feelings as culturally and historically constituted, as happening not "in me" but "au dedans de nous."

This is a very large and opaque "somehow," however, for our idea of our very identity stands between us and the truth we must accustom ourselves to. The size and depth of the gulf of inconceivability we face here can be measured by the inadequacy of the examples by which the paradoxical man makes the gesture of bridging it. First he quotes a speech from Sophocles' *Philoctetes* which would work nicely as an instance of the "simplicity and force" of Greek tragedy (359/141–42), if only it really existed. Actually there are just two very brief moments in Sophocles (*Philoctetes*, 971–72, 1009) where sentiments even remotely similar to those in Diderot's "quoted" speech are expressed. The paradoxical man, that is, can demonstrate the Greeks' nearness to true tragedy only by fabricating it. Which does not mean that the Greeks did *not* have true tragedy, only that there is no way to explain it (however paradoxically) in terms we might understand.

And when the paradoxical man then turns to the Romans, the result is even worse. He does give a reasonable paraphrase (361/142–43) of Regulus's speech to the Senate, in Horace's account (*Odes* 3.5). But that speech, far from showing a radically different spirit, presupposes on the part of its audience exactly the same hypocrisy that we had earlier learned to recognize in contemporary France. If what Regulus (and Horace through him) says is true, then the audience to that speech are guilty of exactly those vices ("le cœur qu'on a") which, *as* an audience, they join together in despising ("le cœur qu'on se suppose"). It may be, therefore, that in Greece or Rome, or both, something much closer to "true tragedy" obtained than in seventeenth- and eighteenth-century France, but there is no way to extract evidence for or against this supposition from any texts of the times in question. Again, this is a matter that lies entirely beyond the scope of system or argument or doctrine, or positive formulation of any sort, which is why the paradoxical man forces his interlocutor into the role of making positive statements, while he himself, by his choice of examples, cryptically casts doubt upon them.

Nature and Language: The Shape of the Social Problem

If we have the *Paradoxe* in mind when we read the *Supplément au voyage de Bougainville*, our attention is immediately caught by several skeptical remarks of speaker A. In response to B.'s account of the "Farewell of the Old Man," he says, "This speech seems to me very direct; but behind its indefinably abrupt and savage quality, I think I detect European ideas and turns of phrase" (Diderot, 2:550–51). And after B.'s recital of the conversation between the chaplain and Orou, we read:

A.: I have great respect for this courteous chaplain.

B.: And I, for my part, have much greater respect for the customs of the Tahitians and for Orou's discourse.

A.: Yes, even though it is modeled a bit on European forms. (2:569)

The point A. is insisting upon, however gently, is that there is no way to make Tahitian thinking available to European minds without first tailoring it to those minds and so losing precisely that radical otherness for the sake of which one had been interested in it—just as it is impossible to explain the "true tragedy" of Greece or Rome to a modern Frenchman except in terms that violate precisely its crucial differentness from French theater. B. himself, in fact, describes in detail (2:551) the process of translation by which a European quality is introduced into reported Tahitian speech.

As in the *Paradoxe*, then, so also in the *Supplément*, the limits of language are an issue: the impossibility of containing, comprehending, or communicating certain particular ideas in certain particular languages, especially European languages. And it is fairly clear that in the *Supplément*, the difficult idea in question is mainly the idea of *nature*.

B., claiming to paraphrase Orou the Tahitian, waxes prophetic: "How far we are separated from nature and happiness! But the empire of nature cannot be destroyed; it will endure despite all attempts to obstruct it" (2:574). And A., despite his generally critical bent, responds, "How compact the law of nations would be if it were modeled rigorously on the law of nature! How many vices and errors would be spared us!" But for all its apparent desirability, "nature" remains thoroughly intractable as a concept. Earlier in the conversation, B. speaks of the "happy" Tahitians and asserts that outside Tahiti "there have never been true morals and perhaps never will be anywhere else" (2:570). A. now draws him out a bit on his idea of morality and then suggests a formulation on which the two men agree: "that once morality is founded on the eternally subsisting relations among men, religious law will perhaps become superfluous, and that civil law must be nothing further than an enunciation of the law of nature." At this point, however, their thinking begins to unravel. They decide to "interrogate" the concept of nature with regard to various aspects of the union of man and woman; and they do manage to agree on a natural basis for the practice of marriage, and even for "galanterie," considered as a necessary prelude to the sex act. But "coquetterie," for B., goes a step too far; he dismisses it as mere falsehood. And yet when A. asks accordingly, "So in your view coquetry is not part of nature?" B. replies, "I'm not saying that" (2:571–72). And shortly afterward, with reference to jealousy—which he has dismissed as a consequence of emotional poverty, greed, fear, injustice, false morality and an undue extension of property rights (2:572)—he says again, "I'm not saying that [that jealousy is not part of nature]. Vices and virtues, everything belongs equally to nature." But then, how can nature possibly operate as a *criterion* of social wholesomeness, as a basis on which to "found morality" (2:571)?

A few moments later, we receive a clear indication of how far we have come, when—in the discussion of another difficult idea, that of "shame," "pudeur"—B. finds himself saying: "Nature, indecent nature if you like, impels each sex indiscriminately toward the other, and in a state of sad and savage humanity, a state that is conceivable but perhaps exists nowhere . . ." (2:573). The vision of "happy" Tahitians has been supplanted by that of a "sad" state of nature. We are immediately put in mind of the vacillating terminology of the *Paradoxe* with respect to the question of convention or naturalness in the self; and as we now therefore expect, the pendulum quickly swings back again. B. works his way from "sad" nature into a tirade against imbalance in the relation of the sexes, a more or less *natural* imbalance arising mainly from women's anticipation of the pain of childbirth. And then, in response to a leading question from A. about how the sex act could become "the principal source of our depravity and our evils" (2:573–74), he returns to the figure of Orou, now blames everything on civilization, and arrives at the glorification of "nature and happiness" quoted above.

The question of nature in general, then, like that of the natural self in the *Paradoxe*, is one that exposes the limits of language. And this point is crucial, because nature is the ultimate touchstone, the ultimate criterion of validity, in all Diderot's social and political theorizing. (What other *ultimate* criterion could there be, that would not already be a result of the theorizing it was meant to validate?) In the *Observations sur le Nakaz*, we read:

> Nature has made all the good laws; the legislator is the one who publishes them. I would gladly say to sovereigns, "If you want to have your laws followed, let them never contradict nature"; I would say to priests, "Let your morality not oppose innocent pleasures." . . . "I want to be happy" is the first article of a code prior to all legislation and to all religious systems. (3:525)

But there are obvious problems with this thinking.

> Natural laws are eternal and universal. Positive laws are only corollaries of natural laws. Therefore positive laws are equally eternal and universal. Nevertheless, it is certain that a given positive law is good and useful in one situation, injurious and bad in some other; it is certain that there is no code that does not need to be reformed in time. This difficulty is perhaps not insoluble. But it must be resolved. (3:513)

And for that matter, how can we ever get to the point of making adequate positive laws in the first place? "I want society to be happy; but I also want to be happy myself. And there are as many ways of being happy as there are individuals. Our happiness is the basis of all our true duties" (3:545). Does this mean that in order to invalidate a law, all I need do is claim that it makes me happy to violate it?

The obvious response to this problem—as every Platonist, and every theologian, knows—is to develop a theory in terms of which one cannot be made *truly* happy by violating a properly constituted law. In the *Encyclopédie*, writing on "Droit naturel" (natural law, or natural right), Diderot in fact takes this course by positing the authority of a "general will" (3:46–47). But by the time of his connection with Catherine II, he has left this device behind. In the *Encyclopédie*, having conceded that the general will cannot be apprehended except by reasoning, he had asserted that whoever fails to carry out such reasoning must be treated as a "denatured being" (3:47), an outcast from the human race. But now he writes:

> The law that requires of a man something contrary to his happiness is a
> false law, and it cannot possibly endure. Nevertheless, one must conform
> to it as long as it does endure.
>   For the legislator, virtue is defined as the habitual conformity of one's
> actions to public utility; perhaps the same definition applies for the
> philosopher, who is supposed to be enlightened enough to know what the
> public utility is.
>   For the general mass of subjects, virtue is the habit of conforming one's
> actions to the law, whether it is good or bad. (3:348–49)

Thus a certain practical equilibrium seems to be secured. The conformity of positive law to natural law, and thence to every individual's happiness, is still a problem, but it is now a problem that we can take our time about working on, in philosophical thought and public advocacy, while in the meantime preserving order by obeying whatever laws actually obtain—as is suggested explicitly at the end of the *Supplément* (2:577).

And yet, how secure is this equilibrium really? War and slaughter, says Diderot to Catherine, cannot be avoided, "because it takes only one *méchant*, one malevolent person, to force the hand of all the good people" (3:347). In fact, even reason may in a sense be on the side of that *méchant*. "It is evident that in a well ordered society, the *méchant* cannot injure society without injuring himself. The *méchant* knows this; but what he knows even better is that he will profit more, as a *méchant*, than he will lose as a member of the society he injures" (3:513). Moreover, even if a reasonably well-ordered society can be preserved for a certain time, how do we know that there is any ultimate hope for our political reasoning, that such a thing as natural law even exists? To return to the *Supplément*, the one piece of certain knowledge we do have about nature is that we are prevented by the limits of our language from forming an adequate concept of it. And how can we be expected to reason—or to communicate our reasoning, which comes to the same thing—beyond the limits of our language? We can buy all the time we like; it will not bring us any closer to the grasp of nature that is required for a truly rational politics.[9]

Drama, Dramatic Theory, and True Society

I think we have now come far enough to understand why Diderot, in the *Paradoxe*, attempts to make a place for the necessarily tacit proposition that theatrical drama, in principle, is capable of skirting the limits of our language and enacting for us a recognition of the lack of natural substantiality, the operation of cultural history alone, of evolved theatrical convention, in what we seem to experience as our own personal self or identity. For just such a skirting or suspension of the limits of language is what would be required in order to achieve a conception of nature sufficiently comprehensive and cogent to found a truly fruitful reasoning on political and legislative matters.

In fact, the theater, as Diderot imagines it, might conceivably itself already be able to produce the needful political conditions. For if we see the basic political problem as a conflict between the "duty" of each individual, to his or her own happiness, and the very idea of a universally applicable natural "law," then the attenuation of the individual in the theater, the recognition that the individual is not an autonomous natural force, but rather—like actual positive laws—an historically evolving convention, obviously makes our situation much more manageable. "The word 'society' suggests a condition of merging, of peace, of the focus of all individual wills upon a common goal, the general happiness. The fact is exactly the opposite. It is a condition of war, war of the sovereign against his subjects, war of the subjects against each other" (3:543). And how is it possible to move from degenerate actuality toward the condition suggested by the word "society"—Diderot compares such movement to a solid body's being propelled upward "against its nature"—if not by way of an incorporation, into all our thought and action, of the *trans-individual* truth of theatrical performance?

I do not mean to suggest that in Diderot's view the theater can be counted upon to have a positive social or political effect. Diderot does not make this claim even for theaters in classical antiquity, supposedly closer than ours to the condition of "true tragedy." In fact, the structure of his thought, as we have followed it so far, positively excludes the possibility of a perfect or ideal theater, hence also the possibility of a fulfillment of the theater's ideal political destiny. For there are, we recall, two basic types of theatrical experience, indicated, respectively, by Diderot's description of the actual theater and by his use of theater as a metaphor: the spectator may either surrender to the illusion of powerful natural feeling or remain intellectually aloof and partake of the preter-individual meaning of the actor's craft as such. And the latter type of experience obviously is more advanced, more loaded with truth, and more potentially productive in a society's political life. But no theater can ever become wholly of the second type, since the very *content* of our intellectual vision, in that philosophically truer theater, is precisely the theater we have supposedly left behind: the spectacle of human beings deriving their imagined inner selves from a tradition of masks. The theater can therefore never become simply or purely a vehicle of truth.

The theater of illusion can exist perfectly well without the theater of truth, but the latter cannot even begin to exist without the former, which means that the political effectiveness of the theater of truth is always limited by its own nature, by its quality as a kind of parasite on the theater that propagates exactly the delusions to which it is opposed. You cannot build or found a theater of truth. If it occurs to you that theater of truth represents perhaps the one slim hope for rational progress in political and social thought, then you must build or found a theater of illusion, in the hope of being able to do something else with it once it is there. This, in any case, the founding of a theater of illusion, is what Diderot does (or at least fervently promises) in his presentation to Catherine, "Dramatic Poets Considered in Relation to National Morals" (3:237–38).

And if we ask, finally, what can be done to promote the theater of truth once a theater of illusion is established—the question that in Hofmannsthal is answered by the technique of adaptation as such, and by a choice of plots that operate as theatrical allegories—it is fairly clear that for Diderot the only possibility is dramatic theory, not theory in the manner of the *Entretiens sur le Fils naturel* or the treatise *De la Poésie dramatique*, which discuss only the theater of illusion, but theory in the form at which Diderot finally arrives with the *Paradoxe sur le comédien*. There is of course a great deal more to be said about the *Paradoxe* than I have said so far, especially about the operation of the dialogue form, the invitation of the reader into something like a dialogic relation with the text, by which those of its implications that refuse to be formulated adequately might nevertheless be coaxed into the open. But the more important point, for present purposes, is that the necessary relation of drama and dramatic theory in Diderot—which is already suggested in the theoretical supplements to *Le Fils naturel* and *Le Père de famille*—provides another instance of the tendency of drama to resist and disrupt the otherwise relatively coherent historical development of poetic and literary forms, which in the late eighteenth century means the emerging idea of artistic autonomy, the sense of the poetic work as a self-contained communicative unit.

Diderot himself, especially in *Jacques le Fataliste et son maître*, follows *Tristram Shandy* and the rest of the eighteenth century in the direction of the ironic novel, that form which, in its incorporated self-commentary, develops the ideal of artistic completeness and self-sufficiency to a level where it is practically indistinguishable from mockery. But in the field of drama, he makes no such formal experiments. The commentary of the *Paradoxe* not only is detached from theatrical practice, and even more from poetic practice, but in its detachment (because its relation to drama is still a *necessary* one) also demonstrates and enacts and enforces the impossibility in drama of full communicative directness or of any supposed organic poetic integrity. The *Paradoxe*, in other words, unmasks drama as the fundamentally defective poetic form that it is, and as the site of our understanding of the defectiveness of literature as a whole.

The Meaning of Plays

For Diderot, then, as for Hofmannsthal, the meaning of a play has practically nothing to do with the meaning of the play's text as we might extract it by any recognized technique of literary interpretation. For Hofmannsthal, the text can suggest allegorically a philosophical understanding of the actor's craft and the situation in the theater. But the character of this understanding—because of its questioning of the *locus* of understanding, in the individual self—is such that it cannot actually be "meant" by a text; it does not exist, strictly speaking, *as* an understanding except in being enacted. And for Diderot the only thing that is required of a play, as text, is that it be suitable for representation in what I have called the theater of illusion. For the theater of truth, which is the theater that really matters, must be built atop an existing theater of illusion, but is built *solely* in the spectator's critically informed response to that theater, with no regard for any specific textual features.

One might be tempted to go further and include Büchner in the pattern, recalling that *Woyzeck*, a text that cannot reasonably be interpreted otherwise than as an expression of the most perfect nihilistic despair, shows an entirely different aspect when one thinks of it in relation to the theater. In the rest of this chapter, I will discuss several more cases in which the meaning of the play has very little to do, except negatively, with the meaning of the text. But we must not be hasty about drawing conclusions from this cluster of instances. To suggest, for example, that drama is "essentially" performance, that a drama never really exists except in the moment of its realization on the stage, would be to overstate the case drastically and, worse, to oversimplify it. For the "meaning" of plays, which I refer to when I say that it is not the meaning of those plays' texts, *is still a textual meaning*, a meaning of the *type* that is associated with texts—not, say, a "gestural" or otherwise nonverbal meaning that we might "read" only with fluctuations in our blood pressure and glandular activity. That the meaning of plays, as I have suggested, cannot be adequately "meant" by a text alone is not an inherent quality of its nature as meaning but rather a result of the quite narrow specificity of what counts as meaning in the historically evolved sphere of literature as we practice it. It is imaginable, for example, that a relatively minor change in the experience of the individual "self" as "reader" could make drama obsolete by making simple text transparent to the theater's otherwise unique mechanism of meaning. But precisely this sort of change is also practically inconceivable, since the meanings to which any text can be made transparent are determined by the implacably conservative unfolding of genre in the hermeneutic sense.

This point is of cardinal importance. When I say—apropos of Diderot, for instance—that certain types of meaning are "beyond the limits of language," I do not mean (where would I get the authority?) that they are unattainable by language as such; I can only mean: "beyond the limits of a particular language or group of languages at a particular historical juncture." (It is suggested in the *Supplément* that the Tahitian language might well contain the concept of nature that is needed in our political theory, and in the *Paradoxe* it appears that classical Greek and Latin might have been infused with the sort of communal spirit that makes "true tragedy" possible.) And when we speak thus of the limits of language, we are speaking, in effect, of the limits of *literature*; we are speaking of "meanings" on the entirely fundamental level where meaning is the same thing as genre, and genre in turn is indissolubly bound to existing tradition. Again, therefore, the first task of dramatic art is to unmask the practice of literature as defective. Plays cannot be replaced by "happenings." The presence of a text in the proceeding is indispensable, the presence of an actual text with its own meaning, whence, by a move of negation, the still basically textual meaning of the play can be given contour.

What such plays have in common—plays in which the meaning of the text is clearly left behind by its dramatic form—is nothing positive, nothing "essential," nothing but the dissociative or disruptive quality (in this case, the separation of meaning from meaning) that attends upon the ever repeated refusal of drama to conform to the category of literature or poetry in which it is nevertheless trapped by its history. In other words, it is by no means necessary, and certainly not a touchstone of dramatic "quality," that we be able to specify a meaning of the play that is not a meaning of its text. But when it happens that we are able to make this specification, we are afforded a very clear avenue by which to approach the problem of drama as a whole.

Prefaces, Stage Directions, and the Like

One of the most obvious cases of separation between the meaning of the text and that of the play is the work of Bernard Shaw. For in practically all of Shaw's plays—certainly in everything from *Man and Superman* on—the prefaces (their mere existence, even if we have not read them) have the effect of detaching the play's polemical or tendentious or expository meaning from the play itself and giving that meaning, so to speak, a more congenial textual home, thus leaving us as spectators to wonder what possible reason we might have had for attending the performance, what possible profit we might hope to derive. Is it the promise of aesthetic pleasure that brings us to the theater? If we agree that the object or stimulus of that non-intellectual pleasure must be some form of *style*, then we are brought up short by Shaw's insistence that "effectiveness of assertion is the Alpha and Omega of style."[10] How shall we now distinguish the aesthetic quality of the play from what is "asserted" in the preface? And even without Shaw's interference, we would find it hard to dispute Harold Bloom's point that "as a critic, Shaw was genial only where he was not menaced, and he felt deeply menaced [not only 'as a critic'] by the Aesthetic vision of which his Socialism never quite got free. . . . Pater insisted upon style, as did Wilde, and Shaw has no style to speak of."[11]

Or we may wish to adopt Christopher Innes's suggestion that "set side by side with the prefaces, the plays are clearly ways of humanizing the issues, giving them an individual dimension."[12] Here, at least, it appears we have Shaw on our side. In the preface to *Saint Joan*, after discussing Joan and "Theocracy," he says, "This, I think, is all that we can now pretend to say about the prose of Joan's career. The romance of her rise, the tragedy of her execution, and the comedy of the attempts of posterity to make amends for that execution, belong to my play and not to my preface, which must be confined to a sober essay on the facts" (GBS, 6:66). The play, that is, will offer us something beyond "prose," something more human, in the sense of emotionally immediate and rich and individual.

Or will it? Only a short space later, Shaw seems to assign the play a completely different function: "For the story of Joan I refer the reader to the play which follows. It contains all that need be known about her" (GBS, 6:69). Actually, of course, the preface contains a great deal more of "the story," "the facts," than the play does. What is Shaw's game with us here? Still further on, in the course of the inevitable comparison with Shakespeare, he boasts: "I have taken care to let the medieval atmosphere blow through my play freely. Those who see it performed will not mistake the startling event it records for a mere personal accident. They will have before them not only the visible and human puppets, but the Church, the Inquisition, the Feudal System, with divine inspiration always beating against their too inelastic limits: all more terrible in their dramatic force than any of the little mortal figures clanking about in plate armor or moving silently in the frocks and hoods of the order of St. Dominic" (GBS, 6:71). But it then turns out that this medieval "atmosphere" consists in the three named institutions' being made "intelligible" to us, in that the three representative figures, Cauchon, Lemaître, and Warwick, are made "more intelligible to themselves than they would be in real life" and say "the things they actually would have said if they had known what they were really doing" (GBS, 6:73, 74).

In other words, Shaw has taken people, "little" people who "were part of the Middle Ages themselves, and therefore as unconscious of its peculiarities as of the atomic formula of the air they breathed," and he has *enlarged* those people, "flattered" them (GBS, 6:72), made them monumental by permitting them to compass intellectually the age they live in; he has thus *personalized* that age and its institutions in precisely the manner he claims to have avoided. Or at least this is true of the play, whereas in the preface, without the outsize human figures to distract us, exactly the "medieval atmosphere" Shaw speaks of, which compels us to attend to institutions, not persons, *does* "blow freely"—in the preface, and *only* in the preface. All Shaw's remarks about what the play supposedly accomplishes, therefore, only face us over and over again with the question of why a performed or performable play is needed in the first place.

The answer to this question—or at least a kind of answer—is provided by what I think is the first of Shaw's works in which he becomes fully aware of the separation between meaning and meaning, *Man and Superman*. Here, more than anywhere else, the play is drained of meaning—as it were, sucked dry—by the abundance of expository and explanatory material that accompanies it, including not only the preface (in the form of an ironic "Epistle Dedicatory") but also "The Revolutionist's Handbook." As spectators, therefore, we find our situation reproduced exactly in Ann Whitefield's last words: "Never mind her, dear. Go on talking" (GBS, 2:733). *What* Jack Tanner (or the play) is saying is not of any special interest to us. In effect, if not in reality, we have heard it all before; at least it is all there, in writing, for us to understand much more thoroughly than we could hope to in the auditorium. As spectators, therefore, we are not so much listening to people talk as (like Ann) *watching* them talk. And the main question we must ask about Shaw is why we are maneuvered into this position, or at least into imagining ourselves in this position.

We can begin by recognizing that the difference between listening to people talk and watching them talk is that in the latter case, the *abstraction* of meaning is absent. We are much more fully present, much more completely involved in the sensory immediacy of our situation, when we are in a sense (like Ann) not really listening, when no part of our mind is drawn forth into the ideal realm of concepts and arguments. We are, that is, more completely *inside the theater*, or at least we have the impression of being so. (There are, incidentally, other authors in whose plays a similar effect can be observed, authors who state their plays' lesson so clearly that we do not need to listen critically to most of what is said on the stage: think of J. M. R. Lenz's *Der Hofmeister* and *Die Soldaten*, or of Apollinaire's *Les Mamelles de Tirésias*.)

But in Shaw's case, paradoxically, this condition of being completely inside the theater is achieved only by way of our possessing a knowledge (concerning the preface, or at least the Shavian practice of writing prefaces) that does *not* belong to the situation that is immediately available to our senses in the theater. We are, in other words, *both* lifted out of our normal existence, fully enclosed within a new sensory reality, *and* required to reflect upon that supposedly excluded normal existence, upon what we have read or what we might read or what we know from our cultural experience is probably available for reading.

Of course, it is not expectable that this contradictory experience will actually happen to us. The most that actually happens to us is probably that we become a bit confused or uncomfortable about the relation between our situation as spectators and our situation, outside the theater, as readers and as part of the reading public. And exactly the same sort of discomfort attends our reading of the stage directions. *Man and Superman* opens:

> *Roebuck Ramsden is in his study, opening the morning's letters. . . . He has not been out of doors yet today; so he still wears his slippers, his boots being ready for him on the hearthrug. Surmising that he has no valet, and seeing that he has no secretary with a shorthand notebook and a typewriter, one meditates on how little our great burgess domesticity has been disturbed by new fashions and methods, or by the enterprise of the railway and hotel companies which sell you a Saturday to Monday of life at Folkestone as a real gentleman for two guineas, first class fares both ways included.* (GBS, 2:533–34)

One recognizes immediately that these sentences are not primarily instructions to a director and actors; they are a detailed description of what is supposed to be going on in the mind of a spectator. Indeed, they are more, for they contain information that even the most perfectly trained spectator could not possibly infer from what he or she sees on the stage—information such as the exact year of Ramsden's birth, which is revealed in the next paragraph. But even without this visually inaccessible information we would recognize that what the "stage direction" requires *cannot possibly be realized in any real spectator's mind*. Obviously we would have to be *taught* to "surmise" and "meditate" in exactly the prescribed form. And even if we have been taught, even if we have read and indeed memorized the stage direction, the only result will be that we will now notice and be irritated by all the little discrepancies between how the stage actually looks and what we had expected. Again, therefore, our quality as reader and our quality as spectator interfere with each other uncomfortably.

Shaw's Audience and Politics

What we have, then, in our relation to Shaw, is an at least mildly uncomfortable or confusing situation, the extreme or perfected form of which would be, for us, the condition of being *both* entirely absorbed in the sensory experience of the theater *and* sufficiently detached to reflect with depth and historical accuracy upon our general cultural situation. This condition, in fact, is occasionally reproduced in the fiction (and on the stage) in Shaw's plays. We have already noted that the preface to *Saint Joan* calls our attention to the figures of Cauchon, Lemaître, and Warwick, who all supposedly possess the ability both to live entirely within the Middle Ages and to command a clear historical perspective upon that period. (Shaw generalizes here by suggesting that such "flattering" of historically specific personages is "inevitable," that it belongs to "the business of the stage" at least in tragedy [GBS, 6:72–73].) And if we agree that in Shaw, as in Diderot, there is a strong movement of separation between the meaning of the text and that of the play, then it seems at least reasonable that the meaning of the play be sought in precisely that perfected form of the spectator's situation—in the condition, again, of being *both* fully involved *and* fully detached with respect to our situation in the theater and, by extension, with respect to our cultural and historical situation in general. Indeed, since that contradictory condition would of necessity imply, on our part, a profound questioning of the status and constitution of what we experience as our individual identity, it follows that the parallel with the meaning of the play in Diderot, with the "secret" knowledge of the actor *as* actor, is quite unexpectedly broad and exact.

Once this parallel is recognized, however, the basis on which it rests is not hard to understand. For Shaw's politics, with allowance made for the century and a half of separation, is practically Diderot's politics all over again. Both men write extensively, in both a speculative and a critical vein, on specific political questions. Both men concede, in the final analysis, that they are unable to formulate either a theoretical model or a practical program for achieving any significant progress in the political sphere. Both men suggest, in fact, that the barrier separating our actual condition from the possibility of political progress is inherently insurmountable by any theoretical or practical means at our disposal: that barrier being, for Diderot, the strictly limited conceptual range of European languages; for Shaw the strict limits that constitute our stage in the evolution of our species, which has yet to produce "a competent political animal" (GBS, 7:42). But despite the impossibility of real progress, neither Diderot nor Shaw is prepared to abandon the struggle with specific political problems, for as Jack Tanner puts it:

> What can be said as yet except that where there is a will, there is a way? If there be no will, we are lost. That is a possibility for our crazy little empire, if not for the universe; and as such possibilities are not to be entertained without despair, we must, whilst we survive, proceed on the assumption that we have still energy enough to not only will to live, but to will to live better. (GBS, 2:776)

And for both Diderot and Shaw, finally, the struggle with the politically impossible appears to involve, in a fundamental way, the form of theatrical drama, this being the main point that emerges from a close reading of the *Paradoxe sur le comédien* and from an appreciation of the simple unflagging tenacity with which Shaw practices the craft of drama once he has discovered it.

This parallel with Diderot, in turn, reinforces the argument I have suggested concerning the relation between Shaw's plays and his prefaces, and the conclusion that Shaw's theater, like Diderot's, is meant to be a place where modern Europeans are exposed with unique intensity to the possibility of a radical questioning of what their cultural history teaches them to experience as their own personal identity. Indeed, one is tempted to ask whether the "superman," or the "competent political animal" yet to be supplied by evolution, is not simply the postidentical individual, the individual who is somehow capable of experiencing the contradictoriness of Shaw's theater—the condition, again, of full sensory involvement coupled with complete intellectual detachment—in its perfected form, the individual, by extension, whose critical awareness (hence political "competence") suffers no interference whatever from that same individual's nonetheless pressing and undenied particular concerns.

As with Diderot, however, so also with Shaw, it is nowhere implied that the special quality of the dramatic theater will somehow of itself create a new breed of politically improved human beings. What I have called the theater of truth, in discussing Diderot, is inseparable from the theater of illusion and can be distinguished from that shallower theater only by a mind thoroughly predisposed in its favor. In Shaw, similarly, we ought probably to say that the highest aim of the theater's contradictory structure is to provide a vessel for improved humanity whenever it should happen to appear, an atmosphere in which the improved human being might quickly and forcefully be made aware of his or her own nature and its attendant obligations.

I do not for a moment pretend to know exactly how seriously we are supposed to take Shaw's evolutionary or "metabiological" speculations. But even if it could be shown with perfect certainty that he did not sincerely believe a single word of this whole side of his writing, his reason for writing those words would still be entirely clear. Whatever else it may be, Shaw's evolutionary religion, or universal heresy, is above all an alternative to "despair." We "must," says Jack Tanner, "will to live better. . . . And with Must there is no arguing" (GBS, 2:776, 780). Shavian evolution is at least a positive doctrine; and even if, at some future time, humanity is improved by forces that have nothing to do with evolution, still that doctrine will have done its part to husband whatever positive energy effected the improvement. Shaw's theater—which means the theater and its texts and its prefaces—is similarly a shot in the dark. And even if the improved human beings for whom it is erected never actually take their places in it, even if they laugh not in it but at it, with superior scorn, still it will have done its part in preserving that modicum of hopeful vitality, that appetite for possibilities, without which they would never have come into being.

The Limiting Case

Tempting as it might seem, with respect to Samuel Beckett's theater, to speak of negative representation, or of a representation of the negative, I think the basic logical difficulties produced by such a conceptual yoking will probably prevent its use in any reasonable historical view of dramatic form—unless, of course, it be the view that with Beckett, the history of drama comes to an absolute end, to a kind of ontological precipice at which the niceties of our accustomed conceptual calculus no longer apply.[13] There is, in fact, probably a case to be made for this extreme view—in spite of Beckett's openness, in the course of his career, to new forms of the dramatic or quasi-dramatic medium, hence by extrapolation his openness to the history of forms as yet undisclosed—but it would be a strictly negative case, therefore irrefutable, and for that reason probably not very interesting. And yet it is hard to read Beckett without thinking of him as the more or less absolute limiting case of something. I will propose that it is useful to understand that "something" as the separation between the meaning of the text and that of the play.

For meaning, in Beckett's dialogue, is neither absent nor negated. It is true that in the case of expressive meaning, our sense of a whole human self as the agent of expression is regularly thwarted; expression thus seems *fragmented*. And in the case of allusive meaning, it is true that the possible interpretive usefulness of relations to other texts, literary and scriptural, is regularly thwarted; Beckett's allusions, in the end, seem *random*. But allusion and expression, along with numerous coherent and recognizable if undeveloped bits of meaning in the form of description and narration, are nonetheless present. And in all Beckett's plays—by contrast, for example, with Eugène Ionesco's plays—there is a kind of pervasive logic in the dialogue, a quasi-musical structure established mainly by the repetition of words and phrases, even if the principle of that logic is available neither to the fictional speakers, as the basis on which to build a self, nor to the audience, as a guide to interpretation.

In fact, if we concern ourselves with stage directions (as we did with Shaw), we find grounds for expecting Beckett's plays to be *more* semantically and semiotically integrated than other dramatic texts. For the relation between stage directions and dialogue ordinarily produces a kind of looseness or openness in dramatic writing. Stage directions say to the director and the actor, make the stage (including the acting bodies) look like this; they say to the reader, try to imagine that the stage looks like this. But dialogue says to both the actor and the reader, use your interpretive powers to imagine from within who the person is who speaks these words, and (for the actor) try to give the impression of *being* that person—or for the Brechtian actor, try to demonstrate to the audience who that person, without knowing it, *really* is. Stage directions and dialogue thus require two basically different forms of response. In Beckett, however, where the interpretive move by which we approach dialogue is regularly thwarted, dialogue becomes just another form of stage direction, a simple command to the actor: say this. W. B. Worthen, referring mainly to the short play *Play*, says, "The direction-text displaces the means of the actors' charismatic self-presentation: it prohibits gesture, movement, facial expression, vocal inflection, tonality and rhythm, even their uninterrupted visibility before the audience. The protagonists are sculpted, hollowed out by the text of the mise-en-scène" (p. 136). And even if the specific prohibitions are not yet there in, say, *Waiting for Godot* or *Endgame*, the tendency that eventually produces them definitely is. In effect, therefore, dialogue and stage directions, for Beckett, tend to become a single continuous text; consequently, there is no real genre distinction between the plays with speech and the "Acts without Words."

This is why Beckett is a limiting case. For in Beckett, if anywhere, the meaning of the text and the meaning of the play ought to be identical, since the text does nothing but say, in the simplest possible form, what is to happen on the stage. And yet there are problems here. Martin Puchner, after pointing out that Beckett cannot describe gestures without "relating [them] to the internal states to which they presumably give expression," argues that this evidently uncomfortable necessity is the source of

a tension within his work, for his characters give the impression of being pawns, automatons, or behaviorist guinea pigs and do not possess a complex of repressions, desires, ideals, a formative past, and debilitating traumata associated with a full interiority. It was the absence or near absence of those interior features that led Beckett to demand that actors not "act" or "mime" in ways that would imitate human beings. But the very language through which Beckett isolates gestures in stage directions ties these gestures back to the expressive unity that is the actor. This twofold or counteractive strategy, which is as much an aesthetic choice as a rhetorical necessity, might be responsible for our sense that the characters in Beckett's plays have been split into speech and gesture and have been awkwardly stitched back together. . . . Beckett's plays don't get rid of human experience, passions, and feelings; rather they use them in the confined space of the parenthesis. When one reads Beckett's stage directions, one realizes that in his universe the passions do exist after all, but they are passions in parentheses.[14]

This is a very accurate and suggestive perception, not limited in its range to those plays in which stage directions name gestures by explicit reference to the emotions. But it also raises questions. For the parenthetical or parenthesized quality of human interiority that Puchner talks about, the reduction of interiority to minimal bits of itself—shall we create a phantom etymology and call them "thymemes"?[15]—bits of interiority that are hardly distinguishable from their outward manifestations as isolated gestures (including the gestures of dialogue, responding in effect to stage directions of the form "say this"), this quality in Beckett *already belongs fully to his texts*, and to the meaning of the texts. And how shall we formulate this textual meaning if not by saying, almost exactly as we have said with reference to Diderot: those parenthesized thymemes represent the truth about human interiority, the truth that the individual human self is not a naturally given unit but rather an artificial composite, cobbled together out of gestures that are developed in the course of theatrical tradition? Does the title of the play *Not I* not contain this whole idea in compressed form, the idea that my identity is in truth a "not I"? In other words, what had been the meaning of the play for Diderot, and in effect for Shaw, has become the meaning of the text in Beckett.

Again, therefore, we are inclined to ask whether the meaning of the text and that of the play have not become identical in Beckett. And if they have become identical, does this not contradict the argument that I first suggested in relation to Diderot, that the shifting of the question of identity to the meaning *of the play* reflects the impossibility—given the present condition of European languages—of containing that meaning adequately in the medium of text alone? I think this concern can be dealt with by asking one further question. Why does Beckett not follow the lead of any number of modern and modernist dramatists and write for puppets or marionettes? Or, in writing for film, why does he not specify animated figures, the filmic equivalent of puppets? Why are his fragmented characters, those "characters" made of nothing but gestures, always represented by actual human beings?[16] Even in the play *Not I*, the Mouth that we see speaking is the mouth of a real person.

The great advantage of the puppet theater for Beckett would be that the thymemes to which human emotional life is reduced in his plays would there be represented by *pure* gestures, by movements that would have precisely that quality of nothing-but-gesture by which the very idea of a thymeme—a minimal, parenthesized bit of interiority—is defined. The use of actual human beings to perform those gestures, on the other hand—even when most of the human being is concealed by costume or lighting—produces a discontinuity in the artistic fabric, at least the constant imminent danger of contradiction; the gesture is always on the verge of losing its purity and presenting itself as the expression of an established individual self. And I would like to suggest that exactly this is the point of Beckett's insistence on real people. The meaning of the text in Beckett is simply the truth concerning the composite artificiality of what we seem to experience as individual identity; the separate meaning *of the play* is that I can never grasp this truth, that it can never actually become the truth for me, that by "Not I," no matter how single-mindedly I insist upon it, I always in the end really (*by* striving to be single-minded) mean "I." The agony of Beckett's characters, in other words, and the agony of his audience and of course of his actors as well, is not that they cannot achieve a stable identity but that they cannot escape the delusion of identity, no matter how transparent that delusion has become; that they can never become sufficiently marionette-like to satisfy their own self-knowledge.

In the *Paradoxe sur le comédien*, we observed a tendency to oscillate between formulations that present acting as the fabric of *mere* convention by which human interiority is constructed in culture, and formulations that presuppose the imitative quality of acting with respect to something like natural interiority. And we recognized that each of these types of formulation requires the other. Thinking through the postulate of imitation produces logical difficulties that lead to an understanding of the fundamental cultural constructedness of the human self. But this "understanding," in turn, is constantly interfered with by precisely the quality of individual selfhood that is constructed and is the indispensable *agent* of understanding, so that an honest admission of our limited condition demands the discourse of imitation after all. In Beckett, quite simply, Diderot's mutually necessary opposites are divided between the meaning of the text and that of the play—without requiring any further component, anything like the gratuitous plot for Diderot or an ultimately gratuitous evolutionary philosophy for Shaw—while the impossibility of achieving a stable reconciliation of those opposites is represented by the simple fact of that separation of meanings.

In Beckett, as limiting case, the separation between the text's meaning and the play's, as it unfolds in Diderot and Shaw, is thus reduced to rudimentary form. But even so, the importance of the text, and of textually conceived meaning, is not reduced in the least. The theatrical process in Beckett could not even begin without the operation of textual meanings. This consideration is of great significance for my concluding arguments, as is Beckett's expressive use of the simple fact of an actual human being's presence on the stage.

CHAPTER EIGHT

Performance and the
Exposure of Hermeneutics

To talk about drama in relation to other literary types requires the concept of "performance," and that discussion, once underway, tends quickly to involve the concept of textual "meaning." Neither of these concepts, however, is particularly well formed or well defined. I will attempt here to clarify both by working them one against the other. And in the process, I will elaborate on the notion (from my Introduction) of the "interpretivity" of performance and take one modest step toward a method for dealing with the slippery question of "what happens" in the theater.

The Basic Opposition

My main point is that there is an inherent *opposition* between performance, in a sense that includes nothing that is not comparable to the performance of drama in a theater, and the whole broad range of theoretical endeavor that can be collected under the heading of "hermeneutics." This point depends, however, on a recognition of the perfect *systematicity* of hermeneutics, a systematicity that underlies even its claim to conduct a radical criticism of its own method; and an important property of this systematicity, which produces the unhappy political consequences of hermeneutics, is its ability to absorb—or, as we say, "always already" to have absorbed and organized—any theoretical position from which it might be called into question as a whole. We cannot talk *about* hermeneutics, it appears, without talking hermeneutics. This chapter, therefore—which appeals to the notion of "performance" as a way of getting outside hermeneutics but is still itself an instance of theoretical criticism—cannot avoid disorienting itself in the weightless gulf of incommensurability between its object and its method. I ask the reader not to ignore this problem but to bear with me until the argument reaches a point where we can turn and attempt to meet it.

It may seem reasonable to suggest that the gulf between performance, in its sensory immediacy, and theory, as a type of text, is mediated by the relation of a dramatic performance to the text being performed. But this relation inevitably disintegrates under the stress of generalization. Either it is itself fully theorized, and so becomes a sign and vessel of the tendency of hermeneutic theory to appropriate performance for its own ends, or else the identity of the "text" is compromised—when we speak of performance, for example, as itself a form of "text"—to the point where the idea of its continuity with the text of theory becomes mere sophistry. Only in particular cases, if at all, is it possible for the relation between a text and its performance to have general theoretical significance. Further on, I attempt to show an instance of this paradox in two plays of Jean Genet, which perhaps thus do, after all, make a kind of anchor to the argument.

In any case, I do not claim to have found a method of deconceptualizing the concept of performance. How can performance be interrogated theoretically in the first place, if not in the form of a concept? The questions that need to be asked are what kind of concept it is, what kind of conceptual problems it creates, and to what extent we can extrapolate from these problems into the extraconceptual or extratheoretical domain that the word "performance" appears to refer to. To approach these questions, I will discuss the relations among performance and four other basic concepts: interpretation, hermeneutics, "hermeneutic space," and ideology. I do not propose to define these terms and build on their definitions; I am not sure that satisfactory definitions are possible. But the relations among the concepts—plus a pair of highly fugitive yet catalytic notions, "meaning" and "understanding"—do produce a measure of clarity about what we are aiming at when we speak of "performance."

Interpretation

Etymologically understood, interpretation in some sense "negotiates" between or among several parties. And in the case of the interpretation (N) of a literary text (T), the move of negotiation is doubled: N negotiates between T and its "meaning" (M) but also between T and our "understanding" (U) of T. These terms in themselves, including "interpretation," are still too vague even to be illustrated; but the structure they produce is interesting. For the negotiating or mediating move is also necessarily a move of *interposition*, which keeps separate the very terms or parties or positions that it claims to bring into contact. It is in fact only by contrast with the idea of "interpretation" that we are inclined to define "understanding" as an *un*mediated apprehension of the *un*mediated identity of the text with its meaning. Therefore, if interpretation claims to operate *in the service of* understanding or meaning, we are tempted to ask whether the result of this service is not mainly to create an ever greater need for interpretation itself, whether interpretation—far from approaching its ostensible goals—in truth only defers them indefinitely.

This is a problem, and not (it is generally agreed) a quibble. For it appears to be anchored in our experience, especially in the experience of *misunderstanding*. How, after all, can misunderstanding happen except in relation to understanding (more or less as defined above), and how can the passage from misunderstanding to understanding be negotiated except by some form of interpretation? It is possible to read certain parts of the history of the theory of interpretation as a direct response to this problem. If final meaning and perfect understanding, for example, belong only to God, then the labor of interpretation, precisely by deferring understanding, by keeping truth at a distance, becomes a sign and an acknowledgment of our corrupt human condition, hence an act of pious humility on our part, hence an expression of understanding after all—understanding in the specially immediate sense of faith. Something of this theological paradox continues to operate even in the professedly secular insistence upon meaning (authorial intention) and understanding (receptive intention) as strictly extralinguistic psychic events—which keeps understanding and interpretation out of each other's hair by positing a category difference, the difference between the verbally mediated and the absolutely present, as elsewhere between the human and the divine.

Hermeneutics

Is this theological move a solution to the problem or merely an avoidance of it? The latter position characterizes what modern theoretical parlance calls "hermeneutics," a discipline which is aimed not at solving problems but at *keeping open* a particular problem complex. There is of course a difficulty here: to what extent is a "problem" really a problem if a specific disciplinary structure is required to maintain it, to keep it open, *as* a problem? We will worry about this question later. For the time being, it is important to keep in mind that when I say "hermeneutics," I do not refer merely to the practice of interpretation. I mean the whole structure of philosophical thought by which hermeneutics not only generates but also *radically criticizes* its own practice.

The basic strategy of hermeneutics is simple. Category distinctions of the sort that produce facile solutions to the problem of interpretation must be eliminated. This is, so to speak, the Occam's razor of hermeneutics: the elimination of all category distinctions that are not strictly necessary.

Gadamer, for instance, declines to posit a category difference even between "understanding" and "the being of that which is understood."[1] And the content of hermeneutics consists mainly of the structures that are generated by the application of this basic strategy. Suppose we subject to hermeneutic criticism the distinction that is created between a text (T) and its "meaning" (M) by interposition of the interpretation (N) that produces M. If we are sufficiently suspicious of our temptation to regard the distinction between T and M as one of category, we are bound to decide that M is itself essentially a *text* (like T), whence it follows that the original text T now operates as an interpretation *of* M, which produces yet another "meaning," M_1, and eventually an infinite series of texts, M_n, that arise as "meanings." Actually the structure here (figure 1) is more like a *fabric*, since the original interpretation N also interprets the series M_n, as the M_n do each other in various combinations.

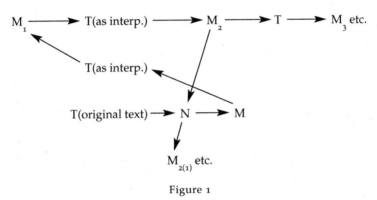

Figure 1

Nor is this idea of an indefinite proliferation of texts as "meanings" at all outlandish. Northrop Frye understands it as belonging to the fabric of social history:

> It is obvious, for instance, that one major source of order in society is an established pattern of words [= T]. . . . Such verbal patterns may remain fixed for centuries: the meanings attached to them will change out of all recognition in that time, but the feeling that the verbal structure must remain unchanged [T as interpretation of its "meanings"], and the consequent necessity of reinterpreting it to suit the changes of history, bring the operations of criticism into the center of society.[2]

And even if the "self-containment" of Frye's "literary universe" cannot be sustained, still it is clear that the principles by which at least the resulting "verbal universe" is held together (especially the ubiquity of the "rhetorical") must operate from *within* that universe, as interpretations—from what position outside could they be imposed?—so that that verbal universe, however different in spirit, is no different in structure from Harold Bloom's decidedly poetic network, in which "the meaning of a poem can only be another poem," even if that other poem is "the poem we write as our reading" or "a poem that never got written."[3] Nor is there any fundamental structural difference from the "space of texts" that grows out of the radical version of "intertextuality" that Kristeva develops in her discussion of Bakhtin.[4]

Or, to move in the other direction, we might criticize hermeneutically the separation that is produced (or uncovered) between text T and our "understanding" U by the intervention of interpretation N. Obviously, N cannot operate as an interpretation without being "understood" as such, which means, if understanding and interpretation are not categorically distinguishable, that it must be interpreted, in its turn, by N_1, and another infinite series or fabric N_n arises.

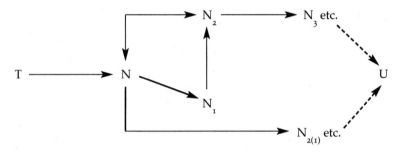

Figure 2

This structure (figure 2), like its sister, also turns out to be not at all unfamiliar if we relate it to the hermeneutic doctrine of "genre," the recognition that our "understanding" of a text cannot even begin until the text has been overlaid with a kind of transparent grid that guides our decisions about how to look at it, a grid which in the final analysis, if genre and interpretation are not categorically distinct, must itself be made of text or of interlocking texts that require understanding. Or perhaps it is easier to visualize the proliferation of interpretations with respect to understanding if we view it from the other direction: every "understanding" requires a preunderstanding (a judgment of "genre," in a sense not categorically distinct from "interpretation"), which in turn requires further instances of pre-understanding, and so on.

Hermeneutic Space

Insofar as it is possible to imagine a totality encompassing all the self-elaborating structures of text generated by hermeneutic thought, I call that totality "hermeneutic space." And with regard to the concept of perform-ance, it becomes important to ask, does hermeneutic space exhaust the whole space of communicable human experience, the whole scene of his-tory? It is fairly clear that Paul de Man's utterances on history as text imply a positive answer to this question. And the idea of "language" in the philo-sophical hermeneutics of Heidegger ("Language is the House of Being") and Gadamer ("Being that can be understood is language": p. 450) which, in a typical hermeneutic move, obscures the distinction between "langue" and "parole," tends in the same direction. But we must not be too hasty in assuming a kind of modern theoretical unanimity on this point. Derrida's "il n'y a pas de hors-texte," for example, stops short of apodictically univer-salizing hermeneutic space; in its context, that statement says only that reading "cannot legitimately transgress the text toward something other than it" (thus that the text, once we are engaged with it, *has no exit*), which is not the same thing.[5]

Hermeneutic space is in fact subject to quite a narrow and exclusive characterization. I have enclosed the terms "meaning" and "understand-ing" in quotation marks; and I have called them "fugitive" and "catalytic" notions: "fugitive" because, in the absence of categorical distinctions, both concepts are obviously *reducible* to "interpretation" and, as ways of looking at the process of interpretation, tend to lose their own identity; "catalytic" because, unless the differences (however tenuous) among "meaning," "understanding," and "interpretation" are maintained, the *communicative* character of hermeneutic space, its quality as a representation of commu-nicative processes, is lost. The concepts "meaning" and "understanding" are thus not merely "heuristic," not merely constructed for the sake of argu-ment. On the contrary, it is possible to argue that meaning and understand-ing are undeniable, and undeniably operative, in hermeneutic space. This hermeneutic theorem, on the *undeniability* of meaning and understanding, or of communication, must be distinguished carefully from the assertion that meaning and understanding *exist*, that they are *actual*. The distinction may seem a small one, but it is important.

"Meaning," as I have tried to make clear in the first diagram (figure 1), is the one step beyond itself at which interpretation always points: interpreta-tion (N) means, or indicates, the meaning (M) of the text it interprets. But this pointing or indicating does not take place somehow *inside* the interpre-tation (N) itself; it takes place only in the process of "understanding." "Understanding" is thus the process or force that calls forth the movement from interpretation (N) to meaning (M); it is the domain in which meaning first arises and can begin itself to be resolved into interpretation. And con-versely, understanding does not exist except as the vessel or receptacle of "meaning"; without "meaning," as the step beyond itself always indicated by interpretation, the whole complicated relation of understanding and interpretation—as developed in the second diagram (figure 2)—would not arise. Meaning and understanding are therefore each radically dependent upon the other. The sign or evidence of their interdependence is the unfolding of the whole fabric of hermeneutic space, and the name of this interdependence is "communication," which, at its most basic, refers not to the supposed transfer of material between minds but to the simple existence of meaning and understanding in an orderly relation with each other. In hermeneutic space, therefore, meaning and understanding, and what I have called "the postulate of communicability," are strictly undeniable.

But on the other hand, *in the real world* it could conceivably be true (1) that meaning and understanding simply do not happen in the type of interaction by which they are hermeneutically defined, that the postulate of communicability does not hold; and (2) that the whole of our verbal or textual existence is nevertheless saturated with the quality of interpretation, that no utterance ever comes into being except as the interpretation of existing verbal material. If (1) and (2) were both the case, however, then it would follow that (2), which we might call the postulate of hermeneutic space, must be absolutely inaccessible to us, absolutely unknowable, and the *critical* aspect of hermeneutics would vanish. We would have no vantage point from which to view our own procedure; interpretation would simply be our pervasive verbal field, no more available to our perception (no more recognizable as interpretation) than a gravitational field, however strong, is available to the perception of a sentient body in free fall. We would still be able to make diagrams like the two above, but those diagrams would be empty, corresponding to nothing in our actual experience. Meaning and understanding, in reality, would not be merely "fugitive," perched precariously on the brink of their reduction to interpretation; they would *already have been* thus reduced. And yet even in this case, we could not deny meaning and understanding without giving up our last pretensions to self-knowledge concerning our position in hermeneutic space. Again, meaning and understanding, in hermeneutic space, are subject to infinite deferral but cannot be denied outright, for without their operation there could be no structure. The chains or fabrics of interpretation, or of the proliferation of texts, would have no leverage by which to articulate their identity as structures; the system would include no differential resistance to entropy.

Hermeneutic space, then, is the space that opens between two strongly opposed statements: (1) that meaning and understanding are undeniable in their operation, but (2) that they are also unattainable, unassertable, impossible to localize or verify, always deferred. The force of this constitutive opposition can be felt whenever the "hermeneutic circle" is spoken of. The understanding of a grammatical or perceptual or artistic "whole," says the circle, requires the prior understanding of "parts," but the parts cannot be understood except by reference to an understanding of the whole. (This is a version of the deferral of understanding.) And for about two centuries now, we have received assurances ad nauseam that this "circle"—either in my primitive statement of it or in any of its more complex forms—is not a vicious circle, not the simple radical refutation of the possibility of understanding that it appears to be.[6] These assurances, however, are based on nothing but the assumption that the possibility of understanding—or the postulate of purposeful and somehow efficacious communication—*cannot* be denied. And this assumption, in turn, is based on nothing whatever. The idea that the denial of understanding itself necessarily claims to be understood, or that "I," the denier of understanding, would never speak in the first place if "I" did not hope to be understood, is vacuous. Must a proposition be understood before it can be correct? Understanding implies precisely the possibility of its proposition's incorrectness. And how can "you" claim to know that "I," in speaking, presuppose the possibility of understanding—always supposing we both understand what "understanding" is? What conceivable discipline of knowledge can establish an original motive for "my" speaking? It is precisely as an exponent of hermeneutics that Wilhelm Dilthey finds himself repeatedly challenged by the dictum *individuum est ineffabile.*[7]

Hermeneutic space, then, is thrown open by the *arbitrary assertion* that meaning and understanding are not only possible but undeniable. That this assertion creates a space for itself, that it does not (and obviously cannot) belong to a preexisting conceptual network, already testifies to its arbitrariness. And it follows by a form of dialectical necessity that hermeneutic space is no sooner thrown open than it is found to contain radical challenges to its own founding assertion: the hermeneutic circle, the hermeneutic criticism of communication, the inexorable hermeneutic deferral of meaning and understanding. But these challenges, once realized (or, indeed, engendered) as *structure*, no longer significantly threaten the founding assertion; they in fact tend now to support and stabilize that assertion, to *clothe* its naked arbitrariness in a developable discursive fabric. It is thus merely systematic self-consistency (not any metasystematic perception or reasoning) that transforms those original refutations of the hermeneutic project into a defense or clothing of it. The hermeneutic circle, we are now told, not only is not vicious but "harbors the positive possibility of aboriginal knowledge" (Heidegger);[8] the criticism of communication now rechristens itself as "hermeneutic conversation" (Gadamer); the deferral of meaning and understanding now means (or is understood as) the very signature of meaning and understanding.

Hermeneutic space thus has the character not of a merely open space but of a system and, in certain obvious respects—to anticipate—the character of a system of political *ideology*. When faced with the problem of persuading "me" to accept it, it operates not from without, by reasons, but from within, by infiltration—by suggesting seductively that in the very act of questioning it or disagreeing with it (thus engaging in a supposedly purposeful debate), "I" already *have* accepted it. In a voice meant to sound like my own conscience, it threatens me with literal excommunication if I should happen simply to answer no to the question of whether efficacious human communication is not after all undeniable. In any event, it is inevitable that hermeneutics as questioning, as the keeping open of a problem, should develop in the direction of system. For hermeneutics itself (in its critical aspect) insists that meaning or understanding always *can* be denied (by being reduced to interpretation, thus deferred) in particular cases. Only on the level of system can meaning and understanding be thought of as undeniable; only the actual coherence of a system—a system of human communication, which is assumed in some manner to work, to make sense, to make progress—can serve as a sign (however delusive) of such undeniability.

Performance and Hermeneutic Space

Let us begin by thinking of a "performance," provisionally, as a social action that is carried out by actual living human bodies and cannot escape being located in hermeneutic space. Hermeneutics asserts not that meaning and understanding do operate for us but only that their operation is undeniable. A similar distinction must be observed between the assertion that performance *is* located in hermeneutic space and the assertion that performance *cannot escape* being located there. (This is, almost exactly, the distinction between saying that performance is always transitive and saying merely that it is always interpretive.) The former assertion (which I do not make), that performance *is* located in hermeneutic space, is generally characteristic of "theater semiotics," the systematic study of signs—but principally of nonverbal signs and codes—in the theater. It cannot be denied, the argument runs, that efficacious communication occurs in the non-verbal area of the theatrical proceeding; at least this cannot be denied without also denying the systematic cogency of theatrical conventions and positing mere chaos. But on the other hand—especially by contrast with the simultaneous operation of language in the theater—that nonverbal meaning and understanding are also marked as unspecified and unlocatable, as deferred, as suspended in the need for a verbal confirmation which systematic constraints (precisely the project of reserving a special semiotic domain for the nonverbal) prevent its ever receiving in full. The theater, in this view, thus pledges allegiance to hermeneutics by reenacting the creation of hermeneutic space (between the undeniable and its indefinite deferral—here with respect to nonverbal communication) and so locates performance unequivocally *in* that space.

Or, to look at it differently, theater semiotics has emancipatory pretensions, which it frequently associates with a questionable reading of Artaud. Language must be dethroned; the verbal text, which brings with it all the deadening moralistic and psychologistic baggage of literary tradition, must be overpowered in the theater by a "physical" stage language in which something like an anarchic "play" of signification is unleashed. But the systematic development of this program by means of *semiotic* categories involves a capitulation to precisely those qualities of verbal language that it rejects. For as Barthes already pointed out in 1964, semiotics, however developed, never frees itself from its original *linguistic* filiation; it exists and shapes itself only as a response to problems in the study of language.[9] In particular, semiotics gains its theoretical leverage by excluding from consideration the ideas of meaning and understanding, at least to the extent that these ideas have a referential component, and focusing upon *difference* as an absolutely primitive notion—which means, however, difference as the *structuring* operation that it is, strictly speaking, only in linguistic systems. One can assert or believe or recognize that two chairs or two gestures are "different," but any useful *semiotic* operation with such differences presupposes a linguistic encoding. And it follows that theater semiotics, in order to carry out its emancipatory move with respect to language, must reintroduce in some form, for leverage against language, the *referential* force of meaning and understanding—the idea, however disguised, that we understand better, or understand differently, in the theater. Which makes it not semiotics, but hermeneutics. Thus performance is situated in a hermeneutic space which, to make matters worse, costumes itself as semiotics and so obscures precisely the critical structures (the radical questioning of meaning and understanding) by which hermeneutics itself ordinarily tries to stay honest.

The Materiality of Performance

Theater semiotics, therefore, at least in its more mechanical versions, ought properly to be called "theater hermeneutics," and as such it is untenable. In the first place, whatever the risk of chaos, experience alone cries out against the idea that performance simply *is* located in hermeneutic space. Experience is an issue here. As I have said, hermeneutic questions would be dismissed as mere quibbles if we did not recognize them as anchored in experience—although hermeneutics itself raises the question of whether that experience is "natural," whether it is not conditioned precisely *by* hermeneutic (originally theological) speculation. And the characteristic experience of hermeneutic space, the experience that inclines us to receive hermeneutics as a philosophically significant pursuit, proceeds in three stages: (1) an initial simplicity, my belief in my ability to understand directly and adequately what I read or hear; (2) the dismantling of this belief by education and debate, the evaporation of understanding into a corrosive atmosphere of mere interpretive opinions which in turn gnaws at the very substance of meaning; and (3) the recognition that this apparently destructive process still has the character of law, of a system within which we can still think and talk fruitfully. But this pattern, this parody of Christian salvation history, which we can identify on widely differing levels in our intellectual experience, does not characterize the experience of theatrical performance unless we arbitrarily trim that experience to fit it.

If we are honest about our experience in the theater—if we do not romanticize or Christianize or forcibly hermeneuticize it or foist upon it, for example, the giddy psychology that has for centuries been foisted upon Aristotle's concept of catharsis—then we must recognize that that experience consists largely of *distraction*, a distraction that is compounded and thrown into relief precisely by its tense relation to our common theoretical understanding of the theater as an instrument for the philosophical or moral *focusing* of attention. (*Hamlet*, for example, becomes the significant theoretical work that it is by doubling the distraction of the "distracted globe" in its structure of plot, dialogue, character, and metaphor.) Our distraction in the theater is in part a result of the sheer number and variety of distinguishable semiotic (potentially significant) assaults on our consciousness, including everything from an actor's minutest accidental stumble (do we *know* it was a nonsignifying accident?) up to our sense of a directorial master plan. It is true that in reading a book and organizing its meaning for ourselves as we go, we must leave out of account the vast preponderance of the signifying units over which our eyes pass. But whereas what we leave out of account in reading is for the time being simply excluded from our experience, in the theater a certain amount inevitably remains or returns before us insistently, physically, as a distraction and interferes with any sense of satisfying closure we might have—at least to the extent of exposing such closure as violence, not progress, not the intimation of a huge self-reconciled hermeneutic systematicity.

(Almost all American schoolchildren, for example, and unfortunately many schoolteachers as well, assume that when Juliet asks "wherefore" Romeo is Romeo, she is thinking of her beloved's whereabouts. The actual meaning of "wherefore" simply does not exist for them; it does not in the least *distract* them in their reading. But if the actress, in speaking that word, has an uncontrollable and audible attack of flatulence, the result is quite different. Even the correct meaning of a word can be utterly absent from our experience of reading; but the fart, however unconnected with any reasonable semiotic description of the artistic proceeding, cannot be expunged from our experience of the performance. And I challenge anyone to find me unable, at practically any point in any dramatic performance, to list from memory at least ten stage events in the past minute of playing that are not equally resistant to a reasonable semiotic resolution. These events may be comparatively small, but they are always there and do not escape notice.)

It is thus the *materiality* of theatrical performance that resists its simple inclusion in hermeneutic space—and in fact, not only the materiality of specific distracting events but the materiality of the whole, since material objects, *as* material, obviously cannot occupy hermeneutic space. The possible objection here, that the theater's materiality, like that of a book, is left behind by the semiosis for which it serves as a vehicle and does not operate *as* materiality, is misguided. The theater's materiality is less comparable to a book's (or, say, a painting's) than to the materiality of what it actually resembles (and in a strong sense *is*), the materiality of a thoroughly heterogeneous *collection* of objects suggesting extrapolation in the direction of "world." It is true, and is in fact a truth that is called strongly to mind precisely by the theater, that the operation of even the world's materiality, as such, is open to question. Can we in real life think of an object, or even merely perceive it, without *already* having semioticized it, encoded it as a signifier, thus emptied it of its strict gross materiality? (This semiotic speculation supports the tendency in metaphysics to equate hermeneutic space with the whole space of experience, the whole scene of history.) But our position with respect to the material objects in the theater is different, for in consequence of the relation of performance and hermeneutic space, we *anticipate* those objects' (and human bodies') semioticization. We expect them to become signifiers, and their sheer materiality (*what* is it that we expect to be semioticized?) plays a role in this expectation that it does not play in real life. A chair in real life is already "a chair" in our perceiving it; its materiality is merely one of many signifiers that participate in that concept. A chair on the stage, by contrast, is always destined to *become* (yet never does finally become) *the* chair in a larger textual or ritual signification, and its resistance to being fully textualized, since it *is* after all a chair— *a* chair—is nothing but its materiality.[10] Objects in a theatrical performance thus have, for us, a greater operative materiality than objects in the real world and offer greater resistance to the engulfing tendency of hermeneutic space. Materiality in daily life is simply a presupposition, an inconspicuous background tone to experience, but in the theater it becomes a positive *disturbance* and gains profile thereby.

Living Human Bodies

This argument from experience can be developed in theory by the stipulation that a performance is an action carried out by actual living human bodies. For the living human body, unlike anything that might play the part of "text" in hermeneutic space, is an arbitrarily self-modifying signifier. That body, on

a performance stage, unquestionably signifies in a manner that invites interpretation. But the present signification of a living human body, no matter
how thoroughly determined by context or costume or makeup, is always
subject to being changed (always able to change itself) unpredictably. On any
given evening it is unlikely that the actress playing Phèdre will illustrate the
words, "que ma présence outrage," in her final speech, by making an obscene
gesture at the audience. But if she decides—for any reason, or for no reason—
to make that gesture, then she *will* do it. The human body is a semiotic explo-
sive. Precisely the discipline of acting keeps us aware that the acting
bodies—by what we vaguely call a "change of mind"—can at any time arbitrarily disorganize the semiotic fabric that their acting creates.

It is, in any case, precisely the idea of situating performance in
hermeneutic space, or textualizing it, that suggests the idea of the living
human body as a *self*-modifying signifier rather than, say, a signifier under
the control of an arbitrary personal will (the actor's). For the latter formulation, besides involving the sort of category distinction that is resisted by
hermeneutics, would make it necessary for us to deal hermeneutically with
a strict, "ineffable," untextualizable individual, which is impossible. Yet on
the other hand, the arbitrarily self-modifying signifier—which is how the
living human body apparently has to be regarded in hermeneutic space—
also *conflicts* with hermeneutic space. The hermeneutic theorem concerning
the role of interpretation in the very constitution of its object does imply
that texts and signifiers, in hermeneutic space, are uncontrollably mutable.
But they are not arbitrarily *self*-modifying. The mutability of entities in
hermeneutic space is testimony precisely to the *structured* or *systematic*
quality of that space, hence to the *subordination* of its elements, not to any
such element's independence. (Other stage effects, incidentally, no matter
how "arbitrary" they may seem to us, do not conflict with our sense of
hermeneutic space but merely complicate it. Only the living human body,
provided we are willing to collapse the distinction between body and person, is strictly *self*-modifying.)

Or suppose, after all, that we do distinguish between the acting body
and its inhabitant, and that we regard the latter not as a hermeneutically
inaccessible individual but simply as the "meaning" of the performance, in
the sense of the *act* of meaning that the body interprets. The trouble is that
meaning in this sense is not subject to the indefinite deferral of hermeneutic
space, because it is trapped in the acting body before us. No matter how far
we extend the series M_n, each M_n is still directly referable to the actor's continuing act of meaning, an act whose immediate *presence* is guaranteed for
us (again) by its arbitrary alterability. (Since we know that the meaning [the
act] can become radically different with no notice whatever—in the next
instant, for example—it follows that that meaning is firmly bound to the
here and now in which we receive it.) And this state of affairs strongly

resists the idea of hermeneutic space. For the indefinite hermeneutic deferral of meaning—hence, from any given point of view, the *absence* of meaning—is required in order to preserve for meaning (and understanding) the
quality of being undeniable. Meaning is supposedly undeniable in its operation, therefore perhaps located somewhere; but it is always located *somewhere else*, somewhere where only its deniability is at issue, where it can
avoid being put to the test of whether it *is* or *is not*. Therefore the actor's living body sticks in the craw of hermeneutic space, and no amount of conceptual labor can swallow it.

To look at it differently, the nonlimitable fabric of M_n associated with an
actor in the theater has no *historical* extension. Every one of its constitutive
interpretive moves must be directly referable to the acting (and speaking)
body before us; otherwise, given the unpredictability of that acting body,
we risk losing touch with it altogether—as we do not, for example, when
interpreting a text. Even if some particular M_n turns out to be, say, an existing literary work or historical event, still that work or event becomes an M_n
only by being "meant" here and now, by the textualized actor, and by being
somehow legible in his or her body. The fabric of M_n thus constitutes, so to
speak, an antipsychoanalysis of the actor, a countertype to psychoanalysis
because the body—which in actual psychoanalysis serves as an *exit* from
the here and now, into the generality of the human species (hence into the
historical space where a hermeneutic system can develop)—has here
become a kind of screen on which the whole hermeneutic-analytic process
is projected.

(I use the term "psychoanalysis" here because psychoanalysis, in one
aspect of its operation—and *only* one aspect—is the closest thing we have to
a hermeneutics that attempts to encompass, if not to penetrate, the "ineffable" individual.[11] For despite the famous topographical diagrams of the
psyche in *The Ego and the Id* and the *New Introductory Lectures*—which are
strictly heuristic—Freudian "meanings" such as ego, id, unconscious,
repression, transference are not actually located in the individual but
escape by way of the interpret*ed* body into a realm of history, tradition, society, and especially language, where they undergo hermeneutic deferral. In
performance, on the other hand, if we adopt the hypothesis of its situation
in hermeneutic space, the interpret*ing* body is a labyrinth by which even
historical and literary meanings are trapped in the present—*if* we adopt
that hypothesis. I am attempting here not to show what performance actually is or does but simply to develop the impossible theoretical consequences of locating it unequivocally in hermeneutic space.)

The M_n, so to speak, thus become a psychoanalysis with no exit from the
here and now, which means that "meaning"—in the sense of a possible
immediate object of understanding—cannot be deferred by the M_n, cannot
be made *absent*, but can only be chased around endlessly in the enclosed

space of just this here and now. And it follows, since meaning still cannot be arrived at but also cannot make the systematic excuse of being deferred, that the futility of this chasing around amounts to a simple *denial of the existence of meaning*. Thus the system of hermeneutic space, in the living body of the actor, is radically warped and compelled to contradict its own founding postulate.

It will be noted, finally, that I have not tried to develop the obvious relation between this argument and my point, in the previous chapter, about Beckett's insistence on living human bodies as opposed to puppets. I think that relation, in its broad outlines, is sufficiently simple and perspicuous to require no special comment (and to go into it in detail would require at least another whole chapter).

The Attraction between Performance and Hermeneutic Space

Performance, then, no matter how we adjust our perspective upon it, *resists* being located in hermeneutic space. (In a terminology used earlier, there is an inescapable category difference—which hermeneutics, by its founding strategy, cannot swallow—between performance and anything imaginable as its "text.") But as I said at the outset, performance also *cannot escape* being located in hermeneutic space. Its mere existence as a concept, the distinction from any action that is not a "performance" because it does not in the same way tempt forth an interpretive response, already implies this impossibility of escape, which I called earlier its "interpretivity." Of course we might have tried any number of other ways to lay hold of the distinction between performances and social actions in general, but the concept of interpretation would have been unavoidable. We should have had to worry about the exact manner in which performance *is* interpretive, and the exact manner in which it *invites* interpretation; and the result would have been a very slippery conceptual situation, since interpretation undeniably operates, in some manner, in every conceivable social event. Hence the usefulness of the notion of hermeneutic space, a space that is constituted by the endlessly proliferating structures of interpretation. The idea that an action is located in hermeneutic space, or that it "cannot escape" being located there, does not produce criteria for distinguishing in practice between performance and other types of social event. But since it is obvious that no such criteria can be found anyway—even though we do generally know a "performance" when we see one—it follows that we must be concerned primarily with the level of systematic pretension in our formulations. And I think the relatively modest formulative move that identifies "hermeneutic space" is justified in these terms.

It perhaps even makes sense to speak of a *force of attraction* between hermeneutic space and all social or public actions in which we recognize the quality of performance. In the case of the dramatic theater, whose exposure to hermeneutics follows as a trivial consequence of its association with literature, that force can be detected only by way of an analysis (as above) of the resistance against which it must operate. But there are cases in which it appears more directly. Public spectacles that involve wild animals, or mortal danger to the performers, or both—bullfights, circuses, rodeos— perhaps have a deep atavistic appeal. But it seems to me that over time, this direct appeal is increasingly confused with the appeal of the interpretive question of why we still stage such spectacles. And in the case of sporting events, especially in the United States, it is clear by now that neither the game itself nor its result really matters any more. What matters is the simultaneous composition and interpretation—under the collective authorship of performers, spectators, and journalists—of a huge historical epic whose terminology (*dynasty, era, legend, record, all-time*) instantly relegates every actual event to the mythical past. The performance, which in this case can perhaps be traced back to forms of ritual combat by which social status (especially of males) was determined, has been almost completely absorbed by hermeneutic space.

This force of attraction, however, originates not in the nature of performance (if performance even has a "nature") but in the nature of hermeneutic space. Hermeneutics has an inherent *need* for performance, an irresistible desire to appropriate and digest it. For the quality of hermeneutic space as a system is correlated with the proposition that meaning and understanding are undeniable, while precisely the structures that that system organizes keep meaning and understanding out of reach by deferring them interminably. The validity of hermeneutics is therefore always in question, and a desire for confirmation of its validity, in the form of *evidence*, is inevitable. But direct evidence in support of the founding proposition (on undeniability) is clearly impossible, which leaves hermeneutics with a hunger for evidence at least of its own systematic cohesion, evidence of successful or efficacious communication. Interpretive discourse itself can sometimes seem to satisfy that hunger, when particular texts, for example, are interpreted as combining into the picture of a historical movement or period, a network of communicated value. But such evidence is always subject precisely to a hermeneutic criticism. Hence the need for more powerful and immediate evidentiary manifestations of communicative success; hence the device of gathering large numbers of people in an enclosed space, of separating some as "performers" and observing with satisfaction that at certain points in the course of an inherently unremarkable action carried out by the performers, all the rest simultaneously laugh or cheer or groan or beat their hands together. (It follows, incidentally, that the most hermeneutically desirable performance situation is one in which absolute enthusiastic unanimity is combined with a communicated content that is of immediate practical importance in the lives of the spectators and might therefore have been expected to yield only a welter of individually conditioned opinions—which adds up, at least in Western terms, to the idea of a fascist, or more generally totalitarian, political demonstration.)

But performance, again, also stubbornly *resists* its appropriation by hermeneutics. How shall we read this situation? Is it simply a matter of recognizing that our historical and cultural condition involves mutually incommensurable tendencies? Or does the relation with performance say something specific about hermeneutics? Might one argue, for example, that hermeneutics betrays a basic unsoundness in its need to nourish itself with a substance (performance) that is ultimately poisonous to it?

Performance Space

All social actions are programmed, at least to the extent that only a certain number of social possibilities are coded (recognizable) as "actions" to begin with. This truth, which is mercifully concealed from us in most social situations, comes strongly into focus when an action unfolds before a company of spectators, and is the basis of our sense of some form of *text* behind every performance. Even if the preexisting text is known to be no more than the rules of a game, or a *scenario* for improvising upon; even if the performance is a solo and subject to strong and unpredictable social interactions with the audience; even if the "text" is in some clear sense not yet existent until the performance is over (in which case the performance would be intransitive), still the relation with a text or program is always implied and, in the vicinity of hermeneutic space (where performance, by definition, finds itself), is inevitably regarded as an *interpretive* relation. Indeed, precisely the dependence of the text on the performance's progress, when this condition obtains, plays into the hands of hermeneutics by suggesting the hermeneutic theorem concerning the role of interpretation in the constitution of its object.

This argument is limited by the consideration that "performance" as such, in a form not yet contaminated by hermeneutics, is never really available as an object of discussion. But it is still clear that hermeneutics and performance enjoy a relatively good fit with each other in respect to the structures, the infinite chains and fabrics of text, that constitute hermeneutic space. In fact, precisely the factors that make performance different from other types of interpretation, or from the verbal-expository form with which we normally associate interpretation, present the spectator more or less *directly* with the same proliferation of texts that for a reader emerges only from speculation on the concept of genre. The materiality of performance, namely, and its execution by living human bodies (or, from our point of view as spectators, the experience of distraction and the recognition of a self-modifying capability in the signs we read), confront us insistently with the fact that the performance (P) is not effectively an interpretation of its text (T) until it is *interpreted* in that sense, since P itself lacks the textlike focus and stability that enable an interpretation (in hermeneutic space) to serve as the text for further interpretation. And yet, even the interpretation (R) of P as an interpretation cannot make P *itself* (in its living bodily materiality, its category difference from the textual) into an interpretation of T but can only state that P "reflects" or "embodies" an interpretation (N) of T. The relation between P and N, however, is categorically disrupted in exactly the same way as the relation between P and T, so that N is in effect another "text" (T_1) of P, which P can interpret only by being interpreted (R_1) to "reflect" another interpretation (N_1) *of* N (= T_1), and so on (figure 3).

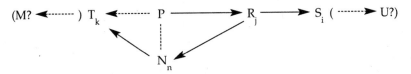

$(M? \longleftarrow) T_k \longleftarrow P \longrightarrow R_j \longrightarrow S_i (\longrightarrow U?)$

N_n

(U = understanding; S_i = spectators; R_i = interpretations of P *as* an interpretation N_n; P = performance; N_n = fabric of interpretations attributed to P; T_k = inferred text[s] of P; M = meaning)

Figure 3

The situation is thus complicated in a typically hermeneutic manner, but with some new twists. For the *social* (not mental) quality of performance introduces a nonlimitable plurality even at the starting point of the hermeneia, with the spectators. Even the individual spectator's interpretation (R) of P receives from the social situation a distinctly *provisional* character (as one among many other possible interpretations), which reinforces the inherently provisional quality of an interpretation whose object is capable of arbitrary self-modification. Thus the fabric of proliferating interpretations and texts is made both larger and more complicated by the addition of parallel possibilities at every stage.

But most important is that this characteristic (let us say) hermeneutoid structure of proliferating text (call it "performance space") *does not appear to require the postulate of an undeniable operation of meaning and understanding.* Performance space has all the advantages of hermeneutic space. Obviously, it defers meaning and understanding indefinitely by interposing interpretation at each step. Thus it may be regarded—at least as plausibly as hermeneutics may, or hermeneutic space—as the execution of a radical critique upon all forms of dogmatic or authoritarian reading. The difference is that in performance space, the operation of meaning and understanding is not required to articulate the hermeneia, to set in motion the proliferation of positions that creates a "space." All that is needed, in performance space, is our recognition of an *interpretive* relation between the performance (P) and its inferred text (T). No force of "understanding" is required to keep that relation open; it is always already opened by the categorical separation between T and the living bodily materiality of P. Moreover, the proliferation of the results of interpretation, by which "meaning" is otherwise both deferred and confirmed, is now anticipated by a proliferation at the level of the target text itself (T_k), so that the question of meaning never necessarily arises. (Of course, the N_n and the T_k are not strictly distinct. The point of the foregoing diagram [figure 3], in fact, is that each N_n inexorably *becomes* a T_k, so that no identity can form at level T which is stable enough to support the question of meaning.) Performance space thus accepts the structure and critical function of hermeneutic space but denies the systematic postulate. It says simply "no" when asked to acknowledge the supersedure of its lengthy and heavy materiality by a supposedly undeniable communicative success.

This argument, and its diagram, are not a final statement of the way performance does operate; they show only a manner in which performance can be regarded. A sufficiently subtle manipulation of concepts could probably produce a similar diagram for hermeneutic space itself, which would bypass its systematic aspect without the intervention of performance. But in its historical actuality, hermeneutics *does* insist on "truth and method," on the ultimate resolution of its critical structures into system, and does hunger for the living human bodies of performance in the hope of corroborating its systematic claims. My point is simply that this hunger is suicidal, precisely on the part of hermeneutics *as system*.

The living, social, bodily materiality of performance renders the hermeneutic postulate on undeniability *unnecessary*—by usurping its function in the articulation (the resistance to entropy) of an antidogmatic space—and so refutes it. Earlier, when I used the metaphor of a body in a gravitational field to illustrate the necessity of the hermeneutic postulate, I should, of course, have said not "body," but "point mass." For in the case of a body, especially a large heterogeneous body, the presence of a gravitational field is apparent in tidal effects. Even if the sun and moon were invisible, their gravitational field could be deduced from the behavior of the oceans. And performance, I contend, is just such a large, material, heterogeneous body in hermeneutic space, a body on which the radically critical structures of that space are revealed as tides, so that the uncomfortable need of hermeneutics to posit as undeniable what it has already radically questioned (meaning and understanding) disappears.

In chapter 2, I discussed the operation of genre, defined as a necessary *condition of communication*, in producing a practically irresistible conservative tendency in literature. And I argued there that the circumvention of this conservative tendency, the production of a truly liberal or revolutionary or (in Trilling's sense) "active" literature, would depend on our being able to dismiss the postulate of communicability (i.e., of the undeniability of meaning and understanding) in literature—which is precisely the principal effect of the unfolding of performance space. It follows that in the dramatic theater, where literature and theatrical performance meet (or collide)—no matter how thoroughly arbitrary or accidental the chain of events that brought them together—we have the point and, as far as I can tell, the only point at which literature operates, *as* literature, in a nonconservative manner. All theater, in other words, is revolutionary theater.

Ideology

The founding postulate of hermeneutics is exposed (by performance) as being nothing of the kind, since the critical structures and functions and insights of hermeneutics do not require it after all but operate (in performance, if not in theory) even if the hermeneutic circle *is* a vicious circle. What we have is a *specious* founding postulate, the imposition upon interpretive activity of a doctored history that serves no purpose but to sanction *system as such*, as long as the system (by its own measurement) is successful or efficacious. We have an intellectual initiative, in other words, that shows all the earmarks of an ideology of political oppression. The very form of the hermeneutic postulate is suspect. As an assertion *only* of undeniability, it hovers between an arbitrary command (you must affirm the operation of meaning and understanding, you would be foolish not to) and a simple constative (meaning and understanding in effect do operate). But this slippery borderline is the home of every repressive political ideology, where naked power costumes itself as reason and knowledge, as merely sensible advice to us on how not to beat our heads against the wall.

The question of how hermeneutics has come to assume the character of an apology in advance for every exploitation of political advantage that successfully clothes itself in an internally justified systematics, is not strictly germane to our inquiry. But the emancipatory rhetoric that develops alongside hermeneutics permits at least a suggestion. Modern hermeneutic theory, in the wake of Kantian philosophy, claims to expose dogmatism by a systematic reflection upon the linguistic and historical conditioning of communication, by understanding texts "better" than their own authors (Schleiermacher).[12] In due course the "human sciences" ("Geisteswissenschaften"), an inherently emancipatory self-knowledge that also avoids the dehumanizing methodological pitfall of an uncriticized analogy with natural science, are sponsored by hermeneutics (Dilthey). And eventually hermeneutics presents us with history itself as a "conversation" in which we can participate fruitfully, as more than mere dupes or victims or rebels (Gadamer).

Hermeneutics, that is, appears as a nineteenth-century systematizing of the eighteenth-century speculative task of human emancipation, in which precisely system had formed the main problem. Even without the extensive logical and historical apparatus of Horkheimer and Adorno, we can satisfy ourselves easily that the whole cluster of concepts that includes emancipation, enlightenment, tolerance, and especially understanding, displays two strongly opposed aspects. All these terms are liberal in tone and, up to a point, liberalizing in operation but are unable to withstand cross-examination on their role in fully developed conceptual or institutional systems. Neither emancipation nor tolerance can produce permanent effects except when enforced from a position of arbitrary political power. Enlightenment, as soon as the demands made upon it become sufficiently systematic, inevitably valorizes the morality (and economics) of white male Christian Europe. And understanding, while I can experience it privately as a moment of liberation, operates systematically as a move of submission to its object. "Tout comprendre, c'est tout pardonner"; or as Ionesco's Dudard puts it before becoming a rhinoceros, "Comprendre, c'est justifier."

Hence, in both Rousseau and Herder, the absence of understanding (or meaning) among the founding principles of language. (Paul de Man overstates the case; he actually reintroduces meaning as a systematic factor, in the very process of insisting that meaning is "empty" for Rousseau.[13] But the case he overstates is valid.) And in the next to last chapter of *The Social Contract*, "Civil Religion," how shall we understand the paradoxical character of Christianity on the basis of which Rousseau attacks it? How shall we explain the combination of passivity, or a lack of decisive commitment, with rigid intolerance, if not as an instance of systematicity in exactly the form that characterizes hermeneutics? (Hermeneutics, in any event, has never really severed its umbilical connection with Christian theology.) Just as the infinite deferral of meaning and understanding gives rise to a system in which meaning and understanding are undeniable—a system that cannot even conceive of the possibility of our saying no to it—so, in Rousseau's view, the deferral of all meaningful judgments concerning our life, the Christian postponement of such judgments until the next world, cuts the ground out from under any attempt to regard that deferral as itself a debatable judgment and so produces perfect intolerance. Nor are the possibilities of performance, as a circumvention of system without a sacrifice of critical penetration, overlooked in the eighteenth century. We think of the political performance envisaged in Rousseau's Assembly of the People, of German dramatic conventions that reflect profoundly upon their realization in the theater, of the attempt in ironic novels to make even reading into a kind of performance.

But by the time Schleiermacher proclaims an "art of understanding," system as problem has been replaced by system as a delusive hope. The use of the term "art," not "science" or "system," changes nothing. In a hermeneutic context the quality of system already follows from the concept of understanding, especially when we are kept at a respectful distance from it by the interposition of a "misunderstanding" that only insinuates the undeniability of its opposite.

Precisely the judicious validity of the hermeneutic criticism of ideology now operates inexorably in favor of an apologetics of oppression. For hermeneutics offers a general systematic critique of the ideological conditioning of communication; it offers emancipation or enlightenment in the form of training in the "art" of reflection upon literary, political, and scientific rhetoric. Ideological conditioning is inevitable in practice, even in critical discourse; hermeneutic space, after all, can never be completely present to us as we read or write or converse, and the particular communicative conventions we are conscious of using—even if only heuristically—are at some level arbitrarily imposed. But hermeneutic training still provides us with an understandable confidence in our ability to prevent at least any single particular ideology (any circumscribed region in hermeneutic space) from gaining ascendancy over us. Therefore, when the reflection we are trained in is turned (as it must be) upon hermeneutics itself, and when its critical force is blunted by the consideration that an attack on its own methodological basis would risk mere chaos, we are not overly perturbed. Our confident grasp of the rhetoricity of our own condition permits us even to accept the prospect that our discipline—threatened with a chaotic tendency that would impair (we fear) precisely its critical or emancipatory effectiveness—*must* seek (or accept) a systematic resolution of its own radically critical endeavors, *must* envision an ultimately successful and efficacious (though never fully summarizable) system of human communication.

The result, however, is that our discipline—in restricting its focus scrupulously to the systematic postulate, in thus leaving open and hoping to keep open, to protect from prejudice, the question of the content of communication—has created a mask of undeniability that is *empty* (since *we* do not claim to have achieved understanding) and is therefore available for use by precisely those ideologies whose coupling with raw political power produces the best available image of communicative success and efficacy, a mask we now find it practically impossible to argue against, since it comes equipped with our own prior sanction. This may seem a rather abstract way of looking at an actual historical situation. But how else does one account for the Heideggers of this world, for individuals of prodigious abstract intelligence who nevertheless manage to accept such things as Nazi ideology?

Genet

Given that an expository treatment of these matters has at best temporary significance, since it will tend to be absorbed eventually into the self-reflexive critical operation of hermeneutics itself, the question arises, can *performance* make a difference in modern hermeneutic culture—or for that matter, in a postmodern (perhaps posthermeneutic), information-driven culture where the mask is taught to exercise power (over all the old victims of oppression) without anyone's actually wearing it, without needing the figure of a Führer? This question itself of course tends strongly in the direction of hermeneutic speculation. (Every performance, *as* performance, shows in effect that hermeneutics does not need systematic resolution in order to sustain its critical power; but this showing, on the level of any possible general cultural efficacy, is available to be appropriated by the self-critical operation of precisely the existing system of hermeneutics.) The question of the cultural role of performance thus hovers on the brink of being itself a *sacrificium intellectus*, an instance of the typical final move toward which radical criticism is impelled by the strength of its own hard-earned negativity, a valorizing—if only (we hope) for the sake of argument—of the "positive" as such, which means: system, success, efficacy, the fruitful, the human, the whole repressive conceptual arsenal we repeatedly forget how to fear. But perhaps the question can in a sense be answered anyway.

The figures in Jean Genet's *Les Nègres*, for example, the people who appear before us on the stage, are characterized by a sharp internal break that is comparable to the distinction between subject of utterance and subject of enunciation.[14] Those people are actually black (as subject of utterance, seen as the speakers of the words they speak), but their discourse—especially when it takes their blackness as an object—evidently presupposes the white subject of enunciation that is also suggested by their names. The structure is thus *layered*. A white subject addresses a white audience by way of the real living bodies of blacks, whose realness is thus reduced to the *function* of a kind of wedge by which white consciousness—or a white conscience, engaged in self-directed "réprobation"—manufactures the distance of representation with respect to itself. In what sense are those black people "real" anyway? "Qu'est-ce que c'est donc un noir? Et d'abord, c'est de quelle couleur?"[15]

A perfected image of this layering is offered in the "court," a white discourse that inhabits black bodies which in turn inhabit white masks. And the blackness of the court, by being presented as invisible, assigns to the blackness of the other figures precisely the quality of *visibility* by which their actual presence as blacks is caught up (and used up) in representation. Thus the whole plot of hermeneutics is enacted. An emancipatory white discourse is enunciated by way of the maskless blacks (led by Mme. Félicité) and reflects critically, by way of the court, on its own inevitable operation as a repressive, colonizing discourse. The systematic perfection of this criticism, however—the successful and total representation, in the court, of the layered structure that otherwise merely includes us, thus the *achievement* of self-knowledge—disarms our reflection *as* criticism (because it is perfect) and so colonizes the staged "Africa" all over again (as it were in spite of us) by reducing it to its functionalized visibility. This beguiling "nécessité" or "harmonie" (Genet 5:97, 133), as Diouf learns to admire it in our hermeneutic reflection, affects even the living bodily materiality of the performance as such, which is layered between its original text and, especially, Archibald's reflections. The fact that Archibald is "really" a black man endows his reflections on performance—on "theater" (5:101–2, 127), on precisely the impossibility of "communication" (5: 85, 148, 155), hence on the overturning of hermeneutics as system—with *an immediate referential validity*, which, however, then operates as a form of textual mastery over the present performance and so reincorporates the performance into a hermeneutic system after all.

Then, however, the fireworks go off, the members of the court remove their masks, and the whole structure—of visibility articulated by invisibility, of totalized self-reflection—collapses. Now, for a moment, the blacks on the stage *are* entirely real and alien. But again, they are "real" with a reality that has already been functionalized as a structural wedge in our hermeneutically systematized self-reflection. Inevitably, therefore, they reassume their masks (now the layering is temporally extended: masked, then unmasked, then masked) and die the death that eternalizes our self-reference in the closure of one of Diouf's "vrais drames," "true dramas" (5:133).

And yet this constant hermeneutic overpowering of performance, this repeated reduction of materiality to representation, this textual bludgeoning of the living bodies on the stage, also *insists* in its repetitiveness on exactly what it bludgeons. It profiles, articulates, thus rescues performance, in all its intractable living materiality; and it does so not merely in the immediacy of the theater but on the level of text or representation, in its own hermeneutic space, whose permanence, as systematic closure, now also makes permanent the unstilled disruption of that very closure.

At least this argument is imaginable, and is perhaps even imaginable with respect to the hermeneutic sanctioning of the oppression of women. I am not sure that Hélène Cixous's *Portrait de Dora*, which springs to mind in this connection, actually mobilizes performance in the realm of the textual. But perhaps Genet's *Le Balcon* does, even without alluding directly to psychoanalysis. Its layered structure is comparable to that of *Les Nègres*. The reality of the women who appear is functionalized as the needful wedge, the interruption or tension, in a masturbatory male discourse that both inhabits their utterances and forms the larger text which they in turn inhabit as signifiers. This structure is then doubled (and anatomized in its paradoxes) by the consideration that the actresses, as actresses, are prostitutes in the same way as are their characters, in performing for payment the textualization of their womanhood. And the ritual ferocity of this pattern of assaults upon the living female body, assaults that include Chantal's and Irma's opposed acts of political complicity, perhaps in the end establishes that body, after all, as a constantly regenerated obstacle or embarrassment to hermeneutics, as the incessant material rebirth of itself in the very bosom of a self-destructively pregnant textuality, as what I would call—if only actual French phonetics were more cooperative—"la gêne née."

Robert Wilson and the Work as an Empty Wavelength for Its Own Public Discussion

Each of the last two chapters concludes by looking at a limiting case of theater. In Genet the bodies of blacks and women, in Beckett the actors' bodies as tokens of personal identity, are subjected to a merciless hermeneutic or textual bludgeoning that in the end reveals not so much the power of text as its failure, its defectiveness, its futility. Thus the way is opened for a form of *literary* discourse—literary in the sense of: self-reflexively scrupulous, hence conceivably honest and efficacious—no longer crippled by the dream of communication (which has been refuted) and by the conservative operation of genre. But what happens when theatrical practice is pushed *beyond* these limiting cases?

Revolutionizing the Theater

All theater, I have said, is revolutionary theater. From its very origin, Western theater has been forced into an unstable and entirely incongruous yet also indissoluble relation with poetry in general, and later with what we now call "literature," a relation that always disrupts—or at least is always capable of disrupting—those literary-historical operations (having to do mainly with genre) that produce in recent centuries literature's else ingrained, if inconspicuous, conservative leaning. I maintain, therefore, that *all* theater is revolutionary in the long run, that the institution as such cannot help being revolutionary, even where the people who use it and the material represented in it are decidedly conservative or reactionary.

In the short term, however, even the theater as an institution can assume a character that has nothing at all to do with revolution. The theatrical projects of Brecht and Artaud, discussed in chapters 3 and 4, are both set up as responses to what their authors perceived (accurately, I think) as a "novelized" nineteenth-century theater that had attempted to be nothing but a faithful enactment of literature in the sense of psychological realism. And in chapter 5, in connection with Büchner's vision of a theater "that never was," it occurred to us that perhaps the actual established theater at any given time, the theater in our very midst, is also somehow not yet fully itself, never fully there as a revolutionary initiative, always therefore itself in need of revolutionizing.

If this is the case—and how can it not be, given that the theater's revolutionary quality is undeniable on the institutional level yet by no means apparent to most practitioners?—if the theater is thus always in need of revolutionizing, can we say anything specific about how this revolutionizing is effected? Do we know enough about the theater to discern and describe a *structure* in the ceaseless process of revolutionizing by which it is constituted as itself in modern social and cultural reality? It is true, in any event, that in the instances examined in this book so far, the emancipatory or antihermeneutic move is accomplished perhaps by stretching established theatrical conventions but never by utterly overturning them. We recognized the significance of theatrical "alienation" for Brecht but also its limitations; and we saw that in *Leben des Galilei* a simple thematic and structural attentiveness to problems of writing does much more than any acting techniques to position the play disruptively with respect to literature and history. Similarly, in *Frühlings Erwachen* and *Murder in the Cathedral*, the choice of subject matter, plus a few audience-orienting devices in structure and dialogue, are alone sufficient to bring into operation the absence of the fictional subject and thereby to recover the whole of what strikes us as an original tragic tension between theater and poetry. In Büchner's texts the game of theater within theater suggests a hermeneutically absurd performance situation, which in turn, I suppose, must to an extent infect any actual theater in which the plays are given. In Hofmannsthal the mere quality of adaptation, as in Shaw the mere existence of supplemental texts, sets in motion the revolutionary theatrical process. And in Beckett and Genet, finally, the bodies of the actors are crucial, not by somehow miraculously escaping the web of textual meanings but precisely by not being able to escape and so forcing the text to expose its own fundamental defectiveness, its morbid need of just those bodies.

What makes Beckett and Genet limiting cases, however, is the clarity with which their work suggests that we have arrived at an absolute end, at the finish of a long *history* of dramatic and theatrical forms—although this history is imagined differently in the two cases. For Beckett, it is the history of separation between the meaning of the text and that of the play, that separation which, at least as early as Diderot, is reckoned necessary in order to make available to an audience the strictly unthinkable (textually nonformulable) truth concerning the theatrical constructedness of all identity. By the time we get to Beckett, this truth—which had begun by belonging exclusively to the play, as that which is shadowed forth by the *simple fact* of performance—has contaminated the text to the point of becoming the text's whole content, whereupon the play, or the simple living body of the actor, is left only with the function of signifying the continued unattainability of that truth, our exclusion even from the domain of our own fully textualized understanding. The living human body on the stage before us is no longer a cryptic window into truth, but merely a token of our entrapment in an identity that excludes us from truth.

In Genet, by contrast, the work's implied prehistory is enacted in the work itself, in the form of a stylized struggle between its textual and material components, a struggle in which precisely the historically definitive victory of the textual, which takes place before us, endows the material component (especially the human body) with its own ineradicable identity *on the textual plane*, as the vanquished Other by which textuality knows or encompasses or textualizes *itself*, so that its victory is also permanently undone, subject to permanent subversion or revolution. (The victory of the material component, if one can even imagine such a thing, would have had no comparable effect, since knowledge or definition has no part in constituting materiality. The simple victory of the material would be equivalent to a mere supervention of Nothingness.)

But in both cases, again, the suggestion of history's having reached a kind of terminus raises the question, what next? Drama, I have argued, is inherently revolutionary and always has been, although its revolutionary quality probably has a greatly increased political dimension in the present age of "literature." And it is a measure of the extent to which this thesis is silently acknowledged to be valid that in the wake of such authors as Beckett and Genet, many critics and practitioners envisage a revolutionary dismantling of the very constitution of theatrical drama, which generally means freeing "theater" from the restrictions of "drama," developing new forms of theater that leave all semblance of drama behind. But is there really any such thing as theater without drama?

Or, to put this question in the terms in which it is most frequently asked, given the development of quasi-theatrical "media"—cinema, radio, television, internet—which burst open the architectural and social forms of the traditional theater: have the traditional narrative or representational procedures of that theater not been rendered obsolete, so that "theater" must now be redefined from the ground up? And are those obsolete narrative and representational procedures really constitutive of "drama"? Interestingly enough, Genet himself takes a position on this question in his prose piece "L'étrange mot d' . . .," where, having paralleled the changed situation of the theater after the arrival of cinema and television to the changed situation of painting after the invention of photography, he continues:

> For as long as we have known the theater, it seems that in addition to its essential function, each play has been stuffed with matters that concern politics, religion, morality or whatever, and transform the dramatic action into a didactic device.
>
> Perhaps—I shall always say perhaps, for I am a man, and one man alone—perhaps cinema and television will do better at filling an educative function. Then the theater will be emptied, perhaps cleansed, of what had congested it, and perhaps then it will be able to grow radiant with its own unique virtue or virtues—which is, or which are, perhaps still to be discovered.[1]

Just as the effect of photography is not to create new tasks for painting but rather to strip away some of its older representational function, thus permitting it to concentrate better on what is truly proper to it, so also in the case of theater the appropriation of narrative and representational functions by the electric and electronic media, which can do such things better, even in thus reducing theater's possibilities, actually *focuses* the theater more tightly upon "its own unique virtue or virtues" (sa ou . . . ses seules vertus).

Therefore, for Genet at least, the educative function—which I have called, from a different angle, the narrative or representational function— does not belong to "drama" at all but even in the preelectric or dramatic theater is a strictly nonessential element (the element, I suppose, that produces the "novelized" drama against which Artaud and Brecht rebel). It follows from this view—or is presupposed by it—that "drama" and "theater" are indissolubly linked, hence that any theater that pretends to leave drama behind is no longer really theater. It does not follow that the theater may not make use of electric or electronic devices. But theater must also maintain its essential link with drama—not "drama" as defined by some idea of narrated action but drama (if the argument of the previous chapter holds) as an antihermeneutics, operating by way of a particular type of tension between language and the actual human body. And this strict yoking of drama and theater, in turn, implies limits, therefore a kind of discernible shape, for theater as a revolutionary initiative. Can we give historical substance to these ideas? Can we establish theoretical criteria for discussing their validity?

"Postdramatic Theater"

At various times in the nineteenth and twentieth centuries, attempts were made to rescue drama from theater, to establish the concept of drama in such a way that the connection with an actual theater was not necessarily implied. In chapter 1, on Aristotle, I discussed one such attempt by Gerald F. Else. But if drama could be successfully detached from theater, it would become, thereby, nothing but a literary genre. The notion and the operation of genre would then no longer be disrupted by drama as a constant nagging incongruity, and the politically conservative tendency of literature would be much strengthened. It is practically certain, I think, that a sense of this danger played a part in motivating the modern dramatic renaissance, the renewal of theatrical drama as a form of high literature, in the late nineteenth and early twentieth centuries.

But again, what next? Once the energy of the modern dramatic renaissance has used itself up, once we get to the end of the line—in Beckett and Genet, or perhaps as early as the last, cryptic plays of Pirandello, or in Dürrenmatt, who several times stages the end of the world—what is the next step forward? Has it perhaps come time to reverse the older, failed remedy and now seek to rescue theater from drama, to rescue sheer performance from the shackles of the literary text? Is it now time to realize literally the idea of absolute or intransitive acting which in Hofmannsthal, paradoxically, arises as a consequence of textual dynamics? If the antihermeneutic or revolutionary move is achieved, as it appears to be, in the constitution of what I have called "performance space," then what has happened to the literary aspect of drama? Is the fundamentally illogical or hypocritical complexity of literature now anything more than a distraction from the inherent political aim of pure performance?

Does it make sense, in other words, to speak of a "postdramatic theater"? This phrase is the title of a book by Hans-Thies Lehmann, which I use as a summary of the best existing affirmative thought on the matter. Lehmann sets forth his basic historical view as follows:

> Certainly the partisans of theatrical revolt [in the period around 1900] break with everything they perceive as traditional, but even in turning toward abstract and alienating stage techniques, they also hang onto the idea of imitation of an action in the theater. Since the late 1970s, by contrast, in the course of the spread and eventual ubiquity of the *media* in everyday life, a new form of theatrical discourse, taking many different shapes, has arisen, which is here called *post-dramatic theater*. This does not imply a denial of the pioneering historical significance of the revolution in art and theater around 1900. . . . The formal idioms that were developed in the wake of the turn-of-the-century avant-garde become, in postdramatic theater, an arsenal of expressive gestures which offers a response, on the part of theater, to a mode of social communication that has been changed under a now universalized information technology.[2]

The idea that "imitation of an action" is an essential feature of drama—I have argued—is already as obsolete for Diderot as it is later for Genet. The same is true of the idea that drama represents "a fictive cosmos . . . whose closure is guaranteed by the drama and its theatrical aesthetics" (Lehmann, p. 44). But Lehmann does not really need these ideas, for he makes another suggestion that is much stronger: that a new form of theater is required in order to respond to profoundly altered conditions of communication in present-day society. I have suggested, it is true, that the very "postulate of communication" is already part of what is denied or circumvented in the dramatic theater. But perhaps it is only terminology that causes a disagreement here; perhaps "communication" as effected by postdramatic theater is no longer communication in the sense of literary hermeneutics.

Lehmann, in any case, summarizes a great deal of material, not all of which is equally useful for defining the postdramatic. The "'dethroning' of the linguistic sign" (p. 161), for example—in a sense broader than just the "depsychologizing" Lehmann speaks of—is already implied in the transition from hermeneutic space to performance space, as discussed in chapter 8. For "the undeniability of meaning and understanding," which characterizes hermeneutic space, is only another way of naming the supposedly unique transparency of the linguistic sign ("Being that can be understood is language," says Gadamer), the special unhesitating assurance with which the word points beyond itself. And that undeniability no longer obtains in performance space.[3] The dethroning of language, moreover, is related in a fairly obvious way to the nonsemiotic prominence of the strictly real in the theater—also discussed in chapter 8 under "The Materiality of Performance"—for which Lehmann has a very elegant formulation: "It is inherent in the very constitution of the theater that the strictly real, which is literally outplayed or covered up ['überspielt,' which plays on 'spielen,' 'to put on a play, to act'] by theatrical illusion, can always reemerge as itself at any time" (p. 175). This—that the real things (including people) on the stage are always in danger of bursting their semiotic shackles—is true of *all* theater. But Lehmann insists, "Not the presence of the 'real' as such, but rather its *self-reflexive* use characterizes the aesthetics of postdramatic theater" (p. 176). If this means, as I think it must, that postdramatic theater distinguishes itself by contriving to *acknowledge* (to call to our attention) the realness of its signs, then the result is a problem. For such acknowledgment must inevitably resemioticize exactly the supposed realness that it indicates (or "means")—it makes realness itself into a meaning—and must therefore end by subjecting the performance *more completely* to linguistic hegemony than classical drama does. Self-reflection, after all, does not happen except in the medium of language.[4]

But Lehmann does provide a very useful formulation. Postdramatic theater, he suggests, is characterized by a collapse of all belief in the "collectivity" traditionally implied by aesthetics, a collapse so complete that it produces a "solipsistic" tendency in spectators: "Therefore, if the new theater wishes to go beyond the strictly uncommitted and private, it must seek new paths toward supraindividual points of contact. It finds these in the theatrical realization of freedom—freedom from subordination to hierarchies, freedom from the need for perfection, freedom from the requirement of coherence" (p. 141). What had once been an audience collectivity, grounded in the more or less unified expressiveness of the work, is now replaced by "a community of disparate, singular imaginations" of people whose "individual perspectives do not combine into a larger whole" (p. 142).

This is a very profound idea: a community or collectivity not grounded in any particular thing or thought or feeling that its members have in common—or even believe or imagine they have in common. But Lehmann makes of it a convincing idea, mainly by way of the media-theoretical notion, common at least since Marshall McLuhan, of information density, of high or low definition.

> In post-dramatic theater, the rule is that the conventionalized rule and more or less established *norm of semiotic density* is violated. There are either too many signs, or too few. In relation to the time or space involved, or to the importance of the subject matter, the observer detects an overabundance, or else a noticeable thinning out, of signs. (p. 151)

And in both cases it becomes impossible for the observer to grasp the work as a whole, as a complete shape or "Gestalt." "There are two limits to *Gestalt*: the wasteland of sheer vast extension and the labyrinth or chaos of excess accumulation. *Gestalt* is the mean between these extremes" (p. 154). The extreme of excess shows itself mainly in the guise of simultaneity, the three-ring-circus-like juxtaposition of actions that have nothing special to do with each other.

> If one asks after the intent and effect of simultaneity, one recognizes: *the fragment character of perception* is made into an unavoidable experience. If understanding is already deprived of its usual foothold in the large connections that make an action, now even the instantaneously perceived happenings escape any synthesis when they happen simultaneously, and our concentration on one makes it impossible to register the others clearly. Moreover, when material is presented simultaneously, it is often undecidable whether the elements are related or simply happen to appear at the same time. (p. 150)

The spectator therefore recognizes that his or her view of the work is radically idiosyncratic and accidental (depending on which fragments he or she has registered, and how), hence likely to have little, if anything, in common with the views of other spectators. And the same is true when the work is characterized by semiotic *sparsity*.

> Postdramatic theater, in the face of the semiotic bombardment of everyday
> life, works with a strategy of refusal. It practices a recognizably ascetic
> thriftiness in the use of signs, it stresses a *formalism* that reduces the abun-
> dance of signs by repetition and drawing out, and it shows an inclination
> toward *graphism* and script, which seems a defense against visual opulence
> and redundancy. . . . This playing with a reduced density of signs is aimed
> at the spectator's own activity, which, given the very scant material it is
> offered, is meant to become productive in its own right. (p. 153)

Again, the spectator's view of the work is radically idiosyncratic and accidental because it is mainly his or her own production, created to fill uncomfortable gaps in the sign system offered by the work itself.

But in either case, when there is too much semiotic material or when
there is too little, the basic condition of a community or collectivity is still
fulfilled. We have still assembled at one place at one time for the purpose of
putting ourselves in a relation to one work. Thus Lehmann's idea of "a
community of disparate, singular imaginations"—which we now take to
mean a community of people whose imaginative grasp of the work that
joins them is, in each individual case, radically idiosyncratic and accidental,
and is known (in each case) to be so—makes perfectly good sense on its
own terms. Here, then, if anywhere—provided the idea can be justified
empirically and politically (in accordance with the basic revolutionary
character of theater)—we can speak of "postdramatic theater."

Theater and Media

It appears that postdramatic theater must meet at least two criteria. It must
be understandable as a response to *unprecedented* conditions of communication in the age of electronic mass media. And its effect must be the creation
of a community of *disparate* imaginations, achieved by way of the strict
inaccessibility of exactly that "work" that furnishes (nonetheless) a communal ground. The strict inaccessibility of the work, in turn, is what differenti-
ates this theater from the dramatic theater, where—even if it should be very
difficult to absorb the whole work at a single performance—the work is still
available for independent study (thus accessible) in the form of a text that is
presumed to imply all its authentic expressive possibilities.

On the question of the relation of theater to media, the basic structure of
Lehmann's thought appears to agree with Genet's:

> Drama and illusion, as a dominant feature, are transferred to the media,
> whereas the actuality of performance becomes the new dominant feature of
> theater. It becomes clear that the opportunity for postdramatic theater lies
> not in the imitation of media aesthetics, not in simulation, but in *the real and
> our reflection upon it*. As an "image-machine," theater's ability to reproduce

reality, however it may be enhanced, is radically limited. As "direct address," on the other hand, theater sets in motion an irreplaceable process that also permits it to disregard and overstep the limits exhibited by film and media. (Lehmann, p. 409)

And borrowing an idea from Heiner Müller, Lehmann understands the theater's "direct address" as a form of human contact on the level of "mortality" (p. 410)—one thinks also of Genet, on the theater and the cemetery (4:9–10, 14)—by contrast with the "hiatus of mathematicizing" in the media, which interrupts any contact among mortal "subjectivities."

The difference from Genet is that for Lehmann, the appropriation by media of the theater's narrative and representational functions removes from the theater what used to be "drama," whereas for Genet, the new theater of the media age—the postnarrative theater—*retains* precisely its true dramatic character: "Le drame: c'est-à-dire l'acte théâtral au moment de sa représentation" (4:13: drama, that is, the theatrical act at the moment of its presentation). The narrative and representational theater-functions that are appropriated by media—assuming, as above, that these are the functions Genet sees as "didactic"—were never really dramatic in the first place; and the future of the theater, for Genet, must accordingly still be sought by *writers*, "les écrivains de théâtre" (4:12).

But these two views, as represented by Lehmann and Genet, are still similar enough to raise the same general question: why does the theater *need* to be stripped of the functions that are assumed by electronic media? In most theater, in fact, those functions are not discarded. The "novelized" theater, or theater as an edifying staged narrative, lives on happily as if there had never been a Brecht, an Artaud, a Genet or Beckett or Lehmann or Robert Wilson, and is not troubled in the least by the superior representational capability of the media, any more than classical music is troubled by the demonstrably greater generational impact of rock. The statement, in other words, that theater in the media age loses its narrative and representational functions names not a fact but a judgment about what contemporary theater *should* do. And in Genet's case, the content of this judgment is fairly clear: the advent of electronic media presents theater (in a sense that is not distinguished from "drama") with an opportunity to purify itself, to rid itself of its externally imposed, "novelized" nineteenth-century character and to become fully and unadulteratedly—perhaps to become *again*, as a vehicle of "myth" (Genet, 4:12)—what it *is* in truth. Genet's project is thus basically an extension of Brecht's and Artaud's.

For Lehmann, and for the theoreticians and practitioners whom I take Lehmann's argument to represent, the necessity of nonrepresentation in contemporary theater is based on an entirely different judgment. What matters here is not the historically grounded and evolved nature of the theater but rather its communicative efficacy in an age dominated by electronic media. And although Lehmann has a great many sources for his idea of how the communicative problem that theater faces is constituted, I think it will be sufficient for present purposes to cite only one of the authors he refers to repeatedly. He is deeply concerned, namely, by Jean-François Lyotard's description of "the postmodern condition": "We may . . . expect a thorough exteriorization of knowledge with respect to the 'knower,' at whatever point he or she may occupy in the knowledge process. The old principle that the acquisition of knowledge is indissociable from the training *(Bildung)* of minds, or even of individuals, is becoming obsolete and will become ever more so."[5]

On this view, the theater as we usually imagine it, as a place where individuals not only enjoy things that happen in their actual physical presence but also learn from those happenings, is obviously subject to the same obsolescence as "Bildung," which means that the whole institution of theater is in danger if it does not change radically. "Those who refuse to reexamine the rules of art pursue successful careers in mass conformism, by communicating, by means of the 'correct rules,' the endemic desire for reality with objects and situations capable of gratifying it" (Lyotard, p. 75).[6] And in order to avoid such "conformism," to communicate on a level that might make a difference historically, it is clear that theater must abandon its narrative and representational ambitions. "Simplifying to the extreme," says Lyotard, "I define *postmodern* as incredulity toward metanarratives" (p. xxiv). But every fictional narrative, in drama or otherwise, is the sign of a metanarrative, a large narrative of legitimation for knowledge and social forms; otherwise, we would dismiss it as empty of literary meaning. Cohesive fictional narrative as such must therefore be dispensed with; theater, for the sake of communication, must now buy into Lyotard's project: "Let us wage a war on totality; let us be witnesses to the unpresentable; let us activate the differences" (p. 82). What could be meant here by "us" if not a "community of disparate imaginations," based on an acceptance of "the fragment character of perception"?

But once postdramatic theater has established a communicative relation with its public, its posture vis-à-vis the postmodern, and especially the media, turns *adversarial*:

> The new technologies and media become, in startling quantum leaps, more and more "immaterial"—"Les Immatériaux" is the name of an exhibition organized by Jean-François Lyotard in 1985 in Paris. Theater, by contrast, is characterized in a special way by "materiality of communication." . . . Theater is a site not only of heavy *bodies* but also of *real social gathering*, where a unique intersection of aesthetically organized life and everyday real life happens. Here, by contrast with all the arts that produce objects and all the

arts that work by way of the media, both the aesthetic act itself (the playing) and the act of reception (theatergoing) take place together as a real
activity here and now. (Lehmann, p. 12)

This difference between theater and media, however, is also a tension and a
danger:

> What must worry the theater is the apparent transition to a form (at pres-
> ent, in content and technology, still primitive) of *interaction* among partners
> distant from each other by technological means. Will such ever further per-
> fected interaction threaten to invade and occupy what is now the domain
> of the theatrical live arts, whose principle is *participation*? (p. 408)

For the time being, says Lehmann, participation still seems to be holding its
own against interaction; "this seemingly almost old-fashioned institution
[the theater], with surprising stability, still makes a place for itself in society
and alongside the technically advanced media" (p. 12). But will this necessarily continue to be the case?

Theater versus Media: Reality, Reflection, and Freedom

Lehmann himself, in his argument, along with the theoreticians and practitioners I take him to represent, is thus obliged to maintain a precarious balance. On one hand, the theater must adapt itself to an audience whose
beliefs and communicative habits are conditioned strongly by electronic
media. On the other hand, it must bring to bear, in the minds of a roomful of
habituated screen-watchers, the quality of the strictly real, of physical and
social immediacy, of the here-and-now, by which it distinguishes itself from
experience in an electronically mediated form. I say "bring to bear" for want
of a better term. In any case, it is clearly not enough for the theater simply to
be real; it is not enough that we simply find ourselves sitting with others in
the same room watching the same performers. The realness of these elements of our theater experience must also be structured and positioned in a
manner that marks it emphatically as alien to our media-conditioned sensibilities. The raw material of reality is constantly reprocessed by the media
anyway, and this reprocessing is something we are perfectly capable of
internalizing and carrying out for ourselves even when the power is off.
Watch—for instance—*Dateline* and tell me that most of the interviewees are
not experiencing their own real suffering as a kind of TV show.

  More than merely the realness of the theater is needed, therefore, and
Lehmann describes that "more" very eloquently:

> A figure steps out onto the stage. It interests us, because the frame of the
> stage, of the staging, of the action, of the scene's visual constellation, displays

it. The peculiar tension with which it is observed is a form of curiosity grown into the craving ["Neu-gier"] for an explanation that is both imminent and withheld. . . . The figure, in its very presence, is nevertheless—absent. Or should we say: virtual? It remains *theatrical* only in the rhythm and measure of an uncertainty that restricts our perception to the form of a seeking. The dimension of not-knowing in theatrical perception—every figure is an oracle—produces its constitutive virtuality. (pp. 442–43)

And with a final invocation of Lyotard, Lehmann makes clear that this other "virtuality," of the theater, this hesitant, uncertain, unsatisfied relation of spectator to image, is how theater resists the dominance of media:

Lyotard determined in 1979, in "La condition postmoderne," that everything that cannot take the form of information, under the conditions imposed by universalized communications technologies, will be dropped from the knowledge of society. This fate could befall the theater, for "theater," in the emphatic and ideal sense in which we are discussing it, in fact transforms, contrariwise, all information into something else, into virtuality. (p. 446)

The theater is still in danger, but its danger is now at least understood as attendant upon its offer of a positive alternative to the world of media representations.

Lehmann suggests, to be sure, that the mere realness of the theater is enough to produce this effect. "Theater-bodies, since they are only 'there' in their interbodiliness ["Zwischen-den-Körpern"], are not containable in any video" (p. 441). But he himself, in a passage we have already looked at, names the ingredient without which realness never becomes theatrical in the first place: "the opportunity for postdramatic theater lies . . . in *the real and our reflection upon it*" (p. 409). Not even the "absolutized body" (p. 164) can operate theatrically without "reflection, which cannot be excluded even by the denial of meaning that theater's presentness entails" (p. 165). And without reflection on our part, we could not possibly experience the "freedom" that constitutes those new "points of contact" by which theater produces a community to resist the threatening "solipsism" (p. 141) of the present age.

Not only the theater's realness but also our reflection upon it is required. Indeed, a particular *kind* of reflection is required of us—not the mere "ah! and oh!" of casual observers (Lehmann, p. 165) but a reflection including sufficient critical sophistication to color our theatrical experience with unsatisfaction or "virtuality." And how, we must ask, is this special kind of reflection going to be enforced, or at least suggested to an audience? How else but by way of some sort of explicit or implied guiding narrative, which is to say in the form of a recognizably *literary meaning*? And what is theater conjoined with literary meaning if not *drama*? Does it follow that postdramatic theater, in order to be precisely what it is, must become dramatic theater all over again?

Talking about Talking about Robert Wilson

This argument does not, by itself, discredit the idea of a postdramatic theater. But it does uncover a paradox in that idea, and it therefore suggests that the concept of "reflection" is too vague, too intangible, to ground a discussion of the exact difference between the operation of theater and the operation of media with respect to the large unfolding of cultural history. This concept appeared to be called for because the theater's strict realness, taken by itself, is not something that can operate in history without first being processed, without being given some form of communicable extension beyond the few moments in which we happen to apprehend it directly. And my suggestion is that a more useful way of dealing with this problem is by way of the concept of *public discussion*. We have, it is true, an ingrained aversion toward speaking of "the work of art" and its public discussion in the same breath, especially if we allow the latter to influence our understanding of the former. But in both principal aspects of the situation I am now discussing, in the history of drama as a fundamentally defective form and in modern civilization as influenced by mass media, the idea of the aesthetic integrity and sanctity of the work of art has long been discredited anyway. And public discussion, after all, is the only relatively objective sign we have of what actually happens in our "reflection" on art.

The public discussion of contemporary theater is an unmanageably broad field, however, and I propose therefore to concentrate on the public discussion of a single artist, Robert Wilson, for two reasons. First, although Wilson definitely belongs to postdramatic theater in Lehmann's sense—his work being characterized, very strikingly, by both the overabundance of signs (simultaneous unrelated actions) and the sparsity of signs (slow motion, minimalism) which prevent "the work" from becoming available—he is still positioned relatively close to the border with dramatic theater; his activity is still primarily directorial and does not yet involve, for instance, a radical architectural or social undoing of the traditional theatrical situation. Therefore, he represents a useful case for understanding the exact nature of that border. And second, just as Lehmann's book enabled me to summarize concisely the theory of postdramatic theater, so also, in Wilson's case, we can reasonably take a single book, by Stefan Brecht, to represent the large public discussion.

Brecht's *The Theatre of Visions: Robert Wilson*, is clearly a work of criticism. It opens with a definition:

Theatre of visions is the staging, with live performers, movements and development in such a fashion as to appear a world or reality or the representation of one by an individual of images occurring to that individual and seeming personally important and significant to him (or her) independently of verbal, intellectual or discursive analysis,—meaningful, but quite possibly the unique significations of their meaning.[7]

It then develops this definition into the idea of a "right-brain dominated theatre" (p. 10). It describes Wilson's own development in relation to this guiding idea: "As Wilson's theatre [19]69–73 can be thought of as the subdominant hemisphere's coup d'état, a theatre of and for the left hand's brain, so his theatre [19]74ff. can be thought of as the right brain's attempt to annex the province of speech" (p. 265). And it arrives at a judgment: "Wilson's attempt to incorporate speech independently of its syntactic and semantic essence into his theatre of visions destroyed it" (p. 267). Wilson, in the end, is "a man of integrity and daring, and a genius, desperately . . . attempting to transcend the limitations of his achievements" (p. 384).

This basic expository plan is filled out with a great deal of subordinate material, including very detailed descriptions of many of the minor and major pieces up to *I was sitting on my patio this guy appeared I thought I was hallucinating*, plus a whole second book's worth of footnotes containing writings of Wilson himself, of associates, reporters, interviewers, critics, and of Stefan Brecht, the commenting author of the whole thing. The curious point about this many-layered structure, however, is how tenuous, insubstantial, often simply nonexistent are the connections out of which it is built.

In the long section on *Deafman Glance*, for example (pp. 54–140), which goes through the whole piece three times, describing and summarizing what happens in enormous detail, then commenting and theorizing, there is no real attempt to elaborate or apply the notion of "right-brain dominated theatre." Most of this section, even when it is closest to being pure description, reads very much like all the art and literature criticism we had gotten used to long before Robert Wilson, covering the whole spectrum from conceptually tidy interpretations of single motifs to dizzying psychological speculations on audience response. Brecht even defends this critical-interpretive approach in a footnote:

Wilson would pretend that his plays have no meaning, or that, at any rate, he does not intend them to have any; at least that whatever meanings they have for him, does not guide his work on them, or at the very least, is not what he aims to put across by them. . . . This pretense informs not only his interviews but his plays. Naturally, as in all art, the meaning is metaphorical [the actual text here has "metamorphorical"]: analogic rather than iconic or abstractively analytic. A man would have to be an idiot to put work into art that didn't make sense to him. (p. 83)

The vehement and tortured prose here, I think, shows Brecht's embarrassment, and thence his awareness of the difficult situation he has gotten himself into. By the mere act of writing about Wilson, he has positioned himself as a seeker of meaning (of sense, order, system, syntax), which clashes with his original claim to treat right-brain theater.

Even the discussion of *Einstein on the Beach*—which opens (pp. 316–59) with a minute-by-minute description of the entire piece (visual and verbal aspects in roman type, musical in italic, exact times of day on 28 November 1976 in the margin)—shows the same lack of a relation between specific perceptions and general argument. Here, where in Brecht's view the "theatre of visions" is collapsing under the stress of an enforced inappropriate combination with language, one expects that the possibility of a critical bridge, in language, between the specific and the general might arise. But Brecht's most general point about *Einstein* is that "Wilson failed to find images for what was on his mind. The themes he hit on do not relate to the content. He changed his style to divorce the spectacle from its content. Watching it, we see the meaningless alternation of meaningless themes, and perhaps the theme of failure" (p. 375). And there is no connection whatever with the overall argument that "language poses a problem for such theatre . . . because it is the form and instrument of definite denotation and of judgment,—of specific signification and commitment to it" (p. 267).

Language, therefore, is not the issue here; the involvement or noninvolvement of language in the theater pieces under discussion is not what determines the extent of disjunction between specific perceptions and general argument. In order to understand what happens in writing like Brecht's on Wilson, I think we have to go back to Lehmann's question concerning the availability of "the work," as a whole, to its spectators. If a direct logical connection could be made between (1) an argument placing the theater piece in a large theoretical or historical context and (2) the interpretation of particular, relatively small segments of the piece, then that connection would serve as a guide by which the spectator might achieve a grasp of the whole work after all, starting from what is offered to his or her perception. Brecht is thus simply doing the best he can; it is (or at least might as well be) a scrupulous attentiveness to the type of artistic situation he is dealing with (as Lehmann would describe it) that keeps him from making the illegitimate conceptual leaps that would be needed to unify his critical position. (Most writers on recent theater in fact drop the pretense of large theoretical argument altogether and present mainly anecdotes and essays, as does Gordon Rogoff's *Vanishing Acts*. And theoretical writers like Herbert Blau generally find ways of exhibiting the details of particular pieces without getting tangled up in their interpretation.)[8]

But then, one might ask, why attempt an argument like Brecht's on Wilson in the first place? Why not leave out the theoretical dimension and concentrate on describing what actually happens in the theater, so as to preserve as much as possible of the realness of that happening in an intellectual medium where it can then be subjected to "reflection"?

Here again we are brought back to Lehmann and to the concept of a "community of disparate [thus free] imaginations," without which the whole idea of postdramatic theater does not make much sense. I have already remarked upon two important consequences of this concept. First, the community it names is not grounded in any particular thing or thought that its members have in common; second, that community must nevertheless be grounded in something beyond the mere physical proximity of its members. And it is fairly clear that that something which grounds or defines the community has to be, in some sense, "the work" that is performed. But "the work," by definition (the definition of postdramatic theater), is not accessible to the spectators as spectators, hence cannot be understood as prior to their spectating and must therefore first be *constituted* by their community, which can happen nowhere except in the piece's public discussion. And that discussion, in turn (like Brecht on Wilson), *must* therefore aim, explicitly or implicitly, at a theoretical or historical contextualizing of "the work" as a whole, even while (like Brecht on Wilson) necessarily failing to establish a connection with the details of audience experience. For only thus does the public discussion itself in effect *become* "the work," at least in a strong enough sense to ground the community of its participants.

Public Discussion and the Work: Hermeneutic Space Revisited

The foregoing argument is simple but important, and its necessity needs to be understood clearly. First, to say that the work is not accessible to the audience in postdramatic theater is not to say that the work does not exist. I pointed out in the previous chapter that every conceivable action or happening that is recognized as a "performance" must be based at some level on a "text" or program, even if this text is imagined as arising only in the course of the performance. The "text" that is in this sense necessarily present is what I have called, in this chapter, "the work," in order to avoid confusion with the idea of a piece of writing that governs the theatrical proceeding. Second, that the work is inaccessible to the audience, therefore, means, more precisely, that its *content* is inaccessible, its quiddity, although its existence is known. Indeed, there is no guarantee that the particular sense impressions that affect a spectator most strongly in a performance actually belong to that content; they could just as well be accidents that no one will ever again associate with this particular work. Third, the work extends beyond the performance; its existence does not end with that of any performance or group of performances. This means simply that "the work" names that aspect of the theater piece's existence by virtue of which we can even begin to speak about it in a general historical or theoretical context. Fourth, the content of the work—since, in effect, it does not exist in the immediacy of performance and could not exist "before" the performance without becoming accessible to at least some spectators—is received by the work only "after" the performance. I put the words "before" and "after" in quotation marks because I am not referring to actual chronology, where of course there is a single space of time that is both after today's performance and before tomorrow's. The point is that no matter how much one seems to know about the work before attending a performance, one is not enabled thereby to make a satisfying connection between what one knows and what one then sees in the theater—for the same reason as that which explains the disjunction between specific interpretations and general argument in Brecht on Wilson. But then, fifth, where can we locate the work's content in the realm of the postperformance? In the mind or memory of the individual spectator? This is precisely where we began by stipulating that the work does *not* achieve its content. Hence the metaphor of *the work as an empty wavelength for its own public discussion.* Only public discussion can give the work its content in a form that surpasses individual spectatorial idiosyncrasy, a form that may, so to speak, be broadcast to the world, exposed to history and theory.

It follows from this argument that in a theater like Wilson's, the work is uncontrollably mutable, subject utterly to the vagaries of public discussion. There is no guarantee—indeed, there is no reasonable expectation—that the work will be tomorrow what is it today. Precisely those works that prove most significant, in the sense of attracting most strongly our interest and response, are also therefore the most discussed, hence the most elusive, the most difficult to pin down, which in turn probably reinforces our sense of their significance. Obviously, there is much to be said about this system of evaluation; but most important for now is that it poses no problems for hermeneutics; it offers no resistance to the operation of hermeneutic space as defined in the preceding chapter. Hermeneutic space, we recall, is constituted by a refusal to accept category distinctions among such concepts as "text," "interpretation," "understanding"; the collapse of the distinction between the work and its public discussion fits here perfectly.

In fact, Wilson's theater furnishes a kind of ideal case—an instance verging on parody—of the process Gadamer calls "fusion of horizons."[9] Public discussion, at any given time, represents Gadamer's "horizon of the present," the complex of historical and theoretical prejudices that necessarily limit our approach to the work, it being understood that this horizon is constantly changing—as one "present" gives way to another—and is assumed to be distinct from that second intellectual horizon within which the work, as an event, was somehow originally itself. Gadamer's argument is that these two horizons, which are kept separate (in "das Spannungsverhältnis zwischen Text und Gegenwart") by the same interpretive project that seeks to bridge their separation, are always nevertheless historically related on a level sufficiently deep that their "fusion" is available to be articulated hermeneutically as "understanding," as the *success* of that interpretive project. And in Wilson's theater, this complicated philosophical speculation appears as a simple fact of experience, since here the public discussion, quite simply, *cannot be mistaken* about the work, of which that discussion itself is the content, the broadcast message. The discussion can of course, so to speak, change its mind, but it cannot be wrong—any more than a valid understanding of the past can fail to be available, in Gadamer's view.

But the main point of the preceding chapter was that the revolutionary quality of theatrical drama, its opposition to the conservative tendency in literature, can be understood in terms of its *resistance* to inclusion in hermeneutic space, a resistance that has to do mainly with the living bodily materiality of the theater. And surely, one would think, this resistance must be even stronger in Wilson's theater, or in other postdramatic theaters, which are much more exclusively "theatrical," much more fully contained in the here-and-now of performance, than drama is. In fact, however, exactly the opposite is the case.

The simple materiality of objects used in the theater is inconsequential in itself, for it is, so to speak, dissolved in the medium of hermeneutic space. Merely by being placed prominently before an audience, the material object becomes a sign, becomes semiotically translucent, loses the full opacity of material substance. (This is what Lehmann calls the "virtuality" of objects in the theater.) The object operates *as* material (and so interferes with the operation of hermeneutic space) only if its materiality is somehow profiled for the audience, somehow thrown into relief. As I pointed out, in chapter 8, this happens principally in the *dramatic* theater, in a theater whose every image and action is understood to be governed by a single literary text, even if we, personally, happen never to have read that text, or even if the director has "taken liberties" with it—liberties that are still, after all, readings of the text in question.

For in the dramatic theater, when a hatrack or a crown or a person is placed before us, we understand that that thing represents not merely "an" object, but *the* object meant by the text. We know that the function of words in a literary text is mainly to evoke or call forth a kind of reality, to *bring into being*, for our imagination, objects and people and situations, as the words of Kleist's Penthesilea literally bring into being the dagger she kills herself with. In the dramatic theater, therefore, the object on stage must obviously stand for *the* corresponding object engendered by the text. But it is equally obvious that the object on the stage is *not* a simple product of poetic imagination; it is not *the* object evoked by the text, but merely *an* object, a prop or an actor, that could easily be replaced by another similar object. And this latter quality of the theatrical object, which is profiled, brought into focus for us, by contrast with its literary aspect, is precisely its immediate material presence here and now. Objects in the dramatic theater, therefore, are *emphatically* material—in effect more operatively material, for instance, than objects in everyday life—and it is this emphatic materiality that clashes with the order of hermeneutic space. In postdramatic theater, however, such emphatic materiality is missing. The objects on stage are still signs, but they no longer have the radical *verbal* dimension that clashes with, and so profiles, their materiality. They are simply exposed to the corrosive atmosphere of hermeneutic space and no longer resist it.

The case of the living human body of the actor is similar. The actor's body—as I noted in the previous chapter—conflicts with the operation of hermeneutic space by being an arbitrarily self-modifying signifier, a signifier which can at any time simply abandon the semiotic order within which it has signified. This concept is of course valid for any theater, dramatic or otherwise. The actor is always in a position, if he or she wishes, to disrupt utterly the semiotic proceeding on the stage. The difference is that in the dramatic theater, this capability on the actor's part is a serious danger, whereas in postdramatic theater, in a strong sense, what the actor happens to do at any given point *makes no difference*, because—again, by definition—there is no clear connection for the spectator between the specific movements he or she sees on the stage and a large overall grasp of the work against which those specifics might be measured. Of course, it is never really likely that any actor, dramatic or otherwise, will do anything but what has been arranged beforehand. That the actor *could* deviate from the script, however, constitutes in drama a direct threat to the very presence of the work—that work which the spectator is encouraged to keep in view constantly and to connect with what happens on the stage—whereas in postdramatic theater the threat is far less serious (since the work is "not yet" there), and the actor, correspondingly, considered as a living human body, is far less emphatically present, far less an impediment to the operation of hermeneutic space.

Theatrical drama, finally, has the effect of opening what I have called "performance space," a semiotic state of affairs that has all the liberal or antidogmatic quality of hermeneutic space, while at the same time avoiding the inevitably conservative hermeneutic postulate of communicative efficacy, the postulated undeniability of meaning and understanding. In particular, performance space is opened by a category difference, an incommensurability, between the mode of existence of the dramatic text and the living bodily materiality of the performance in which we seek an interpretation. And although this difference may still obtain in postdramatic theater, it is certainly not as clearly marked, not as effective in a revolutionary sense, because here the text is less exclusively verbal and the performance (we have seen) less emphatically material or bodily. Moreover, the actual social institution in which the conservative character of hermeneutic space operates most directly and powerfully is the institution of *literature*, which is exactly where the dramatic theater (as itself a literary type) mounts its attack. Postdramatic theater, however, has done as much as possible to sever its connection with literature, which means that whatever revolutionary power it retains is misdirected or undirected. It is as if the mob in 1789 had stormed the Jardin des Plantes instead of the Bastille.

Theater and Its History: The Inevitability of Drama

It may seem arbitrary, on my part, if I now assert that postdramatic theater in the strict sense, as represented by early Robert Wilson, theater that succeeds in terminating absolutely its association with literature—assuming that such a theater is possible—is not really theater at all. It is of course easy to demonstrate that "all theater is revolutionary theater" if one simply excludes from the definition of theater everything (like postdramatic theater) that happens not to be revolutionary in its operation on an institutional level. But I make that assertion nonetheless, and I contend that it makes sense historically.

Long before there was theater, there were religious rituals and public ceremonies that probably looked more or less like theater, with certain principal figures performing prescribed actions in an open space before an audience. But generally, in the Western tradition, we do not regard as "theater" itself anything earlier than a specific sixth-century practice, in the neighborhood of Athens, whose invention is ascribed to Thespis. And I think it has been shown convincingly, as was set forth in chapter 2—especially in the book by Jennifer Wise from which I quoted—that this invention, the invention of theater, was entirely dependent for its possibility upon the prior invention of the *art of writing*, upon a condition of alphabetic literacy in the civilization that produced it.

My own contribution to this discussion, I hope, has been to show that that original bond with the art of writing has remained strong throughout the history of European theater, in the form of a bond with the art of poetry and then with poetry's successor art, "literature"; that that uncomfortable but indissoluble bond has exerted a very strong shaping (and distorting) influence upon our basic idea of poetic genres and their relations; and that even in the twentieth century the resulting unstable hybrid, which we still call by the Greek name "drama," has an important disruptive, subversive, revolutionary function within the otherwise conservative mechanism of literary history, where it sustains, practically single-handed, the possibility of emancipatory literary effects. I claim, on this basis, that to divorce theater from the art of writing is in truth, historically speaking, to divorce it from itself. Indeed, it is conceivable that this claim is not even necessary, that it is *impossible* to divorce theater from writing, that postdramatic theater in an absolute sense simply does not exist.

Let us look again at the case of Robert Wilson. If the foregoing argument holds, then the "work," for Wilson, still belongs to the domain of writing, in the form of public discussion, and the question is whether such "writing" can fill the place of the text in theatrical drama. In a purely structural sense, as I have said, public discussion comes "after" the performance; but in the real world the work's public discussion normally unfolds side by side with a continuing series of performances. And it is entirely possible to imagine that for an audience of participants in the discussion (at least passive participants, as readers), the prop on stage will be perceived, first of all, as *the* (well-known) object that figures in that discussion and will receive its emphatic materiality by contrast with this basically literary perception. It is entirely possible to imagine that the audience's sense of the play's writtenness (as discussion) will be sufficient to profile the actors as arbitrarily self-modifying signifiers. And to the extent that something like this actually happens, the revolutionary quality of the theater will have been restored, but only by way of the understanding that it is in truth a *dramatic* theater after all.

It is, in any case, no part of my business to comment on Robert Wilson's personal or professional politics, or on the actual political effect, short or long term, of his work. My concern is the inherent political character of specific artistic forms—not in the sense that this character is expressed every time the form is used (which would presuppose a necessary relation between form and "content," hence an ideal of artistic perfection and a hermeneutic focus on the work's meaning, hence a simple *exclusion* of the radically defective and antihermeneutic art of theatrical drama) but in the sense that the presence or absence of certain artistic forms in a particular discursive system is an indication of whether certain kinds of political attitude or action are even conceivable there. I have suggested, for example, that without its uncomfortable inclusion of theatrical drama, the institution of literature would be a strongly conservative force in Western politics, regardless of how many liberals or revolutionaries used it to express themselves, so that the very possibility of a "liberal imagination" is yoked to the existence of the theater.

The critical project thus formulated, however, the attempt to understand the inherent politics of artistic form, has a strong tendency to drift toward the abstract and requires therefore to be developed in relation to particular instances, as I have tried to do here in part 2. And it is with regard to particular instances, especially as these approach the contemporary, that the boundaries and distinctions suggested by theory become difficult to sustain.

Robert Wilson is certainly not a dramatist in the sense, say, that Genet is a dramatist. But it does not necessarily follow that what he produces is not drama. Indeed, from *the CIVILwarS* on, his work tends more and more in the direction of what can reasonably be called "adaptation," ranging from the wildly unconventional staging of complete plays and operas to the incorporation and recontextualizing of parts or scraps of existing works.[10] And I see no particular reason not to apply here the same theoretical considerations developed in chapter 6 about Hofmannsthal, which lead to the idea of a theater with no meaning and hence to a denial of meaning and an essentially dramatic attack on the founding postulate of hermeneutic space.

One could perhaps go even further and argue that the whole of Wilson's "theater of visions" is, from the beginning, a theater of adaptation. For the absence or obscurity of motivation in those visions—which every commentator insists upon—has as a consequence that no particular "vision" could ever even be identified as such without being referred to some model in an established artistic vocabulary, a model of which it would then operate as an adaptation. (This vocabulary of models is of course not restricted to the domain of high art, and necessarily has a *verbal* component, since it can arise only by valuation and selection.) In some cases, the model is simple and easily detected, the frequently occurring figure of Medea, for example. In other cases, we should probably have to name a number of models that contribute to a single's scene's identity, perhaps different models for different spectators. Of course, it is true in theory that these considerations apply equally well to the scenes in any traditional play. But if the scene is conventionally motivated, by its function in a plot or as a transparent topical reference, then its quality as adaptation is obscured, whereas this quality is profiled or foregrounded (even if one cannot, at the moment, name a specific model) when all expectable types of motivation are avoided, in Wilson's customary manner.

There are, then, at least two entirely incompatible ways of situating Robert Wilson—or, we might say, borderline postdramatic theater in general—with respect to the notion of revolutionary theater that I have developed in this book. Either (1) the absence of a governing text—hence the relegation of the "work" to the process of public discussion—dilutes the emphatic bodily materiality of the theater to the point where it no longer mounts a significant resistance to hermeneutics and so in effect ceases to be theater; or else (2) public discussion itself, as an evolving body of writing—together with the ultimately literary quality of the tradition that preserves a vocabulary of models for adaptation—is sufficient to produce the effect of a dramatic text, whereupon the theater in question is revealed as dramatic, hence revolutionary, after all. And this evidently undecidable Either/Or is the result of a reasonably consistent application of the idea of dramatic theater as a criterion for judging theater in general.

Does the undecidability of this question imply that the critical category of drama, or dramatic theater, has become obsolete in an age characterized by work such as Robert Wilson's? In fact, it implies exactly the contrary. The categories in terms of which Wilson's work is most commonly discussed raise questions that have fairly easy answers. Continuous fictional action by characters with stable identities? Obviously absent. Referential, allusive, and structural open-endedness, leaving crucial elements to be supplied by the imagining spectator? Obviously present. But what do we learn from this? Such a theater, we hear, produces problems for the spectator—which is true as long as we imagine a spectator whose sensibilities and expectations are still rooted in the nineteenth century. The advantage of the category of dramatic theater, as I have tried to develop it, is that it does, by contrast, tempt forth a *genuinely* (and insolubly) problematic quality of Wilson's theater and of similar theaters—a quality, that is, by which it is possible that that theater will make its true historical mark. I do not claim, by these considerations, to prove that the way I have chosen to look at Western drama and theater, organized around the assertion that "all theater is revolutionary theater," is uniquely correct. But I do think I have shown, by way of the problem it opens in Robert Wilson, that in the twenty-first century this approach to the question of theater remains at least historically reasonable and fruitful. And finally, I think the category of dramatic theater answers the question with which this chapter began, the question of whether we can say anything specific about how the continuous revolutionizing of the theater must work. But that category does not decide particular cases—and as long as the concept "revolutionary" means anything, it cannot be expected to.

Freedom, Consensus, and the Totalitarian Move

An interrogation with regard to the concept and history of dramatic theater, then, renders Robert Wilson's theater not merely perplexing or challenging but problematic in the strict sense, open to question at a level that affects its very right to exist. The consideration, in the argument I have presented, that all drama is problematic in very much the same way—that it is what it is only by being defective (which makes it, so to speak, ontologically questionable)—implies at most the *possibility* of a positive link with Wilson's work, not the *existence* of such a link. But a more immediate question presents itself: Is the problem engendered by Wilson's work an important one? Open-minded theatergoers, as a rule, seem happy enough with what Wilson offers them, and most would probably dismiss any talk of "problems" as an academic game. But is the problem of Wilson merely a problem for academics?

The absence of a demonstrable governing text, in relation to which Wilson's theater might be regarded as interpretation, causes difficulties when one tries to identify "the work," that entity as which the ephemeral theatrical proceeding secures for itself a historical identity and becomes more than a pure "happening." Obviously, the theatrical proceeding must in some sense be reflected upon in order to become historical, but the idea of spectators' individual reflecting (I have argued) is not sufficient. Thus the idea of the work as an empty wavelength for its own public discussion arises; and the admittedly vague notion of "public discussion" serves here as an explanation of how the work might receive a collectively available content (if also a radically mutable content) without benefit of a prior governing text. The notion, as I say, is vague. Its reference is empirical, but its origin is formal: if it makes sense to talk about a "work" of Robert Wilson's, and if that "work" must originate in a space logically *following* the performance, then "public discussion" seems simply to be the most inclusive available name for the content of such an entity.

Thus we find ourselves talking about public discussion without really knowing what it is. Indeed, we *cannot* know what "public discussion" really is; to the extent that it interests us, it is ipso facto still in progress, still unpredictably mutable. Hence the problem of Wilson's theater. As long as public discussion has the quality of "dramatic text" in a degree sufficient to produce a categorical distinction from performance, and so to open "performance space," that theater remains basically dramatic—in the sense of my argument—and evinces a liberal or revolutionary potential. Otherwise, it not only fails to mount an effective resistance against being included in hermeneutic space but in fact commits a kind of positive treason against theater as a historical force, by undermining both the emphatic materiality of its objects and the emphatic living bodily humanity of its actors. And the problem is that although these are strict alternatives, not points on a scale of possibilities, we are still never in a position to decide which of them obtains. We may persuade ourselves from time to time, on the basis of our sense of where public discussion is headed, that we have grounds for either hope or fear, but even if our attitude at the time is justified, we have no grounds for assuming that the situation will not change radically tomorrow.

Wilson's theater thus has indirectly the effect of evoking and profiling the problem of public discussion in general, as a political problem in societies built around representative governments of the Euro-American type. Is public discussion in such societies—including education, publishing, the press, the media, political and cultural debates, legislative compromises, judicial rulings—an expression of our freedom and a field for its exercise, or is it rather a self-driven rhetorical machinery over which we have no control, more or less like a sporting event where our participation consists of cheering when we hear something that suits what we take to be "our" opinions? The question here is as undecidable as the Either/Or Wilson presents us with. Exactly the same quality of unpredictability characterizes public dis-

cussion in both cases—as does exactly the same instability of basic oppositions. "Freedom," or its "defense" or "preservation," is often enough the
central value in arguments that tend clearly toward some form of enslavement; and it is by no means easy to frame an emancipatory rhetoric that
would exclude that tendency without presupposing a degree of mediatic
control that would, if it obtained, make emancipation inconceivable.

But another, more threatening dimension to the problem of public discussion has to do with the question of consensus. If the identity of a
"work" is represented by a single demonstrable text, its public discussion
will normally have the character of *debate*, on matters of interpretation and
evaluation. In the case of a theater like Wilson's, however, where the
work's identity must first be constituted in public discussion, the portion
or aspect of the discussion that concerns that identity will have the character of *automatic consensus*, since the discussion cannot happen in the first
place without consensus about its subject matter. This is why the work's
identity, as I have said, is mutable. The discussion, at any given time, cannot be mistaken on the issue of identity; the consensus must constantly
reconstitute itself. And the problem is, how do we *distinguish* between the
"portion or aspect" of the discussion (the problem is already contained in
the vagueness of these words) where consensus is appropriate and that
"portion or aspect" where debate is appropriate? I have already mentioned one particular form this problem can take: when (for instance) a
postdramatic theater piece is very much discussed, the sheer volume of
discussion is likely to be understood as a sign of value (region of debate),
while at the same time the wide differentness of attitudes in the discussion
makes the work's identity very hard to pin down (region of consensus), so
that we find ourselves assigning value in the same measure as we fail to
grasp what we are assigning it to.

The most dangerous consequence of this problem is what I call "the
totalitarian move." If we agree that a totalitarian society is a rigidly con-
trolled society in which the controlling power or government nevertheless
enjoys the relatively unstinting support of its people—in which, therefore,
even free choice is somehow subjected to control—then the obvious question is how such a situation can possibly arise. Or more specifically, how
could German and Italian fascism, in the 1930s and 1940s, gain the support
of as many intellectuals as quickly as they did? To deal with this question in
detail would take up another whole book (which I have every intention of
writing). But in general terms, what is required for totalitarianism is that
public discussion be framed so as to include prominently a region of automatic consensus and a region of free debate, separated by a boundary that
will inevitably become uncertain and will permit otherwise debatable
issues (this being the totalitarian move) to assume inconspicuously the
mantle of the existentially or historically absolute.

And it is more than just a curiosity that one of the clearest available models of this situation is provided by the institution of literature. We are encouraged to interpret the literary work and to argue about its interpretation and valuation, but only after we have accepted the more or less fictional "premises" on which it is based. Is this acceptance, this automatic consensus, as innocent as it is necessary? Kafka raises this question in, for instance, the story "In the Penal Colony," which we apparently cannot begin to interpret without accepting the existence of the punishment machine, even though that machine, as the narrator carefully describes it, is an obvious physical impossibility. (The prisoner's body, for one thing, cannot be rotated while both his hands are strapped down separately.) And the same question, as it is raised by Wilson's theater—where, in the realm of public discussion, does consensus (the "work") end and debate ("about" the work) begin?—includes the added complication of being subject to changing circumstances. This is important because it exposes the fallacy of arguing that the totalitarian move can be prevented simply by insisting on a *firm* boundary to the region of necessary consensus. Where, in the ceaseless flux of circumstance, is the basis for defining a "firm" boundary? Precisely the act of proclaiming such a definition is a typical form of the totalitarian move.

Is Wilson's theater therefore an *instance* of the totalitarian move, in a cultural arena? Or is it a modeling and therefore an *exposure* of that move to our scrutiny? Does the difference between these two possibilities depend on particular features of that theater, or does it depend entirely on how the public (we, as readers and spectators) shapes its own discussion? Where shall we seek criteria by which to answer these questions? Or should we seek at all? Would the pretense of "answering" questions of this sort be entirely innocent with respect to the questions' content? (This is the problem we found in asking whether Brecht's *Leben des Galilei* is a revolutionary act or a capitulation.) And to what extent do the answers to any of these questions depend either on the large political circumstances in which they are asked or at least on our perception of those circumstances? It is clear, in any case, that we are not in a position to say where Wilson's theater "stands" with respect to the questions it raises. And it is the argument of this whole book that something at least very like such a condition of unpositionability characterizes Western theater from the very beginning.

Conclusion

Assuming agreement on the central point of my various arguments—that an inevitable conservative tendency in literature is counteracted only by the incongruous association of literature with theatrical drama, whence drama receives its enduring revolutionary character and keeps open, in turn, revolutionary or progressive possibilities for literature in general— the main question that remains is how seriously one must take this assertion, how important it is, especially in the contemporary political arena. And this question, in turn, is divisible in two: first, exactly how conservative is literature really, how deeply resistant to genuine novelty? and second, how much real effect does literature—mere literature—have on the rest of our intellectual life?

At least another whole book would be needed to deal with these questions in full detail, but a few basic points are fairly obvious. If we distinguish between higher and lower levels of literature, first of all, then it is clear that the higher levels will be more strongly conservative. When we regard a work as belonging to high literature, we make greater demands on its meaning; we ask that its meaning possess, all at once, greater density, variety, scope, exactness, and depth than that of less pretentious writing. We ask, in other words, that its meaning greatly exceed what a literate but relatively untrained mind could derive from the same sentences if it found them out of context. And the only possible source of this excess, of this difference between the text and itself for different readers, is a highly refined sense of genre, which in turn—as is argued in chapter 2—is the main site and source of conservative inertia in the domain of writing.

It will be remarked, in response to this point, that there is both a general historical tendency and a specific contemporary tendency to break down, or at least to call into question, the division between high and low literature. But what is the effect of this tendency, whether we measure it, say with Auerbach, in the centuries-long process by which styles once regarded as "low" gain artistic stature, or in the relatively recent inclination of sophisticated literary criticism to apply its techniques to what was once regarded as mere popular writing? Is it the effect of this tendency to reduce the demands we make on high literature, or to increase those we make on the humbler instances, to interrogate low or minor literature ever more deeply? Obviously, the latter is the case, which means that the territory of high literature, and hence also the conservative influence of genre, tends in effect to *increase* in our intellectual life as a whole. Is it possible to reverse this process or at least slow it down, to preserve from academic infection at least some specific wilderness areas in our intellectual and literary landscape? Obviously not. The very identification of such areas requires a literary-critical operation and inevitably, in fact, an invocation of the concept of genre.

It is almost certainly impossible to say "exactly how conservative" literature is. At least I do not see how any conceivable point of view is available from which to make that measurement. But given the logically inescapable recognition of a conservative tendency in literature, it appears to follow that that tendency will itself tend over time to become stronger, larger in scope, and by consequence more influential in areas of our life that are not strictly literary. Contemporary popular culture, for instance, especially in film and song, seems fascinated by the perhaps still exotic term "genre"—whether or not this fact means anything. And in case there is some form of actual danger behind these considerations, a short look at the historical aspect of "literature" may give us a somewhat better sense of where we stand.

I pointed out in chapter 2 that the concept of "literature"—redefined in more or less aesthetic terms, and referring to everything that had earlier been known as "poetry" (including practically all drama) plus the novel and a variously defined collection of other fictional and nonfictional prose genres—arose only in the eighteenth century and became fully established only in the nineteenth. Literature in the modern sense was thus born in the lap of the development and establishment of the major modern nation-states of bourgeois-industrial-parliamentary Europe, and I do not think this circumstance was an accident. The evidence after the fact is clear enough: the newborn concept of literature does not really begin to have an important function in intellectual life until it is used to create the idea of *national literatures*, which in turn underpins the increasingly flourishing nineteenth-century production of histories of national literature and makes possible the increasingly common incorporation of national literature into school and university curricula, where it serves the nation-state by indoctrinating its young citizens with the idea of a cohesive and continuous national culture stretching far into the past. Already at the beginning of the nineteenth century, the notion of national literature *as such* is so well established that Goethe feels called upon to conceptualize its opposite in what he calls "world literature."

I speak advisedly when I say that the concept of literature is used to *create* the idea of national literatures. For in reality, there is no such thing as a national literature except in the entirely trivial sense of a collection of all the more or less poetic writings in a given language. Poetry, of course, does have a history and a historical identity, as do all the extrapoetic forms later gathered under the heading of literature. But these histories, to the extent that they are at all interesting in a "literary" sense, to the extent that they engage the evolution of genres and questions of hermeneutics, tend very strongly to develop across or between languages rather than within languages. Critical historiography laughs at us when we claim that one particular narrative is the correct way of looking at this or that aspect of history. But there are plenty of cases where we can assert confidently that a particular narrative grossly distorts history. And one of those cases is the fairytale that shows us a national literature developing in accordance with its own inner principles and occasionally (so we say) responding to external "influences." I do not mean to say that the nation itself—the *natio*, the people, the *Volk*, the tribe—does not exist and does not have historical identity in the form of a culture, although we must be careful about the form of existence we ascribe to it. But precisely the main vehicle by which that culture is meant to be transmitted in the public schools of modern nation-states, the national literature, does in fact not exist in any relation to the technical concept of "literature" that would be deep enough to ground—precisely—a particular form of culture.

As happens with many demonstrably false or misleading ideas, however, the idea of the national literature is remarkably tenacious—tenacious, I suppose, in proportion not only to its obvious patriotic usefulness in public education but also to the amount of desperate industry invested in it by its sincere proponents. To this day, in the United States, the study of literature in broader than national terms is normally called "comparative literature," as if national literatures were the indisputably fundamental units of the discipline. What we have, then, in literature, is a firmly established institution with an inherent conservative tendency which very probably contributes—not directly, but by way of an illegitimate and self-obscuring conceptual operation that makes it difficult to criticize convincingly—to the maintenance of existing national structures and ultimately of nationalism itself in some sense.

Thus, it seems to me, questions of considerable significance are raised. For from the late twentieth into the early twenty-first century, nations and nationality are at issue. Aspects of national interest are increasingly seen to be "globalized"; in Europe, the very breeding ground of the modern nation-state, that political-cultural entity seems almost on the verge of disappearing; the United States, a state without a historical *natio* of its own, has become paradoxically the principal new homeland of nationalism; old and new nation-states are objects of controversy in the former Soviet Union, in the Balkans, among Israelis and Palestinians, and so on. What is the expectable effect of the basically corrupt concept and institution of literature in this situation if not to confuse all the issues to which it bears any relation? Is it really possible to rethink modern nationality or nationalism without studying its very voice, its language, its secret vocabulary, in the form of literature? And is it possible to study literature adequately—at least for political purposes—without getting used to the accidental and (hence?) mercilessly critical perspective afforded us by the dramatic theater?

How Büchner Uses and Conceives of
Thomas Paine (Payne) in Dantons Tod

Does Büchner believe that Paine had been an atheist? In England and America, there were people who considered Paine's deism the equivalent of atheism. But in all the sources we know to have been available to Büchner, there is not the slightest association made between Paine and the concept or doctrine of atheism, or between Paine and any established atheist thinkers or movements. By "all the sources we know to have been available to Büchner," I mean all the sources mentioned in Georg Büchner, *Dantons Tod,* ed. Burghard Dedner, Thomas Michael Mayer, et al., 4 vols. (Darmstadt, 2000) = vol. 3 of Büchner, *Sämtliche Werke und Schriften,* Marburger Ausgabe, ed. Dedner and Mayer, plus references in Herbert Wender, *Georg Büchners Bild der Großen Revolution: Zu den Quellen von* Dantons Tod (Frankfurt/Main, 1988). To be sure, in one source Büchner could have used but is not known to have used, Paine and the militant atheist Anacharsis Cloots are mentioned in connection with one another: it is Paine's own *The Age of Reason,* which I refer to here in the Citadel Press edition (New York, 1988), p. 101. But if Büchner knew *The Age of Reason,* then he of course knew that Paine was emphatically not an atheist. It is therefore extremely unlikely that he believed Paine to have advocated the doctrine of atheism. As Erwin Kobel says in his *Georg Büchner: Das dichterische Werk* (Berlin, 1974), p. 107, "Nun kann man, soweit das nachprüfbar ist, immer wieder feststellen, daß er [Büchner] bei allen historischen Personen seiner Dichtungen über ausgedehnte Kenntnisse verfügt. Daher ist anzunehmen, daß es sich um seine Auslegung von Paine handelt, wenn er ihn als Atheisten auftreten läßt." This much, I think, is definitely correct, although I disagree with Kobel's ultimate conclusion: "daß für ihn [Büchner] also das, was Paine Deismus nennt, Atheismus ist."

Is there any further evidence that by making "Payne" advocate atheism, Büchner is carrying out an interpretation of Paine's thought? Or, to put it differently, does it matter to Büchner that specifically "Payne" is presented as an atheist, or is his purpose merely to have the atheistic perspective represented, by no matter whom? If one assumes, for the sake of argument, that the latter is the case, one can think immediately of two candidates for the position of doctrinaire atheist whom Büchner should have preferred over Paine. The first is Anacharsis Cloots, who was known as a very powerful and eloquent advocate of atheism. It is in fact, in my opinion, almost absolutely certain that the whole action of act 3, scene 1, Payne's atheistic "catechizing" (Büchner, *Münchener Ausgabe* [=GB]:p. 105) of Chaumette, is based on the story of Cloots's spirited preaching of atheism to his fellow prisoners (the Hébertists) as their execution approached. See the passages from A. Thiers, *Histoire de la Révolution française* (Paris, 1825), and Johann Konrad Friederich, *Unsere Zeit, oder geschichtliche Uebersicht der merkwürdigsten Ereignisse von 1789–1830* (Stuttgart, 1826–30), that are quoted in the *Marburger Ausgabe*, 3.3: 62, 216, 269. (Wender, p. 169, does not believe that the figure and actions of Cloots had anything to do with Payne's atheistic advocacy. But his reasons, mainly the difference between "catechizing" and "preaching," are not strong.) The trouble with Cloots, for Büchner's purposes, is that he was executed on 24 March, a week before Danton's imprisonment. But it can be shown, interestingly, that Büchner is *not* in principle averse to fudging dates when it suits him. Hérault-Séchelles [*sic*], in particular, was already imprisoned on 17 March (see *Marburger Ausgabe*, 3.4:33), which means he has no business appearing in act 1, scene 1, unless we assume that this scene takes place a full two weeks before act 3. But this cannot be so, since in the same scene we hear of the execution of the Hébertists (GB, p. 70), which took place on 24 March. Therefore Büchner *could* conceivably have used Cloots for his atheist, despite the historical impossibility. And if not Cloots, then why not Chaumette himself—as Wender (p. 169) suggests? It is true that Chaumette's behavior in prison is described in Büchner's sources (and depicted in the play) as irresolute, submissive, timid; see the passages quoted in the *Marburger Ausgabe*, 3.3:62, 234. But again, if all Büchner wanted was to get the atheism controversy (which was important in his own time: see Wender, pp. 168–69 and n. 42) represented on the stage, he still could surely have found a way to use Chaumette without stretching the truth about his character too much, and certainly without stretching the truth as far as he had to with Thomas Paine. For one historical fact that Büchner certainly knew was that Paine did not speak French and therefore could not possibly have conducted a complex philosophical debate like that in act 3, scene 1! Mme. Roland mentions this fact prominently (see *Mémoires de Madame Roland*, ed. Paul de Roux [N.p.: Mercure de France, 1966], p. 169), as does the article on Thomas "Payne" in the *Galerie historique des contemporains, ou Nouvelle biographie* (Brussels, 1818–26), and we know that Büchner used both these sources (see Wender, p. 16, relaying information from T.

M. Mayer and Anna Jaspers). For all these reasons, it is extremely difficult to imagine that Büchner chose Paine simply as a convenient figure to embody the atheistic perspective; Paine is precisely *not* convenient for this purpose. It must be true, therefore, that Büchner is either making a point *about* Paine (as Kobel suggests) or else making a point *by way of* Paine, a point that gains effectiveness from the audience's specific knowledge of Paine's thought or writings—as I have suggested.

Did Büchner know The Age of Reason? *And how important is it for us to know the answer to this question?* Kobel is of course strongly of the opinion that Büchner did know the book and that his treatment of "Payne" is a demonstration, more or less in the spirit of Pascal (see Kobel, p. 107 and n. 30), that Paine's deism is basically the equivalent of atheism. But the only piece of textual evidence that he offers (p. 108, n. 32) is the parallel between Payne's mockery of Chaumette—"Er traut noch nicht, er wird sich zu guter Letzt noch die Ölung geben, die Füße nach Mecca zu legen, und sich beschneiden lassen um ja keinen Weg zu verfehlen" (GB, p. 107)—and several passages in *The Age of Reason* (pp. 50–51) where Paine lumps together the Christian, Jewish, and Mohammedan religions as objects of scorn. There is, however, at least one much stronger piece of textual evidence that Kobel misses, even though it involves a passage in Büchner to which he pays much attention. Kobel points out (pp. 100–102) that Payne completely reverses his position when he says, "nur der Verstand kann Gott beweisen das Gefühl empört sich dagegen" (GB, p. 107). His aim, up to this point, had been to show that reason *disproves* God, even though feeling (like Chaumette's, "vorhin überkam es mich so" [GB, p. 105]) might be tempted, precisely in its suffering, to reach out for divine support. But if Büchner thus uncovers an inconsistency in Payne's position—and why should atheism be any more capable of logical consistency, hence any more *positive*, than nihilism?—he does so in a way that strikingly echoes and overturns a formulation of Paine's in *The Age of Reason*. In part 1, in the section "Concerning God, and the Lights Cast on His Existence and Attributes in the Bible"—which, like the debate in Büchner, deals with the question of God as first cause and with that of God's perfection—Paine says first, "It is only by the exercise of reason that man can discover God" (p. 70). And then, with reference to Job 11:7—"Canst thou by searching find out God? Canst thou find out the Almighty to *perfection*?"—Paine says, "The two questions have different objects; the first refers to the existence of God; the second to His attributes; reason can discover the one, but it falls infinitely short in discovering the whole of the other" (p. 72). Payne and Paine both make the relatively uncommon assertion that *only* reason can prove God, and both imply (one despairingly, one hopefully) that God's supposed perfection is infinitely beyond our grasp. (If Büchner used the German version of 1794, titled *Untersuchungen über wahre und fabelhafte Theologie. von Thomas Paine,* then he read [p.100], "Aber nur durch den Gebrauch der Vernunft kann der Mensch die erste Ursache, diesen *Gott*, erkennen." Another interesting point in this edition is the translator's footnote on pp. 99–100, which refers to "die kritische Philosophie" [Kant] to explain and develop Paine's ideas on the infinity of time and space. This would support Kobel's suggestion [pp. 96–98] that Büchner is thinking of Kant in criticizing Paine.) The relationship here, especially in view of the inconsistency in Payne's standpoint, is quite complex, but it is hard to deny that a relationship exists. In any case, *The Age of Reason* was available to Büchner in German translation (part 1, Lübeck, 1794; part 2, Paris, 1796), and in French translation (1794, and a falsely dated edition of "1792"). Moreover, if it is true, as I think I have shown, that Büchner has some specific reason for using Thomas Paine in a debate on religion, then how could he *not* have known (or at least known about) *The Age of Reason*, which is Paine's only major work on the subject?

Suppose, however, that Büchner never had access to a copy of *The Age of Reason*. Even in this case, I do not think my main argument would be invalidated. All that is strictly necessary for that argument is for Büchner to have known that Paine was a committed deist, and there are any number of ways he could have come to this knowledge. One of the most probable would be through the use of biographical dictionaries, since, as I noted above, we are absolutely certain that he consulted the *Galerie historique des contemporains*. And if he used the *Galerie historique*, then there is every reason to expect that he was familiar with, for example, the more popular and thorough and widely distributed *Biographie universelle* of Michaud, which in volume 32 (1822) of the 1811 edition has a very long article on Paine (correctly spelled); it correctly describes the subject matter of *The Age of Reason* as "religion naturelle" (p. 382).

NOTES

Introduction

1. W. B. Worthen, "Drama, Performativity, and Performance," *PMLA* 113 (1998): 1093–1107.

2. Jennifer Wise, *Dionysus Writes: The Invention of Theatre in Ancient Greece* (Ithaca, 1998).

3. See Benjamin Bennett, *Theater As Problem: Modern Drama and Its Place in Literature* (Ithaca, 1990), p. 217.

1. Aristotle's Defeat

1. All translations in this book are mine except where otherwise identified. I accept, in this translation, that ἀπαγγέλλοντα and ἕτερόν τι γιγνόμενον (sc. μιμεῖσθαι) are direct alternatives and that an emendation—like Zeller's ὁτὲ δ'ἕτερόν τι κτλ., or even Else's ὁτὲ δ'ἠθός τι εἰσάγοντα—may therefore be necessary. If, on the other hand, one reads (either literally or in effect) ὁτὲ δὲ πάντας ὡς πράττοντας κτλ. (with Rostagni)—which would oppose the whole idea of reporting (ἀπαγγέλλειν), including the reporting of direct speech, to the idea of imitating carried out by a group (οἱ μιμούμενοι) among whom individual roles are distributed—the focus on defining dramatic/theatrical form is only increased. In any event, I cannot see how Else can take τοὺς μιμουένους to refer to *"the dramatic characters."* Already in 48a1, Ἐπεὶ δὲ μιμοῦνται οἱ μιμούμενοι πράττοντας κτλ., it is clear that "dramatic characters" are the *objects* of imitation. See Gerald F. Else, *Aristotle's Poetics: The Argument* (Cambridge, Mass., 1963), pp. 92, 94.

2. See note 1, on Else's understanding of τοὺς μιμουένους. Elsewhere, of course, Aristotle uses the more normal Attic ὑποκριτής to refer to the actor—49a16, 49b5, 50b20, 51b37, 56a26, 59b26, 61b34—but in none of these places is the concept of imitation at issue.

3. Else, *Aristotle's Poetics*, pp. 603–5, argues with numbers that when Aristotle wants poems that are "shorter than those of the ancients" (59b20–21), "the ancients" must mean Homer.

4. John Jones, *On Aristotle and Greek Tragedy* (London, 1962), comes very close to making this general point in his argument against the "importing" into Aristotle of a later European idea of the "tragic hero" (pp. 12–20), which includes reference to Aristotle's use of the plural where his translators prefer the singular. And in his argument on *praxis*, he comes even closer: "The gulf between our preconceptions and the express doctrine of the *Poetics* can only be bridged through the recovery of some of the lost human relevancies of action. Aristotle is assaulting the now settled habit in which we see action issuing from a solitary focus of consciousness—secret, inward, interesting—and in which the status of action must always be adjectival: action qualifies; it tells us things we want to know about the individual promoting

it; the life of action is our ceaseless, animating consideration of the state of affairs "inside" him who acts, without which action is empty and trivial, an effluvium. This movement from adjectival action to the substantive self would seem, were it conscious, not merely natural but inevitable. Were it conscious, however, we should have to admit that we are first rejecting Aristotle's injunction to make character serve action, and then replacing it with its opposite" (p. 33). Jones also speaks of Aristotle's "carving of identity situationally" (p. 43), which I take to mean permitting identity to arise only in the interactive situation. And he suggests, finally, that although Aristotle does not explicitly discuss masks, he has constantly in mind their presence and function: "The distinction between the composing dramatist who imitates human beings and one who imitates an action rich in human interest [see Jones, pp. 34–35, *Poetics*, 55a29–32] is paralleled by a second distinction between the actor who impersonates his mythico-historical original and the actor-mask who appropriates to that original his share [!] of the play's action. The actor-mask is tethered to his original lightly, to ensure recognition, while his masking energies drive him on through the stage-event" (p. 46).

5. See Else, *Aristotle's Poetics*, pp. 357, 420–21, 450–52, and, e.g., D. W. Lucas, commentary in Aristotle, *Poetics* (Oxford, 1968), p. 155.

6. Of course, there is no passage in the existing text of the *Poetics* that actually carries out this reading of *Oedipus*. But if one were absolutely bent on defending Aristotle's consistency by attributing this reading to him, one might still claim to see the pattern into which that missing passage would have fit. In his first lengthy discussion of recognition (ἀναγνώρισις 52a29–b8), Aristotle cites *Oedipus* as an exemplary instance twice near the beginning (52a24–26, 32–33) and *Iphigenia among the Taurians* at the end (52b5–8). And when he returns to the topic later on, he cites the same two plays as principal examples of the best type of recognition, which arises directly from incidents in the action (55a16–19). But between these two passages, where recognition is discussed in its function of preventing *pathos*, *Iphigenia* is still present as an example, but *Oedipus* is missing (54a4–9). There is thus something that looks like a break in the pattern here. And that the absence of references to Sophocles' play at this point might conceivably be accidental—not due to Aristotle himself—is also suggested by the lines immediately following: "For this reason, as has already been said, tragedies are written about only a few families" (54a9–10). In the list of tragic families that Aristotle is referring back to (53a19–21), Oedipus is named second, after Alcmeon.

2. Genre and Drama

1. Paul Hernadi, *Beyond Genre: New Directions in Literary Classification* (Ithaca, 1972), p. vii.

2. I realize there is controversy on this point, although frankly I cannot see any other way of reading the following passages from the *Ästhetik*, in Georg Wilhelm Friedrich Hegel, *Sämtliche Werke*, ed. Hermann Glockner, 20 vols. (Stuttgart, 1927), 12:32, 131 (Einleitung); 13:237–38 (end of part 2); 14:580 (end of part 3). But for the present argument, only the contrast of Hegel's systematic rigor with the procedure of relatively recent genre theory is required.

3. Northrop Frye, *Anatomy of Criticism: Four Essays* (1957; New York: Atheneum, 1966), pp. 11, 12.

4. The relevant ideas in Dilthey are well known and are perhaps best expressed in *Der Aufbau der geschichtlichen Welt in den Geisteswissenschaften*, where the natural sciences are described as requiring a suppression of the experiential quality ("Erlebnischarakter") of our relation to the world, whereas the human sciences embrace experience and aim at "das fernere Ziel einer Besinnung des Menschen über sich selbst." See Wilhelm Dilthey, *Gesammelte Schriften*, ed. Bernhard Groethuysen et al. (Stuttgart and Göttingen, 1966 ff.), 7:82–83. There are, Dilthey argues, exactly two ways of looking at humanity: either as "eine physische Tatsache" subject to natural-scientific treatment, or "sofern menschliche Zustände erlebt werden, sofern sie in Lebensäußerungen zum Ausdruck gelangen und sofern diese Ausdrücke verstanden werden" (7:86). Frye postulates, without any justification, a form of verbal existence somehow prior to expression and understanding.

5. On genre in the hermeneutic sense, see E. D. Hirsch Jr., *Validity in Interpretation* (New Haven, Conn., 1967), pp. 68–126, 262–64. The concept is never fully worked out by Schleiermacher but occurs in a number of suggestive contexts. Hirsch (p. 263) quotes, "Das Ganze wird ursprünglich verstanden als Gattung," from Friedrich D. E. Schleiermacher, *Hermeneutik*, ed. Heinz Kimmerle, 2nd ed. (Heidelberg, 1974), p. 47. This idea of genre as a *first* step in understanding "the whole" of the text to be interpreted is developed when Schleiermacher suggests that the very *identification* of the whole—is the given text one whole or several wholes?—depends on genre (Schleiermacher, p. 145). We also read that a single author may be considered "several authors" if he writes in different genres (p. 67), and that genre is the basic comparative study that balances the necessary "divinatory" element in interpretation (pp. 151–52).

6. T. S. Eliot, "Tradition and the Individual Talent," in his *Selected Essays: New Edition* (New York, 1960), p. 5.

7. See Hans-Georg Gadamer, *Wahrheit und Methode: Grundzüge einer philosophischen Hermeneutik*, 3rd ed. (Tübingen, 1972), pp. 350–60, 437–41.

8. Sir Philip Sidney, "A Defence of Poetry," in *Miscellaneous Prose of Sir Philip Sidney*, ed. Katherine Duncan-Jones and Jan van Dorsten (Oxford, 1973), p. 76.

9. Lionel Trilling, "The Meaning of a Literary Idea," in his *The Liberal Imagination: Essays on Literature and Society* (1950; Garden City, N.Y., 1957), pp. 291–92.

10. Jacques Derrida, "La Loi du genre," *Glyph: Textual Studies* 7 (1980), 176–201, esp. 184–86 on the genre of genres.

11. From the two-strophe version of Hölderin's ode "An die Deutschen."

12. Gérard Genette, "Genres, 'types,' modes," *Poétique* 32 (Nov. 1977): 417, speaks of a "confusion entre modes et genres" in much European literary theory, where by "mode" he means "mode d'énonciation," whereas "les genres proprement dits venaient se répartir entre les modes en tant qu'ils relevaient de telle ou telle attitude d'énonciation: le dithyrambe, de la narration pure, l'épopée de la narration mixte, la tragédie et la comédie de l'imitation dramatique." I prefer to speak of *types of genre* for a number of reasons. In the first place, even in Genette's own terminology, it is simply not true that "chaque genre se définissait essentiellement par une spécification de contenu que rien ne prescrivait dans la définition du mode dont il relevait." The implication that what Genette calls "mode" does not have a deep shaping effect on the work's content, hence on what Genette calls its "genre," is absurd—even if, in accordance with my separation of hermeneutic genre, I cannot claim to identify that effect. And of course, once we start talking about "literature" (letters, writing) rather than "poetry," the place of "enunciation" becomes as much a matter of interpretation as the work's "contenu." In the second place, by understanding "contenu" as the defining characteristic of "genre," and by permitting this idea (as he does) to fix itself anywhere one pleases on the scale between theme and meaning, Genette himself confuses historical-prescriptive and hermeneutic genre. In the third place, Genette actually believes (as he must, in order to keep his categories separate) in the strict legitimacy, the objective "linguistic" validity (in the sense of scientific, "anthropological" linguistics) of Plato's triad of "modes," whereas he considers "genre" a strictly "literary" or "aesthetic" category (pp. 418, 421). But one has only to look at Frye's system of "radicals," for instance, to recognize that there are plenty of other "anthropological" possibilities, and that the idea of "structural genre" therefore makes much more sense, by embracing those other possibilities and by recognizing the elusive but inevitable interaction with hermeneutic genre. Derrida, "La Loi du genre," pp. 180–84) gently dismantles Genette's argument.

13. See Theodor W. Adorno, *Ästhetische Theorie* (in *Gesammelte Schriften*, vol. 7), ed. Gretel Adorno and Rolf Tiedemann (Frankfurt/Main, 1970), p. 335: "Vielmehr wird sie [die Kunst] zum Gesellschaftlichen durch ihre Gegenposition zur Gesellschaft, und jene Position bezieht sie erst als autonome. Indem sie sich als Eigenes in sich kristallisiert, anstatt bestehenden gesellschaftlichen Normen zu willfahren und als 'gesellschaftlich nützlich' sich zu qualifizieren, kritisiert sie die Gesellschaft, durch ihr bloßes Dasein, so wie es von Puritanern aller Bekenntnisse mißbilligt wird."

14. On Goethe's antinationalism, see David Barry, "Faustian Pursuits: The Political-Cultural Dimension of Goethe's *Weltliteratur* and the Tragedy of Translation," *GQ* 74 (2001): 164–85. Radical antinationalism is a clear consequence of the argument on "Politik" in Fritz Breithaupt, *Jenseits der Bilder: Goethes Politik der Wahrnehmung* (Freiburg im Breisgau, 2000). And this view of Goethe is also a main argument of Benjamin Bennett, *Goethe as Woman: The Undoing of Literature* (Detroit, 2001), in which an extended interpretation of the essay "Literarischer Sansculottismus" appears on pp. 150–59.

15. Paul de Man, "Literary History and Literary Modernity," in his *Blindness and Insight: Essays in the Rhetoric of Contemporary Criticism*, 2nd ed. (Minneapolis, 1983), pp. 164–65.

16. Martin Heidegger, *Über den Humanismus* (Frankfurt/Main, 1949), pp. 5, 9, 21, 45, 26.

17. On a similar relation, in temper and tendency, between Frye and Wolfgang Iser, see Benjamin Bennett, *Beyond Theory: Eighteenth-Century German Literature and the Poetics of Irony* (Ithaca, 1993), pp. 15–16, n. 2.

18. See note 12, on Genette.

19. See, e.g., M. M. Bakhtin, "Discourse in the Novel," in *The Dialogic Imagination: Four Essays by M. M. Bakhtin*, ed. Michael Holquist (Austin, Tex., 1981), p. 263: "The novel orchestrates all its themes, the totality of the world of objects and ideas depicted and expressed in it, by means of the social diversity of speech types and by the differing individual voices that flourish under such conditions. Authorial speech, the speeches of narrators, inserted genres, the speech of characters are merely those fundamental compositional unities with whose help heteroglossia can enter the novel; each of them permits a multiplicity of social voices and a wide variety of their links and interrelationships (always more or less dialogized). These distinctive links and interrelationships between utterances and languages, this movement of the theme through different languages and speech types, its dispersion into the rivulets and droplets of social heteroglossia, its dialogization—this is the basic distinguishing feature of the stylistics of the novel." There are, in any case, plenty of theorists who do not make a genre distinction between drama and narrative. For Käte Hamburger, *The Logic of Literature*, trans. Marilynn J. Rose, 2nd ed. (German orig. 1968; Bloomington, Ind., 1973), for example, both drama and narrative belong to "The Fictional or Mimetic Genre," and drama is basically fiction in which "the narrative function has become nil" (Hamburger, p. 200). On the fairly common idea, in the late eighteenth and early nineteenth centuries, of a "historical" or "pragmatic" genre that includes both narrative and drama, see Georg Jäger, "Das Gattungsproblem in der Ästhetik und Poetik von 1780 bis 1850," in *Zur Literatur der Restaurationsepoche 1815–1848*, ed. Jost Hermand and Manfred Windfuhr (Stuttgart, 1970), pp. 374–75.

20. Bennett, *Theater As Problem*, p. 2.

21. John Snyder, *Prospects of Power: Tragedy, Satire, the Essay, and the Theory of Genre* (Lexington, Ky., 1991), speaks of "Tragic Genre" (p. 83), "Satiric Semigenre" (p. 138), and "the Essay as Nongenre" (p. 149).

22. I make a similar point with reference to Pirandello in Bennett, *Theater As Problem*, pp. 203–5.

23. Wise, *Dionysus Writes*, p. 213.

24. See Plutarch *Solon* 29, 4–5.

25. This basic point, or a significant segment of it—that the period in which "literature" arises also sees a rather sudden and strong (and revolutionary) dramatic "movement" in Germany, which in turn is a kind of seed for modern drama as a whole—is my argument in Benjamin Bennett, *Modern Drama and German Classicism: Renaissance from Lessing to Brecht* (Ithaca, 1979). And the eighteenth-century part of this argument is developed further in Bennett, *Beyond Theory*, esp. chap. 6, "The Genres of Mind and Contract: The Theater, the Novel, and the Jews" (pp. 269–326).

3. Brecht's Writing against Writing

1. Herbert Blau, *To All Appearances: Ideology and Performance* (New York, 1992), pp. 42–43.

2. Susan Sontag, *Against Interpretation and Other Essays* (New York, 1966), p. 173.

3. Jacques Derrida, *Writing and Difference*, trans. Alan Bass (Chicago, 1978), pp. 244–45.

4. See esp. Julia Kristeva, *Revolution in Poetic Language*, trans. Margaret Waller (1974; New York, 1984).

5. See esp. Theodor W. Adorno, "Engagement," in his *Noten zur Literatur III* (Frankfurt/Main, 1965), pp. 109–35. I am not entirely sure why Brecht gets under Adorno's skin the way he does, but Adorno never discusses him so much as he keeps coming back to him, scratching him like an itch, trying to give him his due but always in effect dismissing him unread yet once more. His treatment of Brecht manages to be at once both fastidious and spasmodic, and reading it is like watching a woman get raped by a gynecologist. See also, e.g., Adorno, *Ästhetische Theorie*, pp. 48, 225 (with a long quotation, which is then dismissed as "eine blague"), 360, 366–67.

6. References to Brecht's play are by page number in Bertolt Brecht, *Werke*, 30 vols., Große kommentierte Berliner und Frankfurter Ausgabe, ed. Werner Hecht et al. (Berlin and Weimar; and Frankfurt/Main, 1988ff.), vol. 5: *Stücke 5*.

7. On "Horizontverschmelzung," see Gadamer, *Wahrheit und Methode*, pp. 289–90. On reception, see Hans Robert Jauß, *Literaturgeschichte als Provokation* (Frankfurt/Main, 1970), esp. the essay "Literaturgeschichte als Provokation der Literaturwissenschaft" (1967), pp. 144–207. An extremely complicated but sometimes useful general treatment of reception theory is Gunter Grimm, *Rezeptionsgeschichte: Grundlegung einer Theorie* (Munich, 1977).

8. Jauß, *Literaturgeschichte*, p. 183.

9. De Man, *Blindness and Insight*, p. 165.

4. Brecht, Artaud, Wedekind, Eliot

1. Frye, *Anatomy of Criticism*, p. 247.

2. Antonin Artaud, *Selected Writings*, ed. Susan Sontag, trans. Helen Weaver (Berkeley, Calif., 1988), p. 267.

3. I quote, for convenience, from Bertolt Brecht, *Schriften zum Theater: Über eine nicht-aristotelische Dramatik* (Frankfurt/Main, 1957), p. 29.

4. Dorrit Cohn, *Transparent Minds: Narrative Modes for Presenting Consciousness in Fiction* (Princeton, 1978), p. v.

5. André Breton, *Manifestoes of Surrealism*, trans. Richard Seaver and Helen R. Lane (Ann Arbor, Mich., 1972), pp. 6–10.

6. Umberto Eco, *A Theory of Semiotics* (Bloomington, Ind., 1976), pp. 6–7.

7. Percy Lubbock, *The Craft of Fiction* (1921; New York, 1957), p. 166.

8. Frank Wedekind, *Werke*, 2 vols., ed. Erhard Weidl (Munich, 1990), 1:530.

9. T. S. Eliot, *The Complete Poems and Plays: 1909–1950* (New York, 1952), p. 183.

10. See Gotthold Ephraim Lessing, *Werke*, 8 vols., ed. Herbert G. Göpfert (Munich, 1970–79), 4:240, in no. 2 of the *Hamburgische Dramaturgie*. Lessing denies, on theoretical grounds, the possibility of Christian tragedy, then hedges: "Bis ein Werk des Genies, von dem man nur aus der Erfahrung lernen kann, wie viel Schwierigkeiten es zu übersteigen vermag, diese Bedenklichkeiten unwidersprechlich widerlegt . . ."

5. The Theater That Never Was

1. Page numbers alone refer to Georg Büchner, *Werke und Briefe*, Münchener Ausgabe, ed. Karl Pörnbacher et al., 6th ed. (Munich, 1997).

2. Numbers with "T" refer to pages in Georg Büchner, *Complete Plays and Prose*, trans. Carl Richard Mueller (New York, 1963). I have sometimes modified Mueller's translations.

3. See the Appendix on Büchner and Thomas Paine.

4. For the actual use of the word "Komödie" in this way, see Büchner, *Werke und Briefe*, pp. 273, 277 (letters to his family). Other letters that show the same mocking attitude include

those to his family, Straßburg, 1832 (p. 274), Straßburg, June 1833 (p. 280), Gießen, 19 November 1833 (p. 283), Gießen, 25 May 1834 (p. 292); to August Stoeber, 9 December 1833 (p. 285); to Karl Gutzkow, March 1835 (p. 299); to an unidentified recipient, Straßburg, 1835 (p. 302).

5. The hopelessness of social reform is a recurrent theme in Büchner's thought. In 1836, for example, he writes to Gutzkow: "Übrigens; um aufrichtig zu sein, Sie und Ihre Freunde scheinen mir nicht grade den klügsten Weg gegangen zu sein. Die Gesellschaft mittlest der *Idee,* von der *gebildeten* Klasse aus reformieren? Unmöglich! Unsere Zeit ist rein *materiell,* wären Sie je direkter politisch zu Werke gegangen, so wären Sie bald auf den Punkt gekommen, wo die Reform von selbst [!] aufgehört hätte. Sie werden nie über den Riß zwischen der gebildeten und ungebildeten Gesellschaft hinauskommen" (*Werke und Briefe,* p. 319). The idea here, that reform is rendered impossible by the gulf between educated and uneducated classes, enables Büchner to suggest a concrete political program. "Ich glaube, man muß in sozialen Dingen von einem absoluten *Rechts*grundsatz ausgehen, die Bildung eines neuen geistigen Lebens im *Volk* suchen und die abgelebte moderne Gesellschaft zum Teufel gehen lassen" (p. 320). Never mind how this "new intellectual life" is going to be nonmodern or non–middle class. The more essential form of the dilemma is the one that arises in Büchner's thought on the theater and theatricality.

6. Hofmannsthal's Theater of Adaptation

1. Hugo von Hofmannsthal, *Gesammelte Werke in zehn Einzelbänden,* ed. Bernd Schoeller (Frankfurt/Main, 1979-80), *Dramen III* p. 105. Further references to the series in this edition are noted by the abbreviations D (Dramen), R (Reden und Aufsätze), and E (Erzählungen, etc.), plus volume and page numbers.

2. Karl Pestalozzi, "'Daß du nicht enden kannst, das macht dich groß . . .': Hofmannsthals Schwierigkeiten mit Dramenschlüssen," in *Hofmannsthal-Forschungen,* Bd. 7, ed. W. Mauser (Freiburg im Breisgau, 1983), p. 99.

3. See Benjamin Bennett, *Hugo von Hofmannsthal: The Theaters of Consciousness* (Cambridge, U.K., 1988), pp. 75–79.

4. Compare the point made in the last section of chapter 5, that theater is both nothing but reality and nothing but fantasy.

5. See Bennett, *Hugo von Hofmannsthal,* chapters 15–16, esp. pp. 293–99, for a related argument: that the ethical aspect and the metaphysical aspect of the thinking of the *Großes Welttheater* are conducted in such a way as to produce oppositions by which anything that might qualify as the play's meaning is reduced to an absolute minimum.

6. See Denis Diderot, *Œuvres Esthétiques,* ed. Paul Vernière (Paris, 1968), p. 311.

7. See Bennett, *Hugo von Hofmannsthal,* p. 70 et passim.

8. On Hofmannsthal's paralleling of himself and Goethe in this respect, see ibid., pp. 303–4.

9. This point, concerning Hofmannsthal's sense of a pressing political danger, could be developed with the aid of the perceptions on Freud and mass psychology in Thomas A. Kovach, "*Acheronta movebo*: A New Light on the Figure of the Physician in Hofmannsthal's *Turm,*" in Erika Nielsen (ed.), *Focus on Vienna 1900: Change and Continuity in Literature, Music, Art and Intellectual History* (Munich, 1982), pp. 77–83.

7. Diderot, Shaw, Beckett

1. The French text I use is from Diderot, *Œuvres Esthétiques;* numbers alone in parentheses refer to pages in this volume. When a parenthesis contains numbers separated by a slash—e.g., 306/103—the second number refers to Denis Diderot, *Selected Writings on Art and Literature,* trans. Geoffrey Bremner (London: Penguin, 1994). English translations from the *Paradoxe* are Bremner's unless otherwise noted.

2. This book, which appeared in 1769, is Antonio Sticoti's translation and abridgment of John Hill's *The Actor* (1750, 1755), which in turn is a translation and adaptation of Pierre Rémond de Sainte-Albine, *Le comédien* (1749). Diderot reviewed Sticoti's book in the *Correspondance littéraire* of 15 October and 1 November 1770.

3. For this argument in *Le Rêve de d'Alembert*, see Denis Diderot, *Œuvres*, ed. Laurent Versini, 5 vols. (Paris: Robert Laffont, 1994), 1:660–61, where in fact the "grand comédien" is mentioned as an example. This volume is cited by volume and page.

4. See note 5 below for more on this question.

5. Richard Sennett, *The Fall of Public Man* (1977; New York, 1992), in an excellent historical contextualization of Diderot's thought, still fails to understand the *Paradoxe* radically enough when he attempts to rescue the idea of natural feeling: "The world where people react directly and spontaneously to each other is a world where expression is often perverted; the more natural the expression between two people, the less reliably expressive they will be." Therefore, Sennett suggests, precisely the conventional and by consequence *repeatable* sign does more to preserve natural feeling. And in attributing this view to Diderot, he tries to get around the paradox of the great man by saying, "A feeling can be conveyed more than once when a person, *having ceased to 'suffer it,'* and now at a distance studying it, comes to define its essential form" (pp. 111–12; my emphasis). The actor, in other words, knows about feeling because he *has* felt, and now remembers his feeling. But Diderot repeatedly takes steps to block this interpretation of the *Paradoxe*. The actor is a "constant observer" not of *his* "sensations," but of "ours" (307/103); the actor's "own potential," his "propre richesse" (which would presumably include memories of past feeling), is not enough to support the variety and magnitude of his imitative tasks (307/104); poets (like actors) are "keen observers" not of themselves but of "what's going on around them" (309–10/105); great actors are "the least emotional of beings" (les êtres les moins sensibles: 310/106); it is better if the actor does not need to separate "self from self," which means, if he has no self (318/113); the great actor "is nothing, possesses nothing which is proper to him or distinguishes him" (347–48/133); one possibility for being a good actor is to be "born without character" (357/140). And we have already discussed the passage (375/153) where Diderot does concede that the actor may have feelings, but then denies that these feelings are the basis for his imitation. It simply cannot be maintained that for Diderot the actor's success in imitating feeling is explainable by the access that he gains to natural feelings in the process of recalling his own.

6. It goes without saying that this reading of the *Paradoxe* implies, in Diderot's thinking, a very great development beyond, say, *Le Fils naturel* and the *Entretiens*, or the "Éloge de Richardson." But there is perhaps also an element of continuity, which is suggested by the central concept in Marc Buffat, "La matérialité du théâtre," in *Diderot: l'invention du drame*, ed. Marc Buffat, pp. 77–88 (n.p.: Klincksieck, 2000). Buffat begins by asserting (p. 77) that among the principal characteristics of the "drame," for Diderot, are "l'intensité de ses effets et ce que l'on pourrait appeler le primat de la matérialité: voix, gestes, objets." The problem, however, is that the "intensity" Buffat speaks of is primarily an *emotional* intensity—characters' emotions, responded to by spectators' emotions—and natural emotions, while they may have material manifestations and effects, are not in themselves material. Buffat shows clearly his awareness of this problem in his attempts to get around it, especially in "l'idée . . . que cette intensité paroxystique est une matérialité, qu'il existe donc une matérialité de l'affect, de l'émotion, et plus généralement du psychisme" (p. 84). In the case of Diderot's "drame," Buffat continues, "Nous n'avons pas affaire à un sujet qui parle, c'est-à-dire se maîtrise, mais à un sujet submergé par une passion qui est cri, voix ou geste, c'est-à-dire matérialité" (p. 85). As I say, Buffat, in claiming to solve this problem, actually only states it. But if we concede that his statement of it is correct (he is well supported in this by the passages he quotes)—if we agree, that is, that closing the gap between materiality and emotion is a central concern for Diderot in his thinking on the theater (or between the physical and the moral "world" [310/105])—then we can see the *Paradoxe* as, at last, a culmination of that thinking. For if what we experience as natural feeling is in truth, or in its

true origin, theatrical convention, then it follows that emotion *is* material after all, that "passion," as Buffat says, "*est* cri, voix ou geste."

7. There is, to be sure, a similar passage in Diderot's discourse *De la Poésie dramatique*: "La parterre de la comédie est le seul endroit où les larmes de l'homme vertueux et du méchant soient confondues. Là, le méchant s'irrite contre des injustices qu'il aurait commises; compatit à des maux qu'il aurait occasionnés, et s'indigne contre un homme de son propre caractère. Mais l'impression est reçue; elle demeure en nous, malgré nous; et le méchant sort de sa loge, moins disposé à faire le mal, que s'il eût été gourmandé par un orateur sévère et dur" (196). But precisely this passage allows us to measure how far Diderot has come in the *Paradoxe*, where the idea that the *méchant* is improved by the theater is completely absent. The *méchant* deposits his vices at the door, true enough, but then he simply picks them up again when he leaves, "car nous ne sommes pas devenus meilleurs" (354).

8. Marian Hobson, *The Object of Art: The Theory of Illusion in Eighteenth-Century France* (Cambridge, U.K., 1982), in the course of an entirely fundamental discussion of all forms of art—not the least of whose implications is that the very category of "art" assumes its modern identity in the period under consideration—argues that the notion of "illusion," as applied to drama, undergoes a basic change in the eighteenth century. "'Illusion' . . . expressed the magical effect of spectacular opera: an effect compounded from a series of rapidly changing sense impressions, of *ravissement*, of surprise; but an effect which incorporated as an essential the awareness of the spectacle's unreality. Increasingly, however, the same term was used to criticise spectacular theatre: not merely was the awareness to be denied, it was to be excluded from the spectator's experience, so that a fundamentally different type of impression was to be created, one not of rapid oscillation between awareness and involvement but of absorption into the theatrical performance. 'Illusion' has then contracted, and awareness is to be excluded" (p. 147). With respect to this view of aesthetic development, Diderot, at least early Diderot, is an obvious instance in his insistence that "passive and involuntary error" (p. 150) characterize the spectator, upon whom "the mistake [mistaking the stage illusion for reality] is *imposed*" (p. 151). And in Diderot, therefore, we expect to encounter the problems associated with this view. What Hobson calls the characteristic "oscillation" of theater, "whereby the audience is deceived with truth, but this truth is itself only an appearance of truth" (p. 152), cannot simply be "excised" from the theatrical situation, no matter how much Diderot may want to accomplish this excision. "For if Diderot no longer locates the oscillation in the art object . . . he still places a comparable ambivalence at the heart of the relation between artist and consumer. The falsity of art is not located so much in the art work, as in the imbalance of the relation between spectator and author. The artist, the playwright, tricks the consumer" (pp. 152–53). But in his later work, especially the *Paradoxe*, Hobson appears to give Diderot credit for a more complete and nuanced aesthetic position, in that for the actor, the "unbridgeable gap . . . between what is felt and the gesture which expresses it" makes room for what she calls a structure of "relay from appearance (the manifestation of emotion), to what appears (the signs of emotion) which is in turn appearance (in that the signs are imitated)" (p. 204). I think I would go further than this. When Diderot speaks of "une imitation qui agrandisse tout dans leurs têtes [in the minds of the spectators] et qui devienne la règle de leur jugement" (358), I think he has moved far beyond the idea of illusion as a mistake of which the audience is unconscious. The insistence here upon "jugement"—like the association of "jugement" with "sentir" that was discussed earlier—implies much too strongly an involvement of awareness, and self-awareness, in our reception of "imitation." And if the awareness in question comes anywhere close to the level of philosophical contemplation suggested by Diderot's use of the theater as metaphor, then the whole problem of an entirely absorbing theatrical illusion is solved. For now, precisely by way of consciousness, we have come to recognize that the actor's putting-on of a convention-bound identity not only represents truth, but *is* truth, quite literally—thus an extreme instance of truth as adequation—a truth of which our understanding, therefore, is measured precisely by our "absorption" in it, which is the same thing as our ineluctable incorporation or embodiment of it. We *are* the truth we know, and we know it only by being it.

9. Lester G. Crocker is known and admired as a critic's critic, a commentator whose commitment to the authors he comments on is always reined in well short of idolatry. But in his assessment of Diderot's political thought, in *Diderot's Chaotic Order: Approach to Synthesis* (Princeton, 1974), I think he is overskeptical. Time and again, he compares Diderot unfavorably to Rousseau in the domain of politics (pp. 119–28, 134), insisting that although Diderot may see the *problem* of a rational politics, he lacks the theoretical clarity and energy to work through that problem to some form of cogent solution. "Diderot's weakness as a political philosopher lies partly in his inability to cut through this basic antithesis of the human condition [individual interest versus social interest] to a new ground on which it can be surpassed" (p. 128). But *can* this antithesis be "surpassed" or transcended or even mollified? Crocker himself, with reference to the passage quoted above in which Diderot develops the "difficulty" of changeable positive laws (3:513), admits: "But it [this difficulty] may be insolvable—in fact the whole political problem may be insolvable. Whatever precautions we may take to assure the rule of law and equality before the law, they will fail. . . . The value of enlightenment is after all limited" (p. 145). And if the problem really is insoluble, shall we prefer that thinker (Rousseau, perhaps) who best gives the best *impression* of having found a rational solution to it? Or shall we find it more honest to remain faced with the problem in as raw and immediate a form as possible, in a form that (as I suggest) allows the mere idea of a solution to arise only at a point admittedly beyond our ability to form a rational concept of it? A point, that is, in what we might call the strictly aesthetic domain. Nor is this structure of thought unique in Diderot (assuming it does characterize his political writing). Jonathan M. Hess, *Reconstituting the Body Politic: Enlightenment, Public Culture and the Invention of Aesthetic Autonomy* (Detroit, 1999), shows very clearly that especially for Kant and Karl Philipp Moritz, the very idea of an aesthetic domain arises as the attempt to bridge an otherwise strictly untraversable gap in rational political theory.

10. Bernard Shaw, *Collected Plays with Their Prefaces*, 7 vols. (London: Bodley Head, 1970–74), 2:527 (cited by "GBS" plus volume and page).

11. Harold Bloom, introduction to *George Bernard Shaw's Saint Joan* (New York, 1987), p. 3.

12. Christopher Innes, "'Nothing but talk, talk, talk—Shaw talk': Discussion Plays and the Making of Modern Drama," in *The Cambridge Companion to George Bernard Shaw*, ed. Christopher Innes (Cambridge, U.K., 1998), p. 168.

13. W. B. Worthen, *Modern Drama and the Rhetoric of Theater* (Berkeley, Calif., 1992), to take an example of responsible and readable and illuminating criticism, frequently uses the *verb* "empty," or its equivalents, in discussing Beckett. We hear that protagonists are "hollowed out" (p. 136), that speech is "emptied" (p. 137), that the spoken text is "emptied" (p. 140), that the text has power "to evacuate" characters and spectators (p. 142). But when Les Essif, *Empty Figure on an Empty Stage: The Theatre of Samuel Beckett and His Generation* (Bloomington, Ind., 2001), then goes a step further and insists on a philosophical notion of "emptiness" (pp. 15–33), which is supposed to be the object of Beckett's "pursuit" (pp. 60–88), the result, it seems to me, is a rather catastrophic loss of critical clarity. Still worse, and more obfuscating, is Adorno's well-known essay "Trying to Understand *Endgame*," in his *Notes to Literature*, ed. Rolf Tiedemann, trans. Shierry Weber Nicholsen (New York, 1991). Adorno says, for example (p. 253): "The Beckettian situations of which his drama is composed are the photographic negative of a reality referred to meaning. They have as their model the situations of empirical existence, situations which, once isolated and deprived of their instrumental and psychological context through the loss of personal unity, spontaneously assume a specific and compelling expression—that of horror." In the very process of claiming to carry Beckett absolutely beyond existential philosophy, Adorno thus simply reexistentializes him with the idea of "horror," which is as egregiously inappropriate as the supposed parallel with Leonhard Frank that he develops in the next couple of sentences. In truth, I argue, if there is any "horror" in Beckett, it arises from the *inability* to achieve "loss of personal unity." For Adorno, Beckett is mainly an excuse to make pronouncements about the postwar age. For instance, "Any alleged drama of the atomic age would be a mockery of itself, solely because its plot would comfortingly falsify the historical horror of anonymity by displacing it onto

human characters and actions and by gaping at the 'important people' who are in charge of whether the button gets pushed. The violence of the unspeakable is mirrored in the fear of mentioning it. [Is the very idea of 'mirroring' not a comfort?] Beckett keeps it nebulous [assuming that 'it' is Beckett's 'it']. About what is incommensurable with experience as such one can speak only in euphemisms, the way one speaks in Germany [only in Germany?] of the murder of the Jews" (pp. 245–46). And yet, Dürrenmatt, in *Die Physiker*, without pretending to legislate about "experience as such," and with no compunction about showing the person who can push the button, does after all write the drama that Adorno declares impossible. See Bennett, *Theater As Problem*, chap. 6.

14. Martin Puchner, *Stage Fright: Modernism, Anti-Theatricality, and Drama* (Baltimore, Md., 2002), pp. 165, 166. The argument develops an idea from Enoch Brater, "The 'Absurd' Actor in the Theatre of Samuel Beckett," *Educational Theatre Journal*, 27 (1975): 197–207.

15. There is of course no Greek verb θυμέω related to θυμός, that would produce a noun such as θύμημα from which one could derive "thymeme." But then, the technical term "phoneme," from φώνημα, has a lot to answer for anyway, in analogous formations like "morpheme" and "lexeme," where the –eme is taken to mean "basic indivisible unit of." A verb θυμόω does exist, and an associated noun θύμωμα, which refer to anger, an idea that may not be all that inappropriate for Beckett.

16. Essif, *Empty Figure*, pp. 190–92, for example, argues that Beckett's characters are exceptionally "marionette-like," but he does not then ask the obvious question.

8. Performance and the Exposure of Hermeneutics

1. Gadamer, *Wahrheit und Methode*, p. xix.

2. Frye, *Anatomy of Criticism*, pp. 349 and (next sentence) 350.

3. Harold Bloom, *The Anxiety of Influence: A Theory of Poetry* (Oxford, 1973), pp. 94, 96.

4. Julia Kristeva, Σημειωτικὴ: *Recherches pour une sémanalyse* (N.p.: Éditions du Seuil, 1969), esp. pp. 84–85 (and see her index, p. 316).

5. See Jacques Derrida, *Of Grammatology*, trans. Gayatri Chakravorty Spivak (Baltimore, Md., 1976), p. 158.

6. See, e.g., Schleiermacher, *Hermeneutik*, pp. 84, 86, on the basic hermeneutic circle as an "apparent" circle, and pp. 141–48, on the problem, in general, of understanding the whole from the parts and the parts from the whole. On another form of the circle, having to do with the problem of how one learns ancient languages, see p. 134.

7. Wilhelm Dilthey, *Gesammelte Schriften*, 1:29; see also 13/1:1, where that dictum (quoted from a letter of Goethe) is used as the epigraph for book one of *Leben Schleiermachers*.

8. Martin Heidegger, *Sein und Zeit*, 11th ed. (Tübingen, 1967), p. 153, in § 32.

9. Roland Barthes, "Présentation," *Communications* 4 (1964): 1–3.

10. For a more complete theoretical development of these issues, with respect to the carrot in *Waiting for Godot*, see Benjamin Bennett, *Theater As Problem*, esp. pp. 70–73, 199–202, 214–15.

11. For a fuller discussion of the relation of psychoanalysis to hermeneutics, and especially of the sense in which the two are *opposed*, see Bennett, *Goethe as Woman: The Undoing of Literature* (Detroit, 2001), pp. 219–23.

12. Schleiermacher, *Hermeneutik*, pp. 83–84, 87.

13. On the "empty" quality of meaning in Rousseau, see Paul de Man, "The Rhetoric of Blindness: Jacques Derrida's Reading of Rousseau," in his *Blindness and Insight*, p. 127. But then de Man goes on to assert that "Rousseau's theory of representation is not directed toward meaning as presence and plenitude but toward meaning as void." And this notion of directedness toward the void, which the balance of de Man's argument depends on, especially his denial (p. 139) of "blind spots" in Rousseau, allows the void itself to operate as meaning, as interpretation's one step beyond itself by which the supposed self-reflexive systematicity of Rousseau's text (and of de Man's) is coaxed into being.

14. As far as I can tell, the difference between "utterance" (*énoncé*), meaning the actual words spoken, and "enunciation" (*énonciation*), meaning the act of speaking those words, is commonplace in linguistics, whereas the distinction between *subject* of utterance and *subject* of enunciation—which suggests an intersection between linguistics and psychoanalysis—is much trickier and, as we might expect, operates frequently in the thought of Julia Kristeva. See, e.g., her "From One Identity to an Other," in her *Desire in Language: A Semiotic Approach to Literature and Art*, ed. Leon S. Roudiez (New York, 1980), pp. 127–28, where the subject of enunciation is seen as arising "between signifier and signified" or her *Language: The Unknown: An Initiation into Linguistics*, trans. Anne M. Menke (New York, 1989), pp. 274–75, where the relation of psychoanalysis to linguistics is discussed. Most people, including Kristeva, agree that the chapter "Subjectivity in Language," in Emile Benveniste, *Problems in General Linguistics*, trans. Mary Elizabeth Meek (1966; Coral Gables, Fla., 1971), pp. 223–30, is a crucial piece of pioneering work on the subject of enunciation.

15. Jean Genet, *Œuvres complètes*, 5 vols. (N.p.: Gallimard, 1951–53), 5:85, 96, 79.

9. Robert Wilson

1. Genet, *Œuvres complètes*, 4:11–12.

2. Hans-Thies Lehmann, *Postdramatisches Theater* (Frankfurt/Main, 1999), pp. 22–23.

3. For a more strictly linguistic argument on the dethroning of language in the dramatic theater, involving the idea of reversibility in the operation of both reference and signification, see Bennett, *Theater As Problem*, pp. 194–216.

4. Lehmann's instinct is perfectly sound. The theater is itself only by being revolutionary, and it is revolutionary only by being repeatedly revolutionized. But the idea of such revolutionizing is questionable if it proceeds by ignoring or minimizing the achievements of the theater it starts out from, as Lehmann does when he dismisses the "illusion-breaking" devices used in practically all Western drama by saying that they are meant to be "integrated so inconspicuously into the fictive cosmos that [they] do not become disturbingly noticeable" (*Postdramatisches Theater*, p. 171). One asks, why were such devices used in the first place, if they were not meant to be noticed? In the history of Western staging, moreover, the "fictive cosmos," in the form of a stage world (with no spectators permitted to sit in it) set off by footlights before a darkened auditorium, is fully established only in the nineteenth century and then quickly unestablished in the twentieth. And when Lehmann suggests that an ethical questioning of the spectatorial attitude is inherently postdramatic (pp. 176–77), he is, in effect, making Büchner postdramatic.

5. Jean-François Lyotard, *The Postmodern Condition: A Report on Knowledge*, trans. Geoff Bennington and Brian Massumi (1979; Minneapolis, 1984), p. 4.

6. When Lyotard speaks of "reality," of course, he means *not* what Lehmann means by "the (strictly) real" but rather precisely an *unreal* (imaginary) structured sense of the world-as-totality, for public consumption.

7. Stefan Brecht, *The Original Theatre of the City of New York. From the Mid-6os to the Mid-7os: Book 1: The Theatre of Visions: Robert Wilson* (Frankfurt/Main, 1978), p. 9. There are of course plenty of later books on Robert Wilson, but none have quite the same quality of immediate public discussion, combining extensive minute description (holding the work fast) with the attempt to attain critical distance.

8. See Gordon Rogoff, *Vanishing Acts: Theater since the Sixties* (New Haven, Conn., 2000); Blau, *To All Appearances*; and Herbert Blau, *The Audience* (Baltimore, Md., 1990).

9. Gadamer, *Wahrheit und Methode*, pp. 289–90.

10. Arthur Holmberg, *The Theatre of Robert Wilson* (Cambridge, U.K., 1996), pp. 22–40, places a break in Wilson's career at this point, too, mainly with regard to the use of language.

Index

DATE DUE

GAYLORD

PRINTED IN U.S.A.